# THE TRANSCONTINENTAL RAILROAD
## CROSSING THE DIVIDE

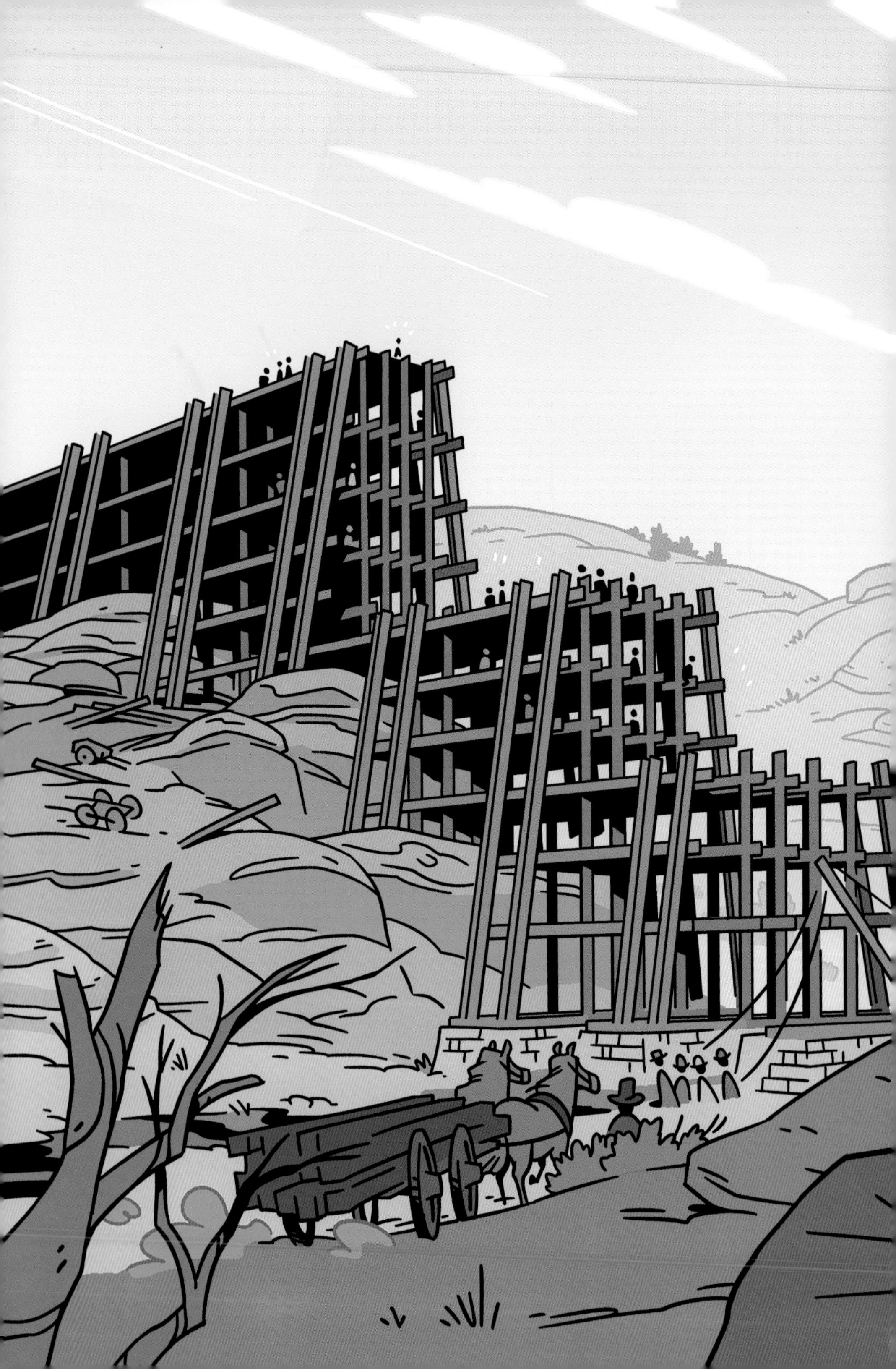

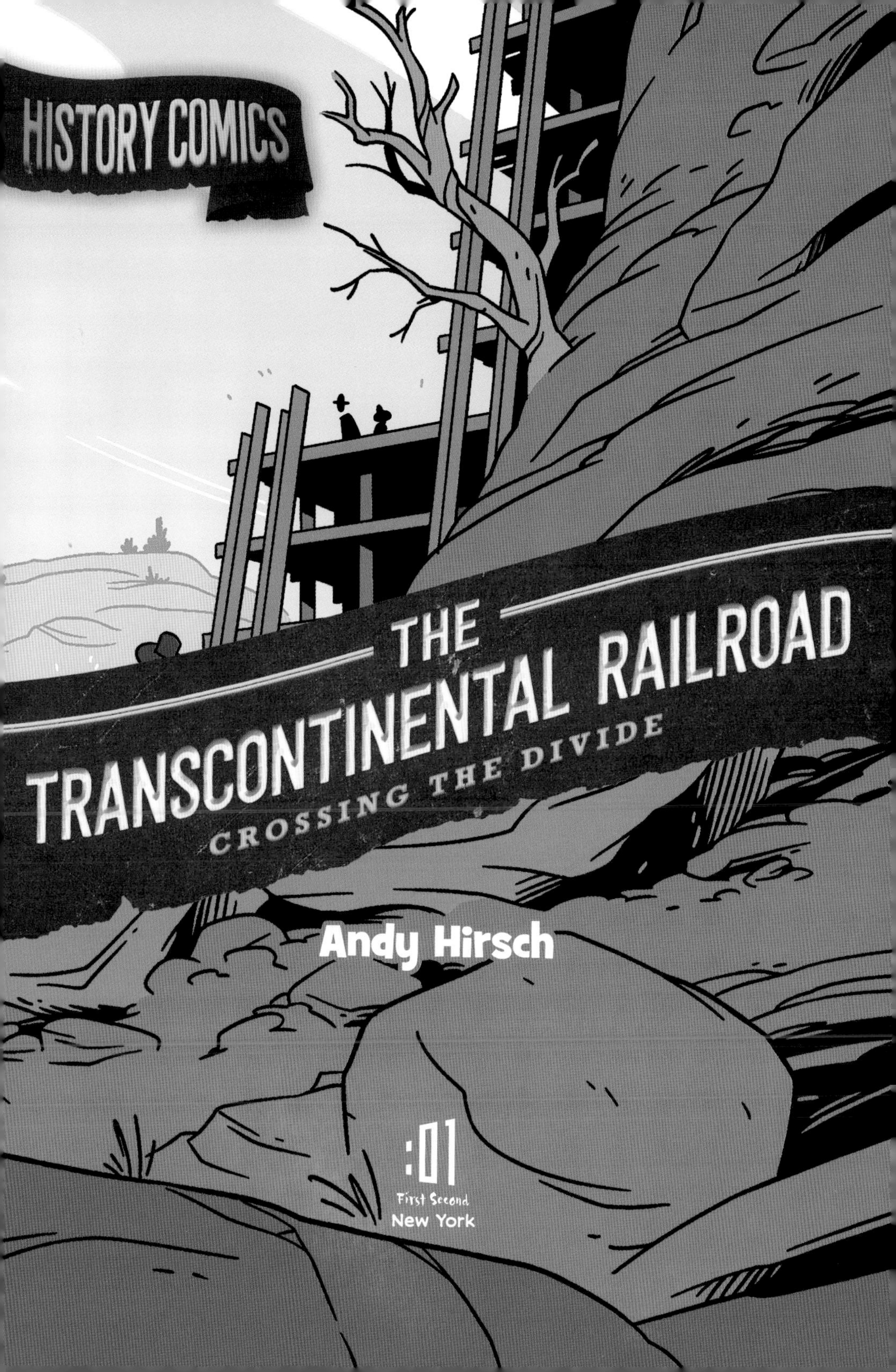

HISTORY COMICS

# THE TRANSCONTINENTAL RAILROAD

## CROSSING THE DIVIDE

Andy Hirsch

:01
First Second
New York

**First Second**

Published by First Second
First Second is an imprint of Roaring Brook Press,
a division of Holtzbrinck Publishing Holdings Limited Partnership
120 Broadway, New York, NY 10271
firstsecondbooks.com
mackids.com

Library of Congress Control Number: 2022902085

Our books may be purchased in bulk for promotional, educational, or business use.
Please contact your local bookseller or the Macmillan Corporate and Premium Sales Department
at (800) 221-7945 ext. 5442 or by email at MacmillanSpecialMarkets@macmillan.com.

First edition, 2022
Edited by Dave Roman and Benjamin A. Wilgus
Cover design and interior book design by Sunny Lee and Madeline Morales
Series design by Andrew Arnold
Production editing by Avia Perez
With special thanks to Elise McMullen-Ciotti and Alex Lu
Railroad history consultant: Ryan Dearinger

Drawn in Clip Studio Paint. Colored in Adobe Photoshop CC.
Lettered with Soliloquous font from Comicraft.

Printed in China by Toppan Leefung Printing Ltd., Dongguan City, Guangdong Province

ISBN 978-1-250-79477-2 (paperback)
10  9  8  7  6  5  4  3  2

ISBN 978-1-250-79476-5 (hardcover)
10  9  8  7  6  5  4  3  2  1

Don't miss your next favorite book from First Second! For the latest updates go to
firstsecondnewsletter.com and sign up for our enewsletter.

Do you have a toy train? Growing up, my brother and I had plastic train sets, painted wooden cars that felt heavy and rolled nicely on wood tracks, and, our favorite, an electric set that we set up with curved tracks, bridges, tunnels, and switches. Our engine had a light, so we could run it in the dark. It puffed artificial smoke. We had a miniature sawmill, houses, and even a little church with a ringing bell. We built a whole alternative world of imagination and play.

Real trains fascinated me, with their power, noise, speed, smoke, and ability to carry many people and things long distances. I could hear the trains running near my home any time of the day or night. I even traveled in a train across the entire country when I was young. What an adventure to sit there over days of travel and watch the mountains, deserts, and towns pass by! I went from California to Chicago, a trip I'll never forget. Chicago had more train tracks around it than I had ever seen.

Later in life, no matter where I went—Kansas, New Jersey, Georgia, Washington, Massachusetts, and even Hawaii—there were trains carrying people, goods, timber, coal, oil, cars, wheat, and who knows what else.

The national network of railroad lines that was built in the mid-ninteenth century formed the country's first infrastructure, a construction and technology network that helped social and economic interaction on a mass scale. Even today, when we have the internet, which is our modern infrastructure, we still depend on the railroad.

The railroads dramatically changed everyday life, business, politics, and culture. Coal and iron ore in the West could get to factories in the Midwest and East. Railroads changed the way we ate, the way we thought about the country, and the way we could vacation. It even changed the way we thought about distance, now that every part of the country was within reach. America was never the same, especially after the completion of the transcontinental railroad in 1869. A person could go from one coast to the other in a week instead of months of dangerous travel. What we even thought about time, such as what could be accomplished in an hour, changed forever.

Immigrants in New York could quickly get to California. Midwesterners could consume New England lobsters and Oregon pears. Vacations to national parks were within reach of millions of people.

We take all this for granted today, but building the railroad infrastructure took a long time, much hard work, and the efforts of tens of thousands of workers from all walks of life.

Many people were worked to the bone; some even sacrificed their lives for our modern conveniences. Imagine constructing a railroad line, with all the clearing of the land, digging, tunneling, building bridges, and laying the heavy ties and track.

The railroad fueled our imaginations, with its sounds, powerful locomotives, and lengths of cars, and became part of our daily lives. We could not have the lives we have today without them. Cars, trucks, and even airplanes can't carry the loads that trains can.

Studying the past helps us understand our present. The world today is a continuation of history and without considering it we can't fully appreciate our current destination and where we are going next.

On my trip across the country when I was a young boy, I remember looking out at the rugged, towering mountains of the Sierra Nevada range that separates California from the rest of the country. I remember wondering how it was humanly possible to clear the way and lay tracks for the railroad through such imposing terrain, including tunneling through the granite cliffs. I wondered how workers survived the blistering heat of the deserts of Nevada and Utah. How did they endure the work to get the rail line through the endless plains of Nebraska, across the mighty Mississippi and Missouri and other grand rivers, and into the crowded cities of the Midwest and East? Hopefully reading this book will give you some insight into what it was like on the ground,

as human hands assembled almost two thousand miles of railroad track.

My toy electric train is packed away somewhere but I'm thinking of pulling it out from storage to share with my daughters. A real passing train leaves them in wonder and even a short ride from our town to the big city for a day's adventure is an exciting experience! All aboard!

—**Gordon H. Chang**,
author of *Ghosts of Gold Mountain: The Epic Story of the Chinese Who Built the Transcontinental Railroad*

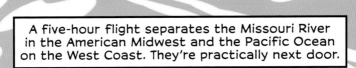

A five-hour flight separates the Missouri River in the American Midwest and the Pacific Ocean on the West Coast. They're practically next door.

Somehow those same 1,500 miles are far wider in the early 1800s.

A journey by land sends you across arid plains, through Native American nations, over mountains, and far from help when trouble finds you.

Trouble **will** find you. It's got most of a year to do so.

Going west is *terrible!*

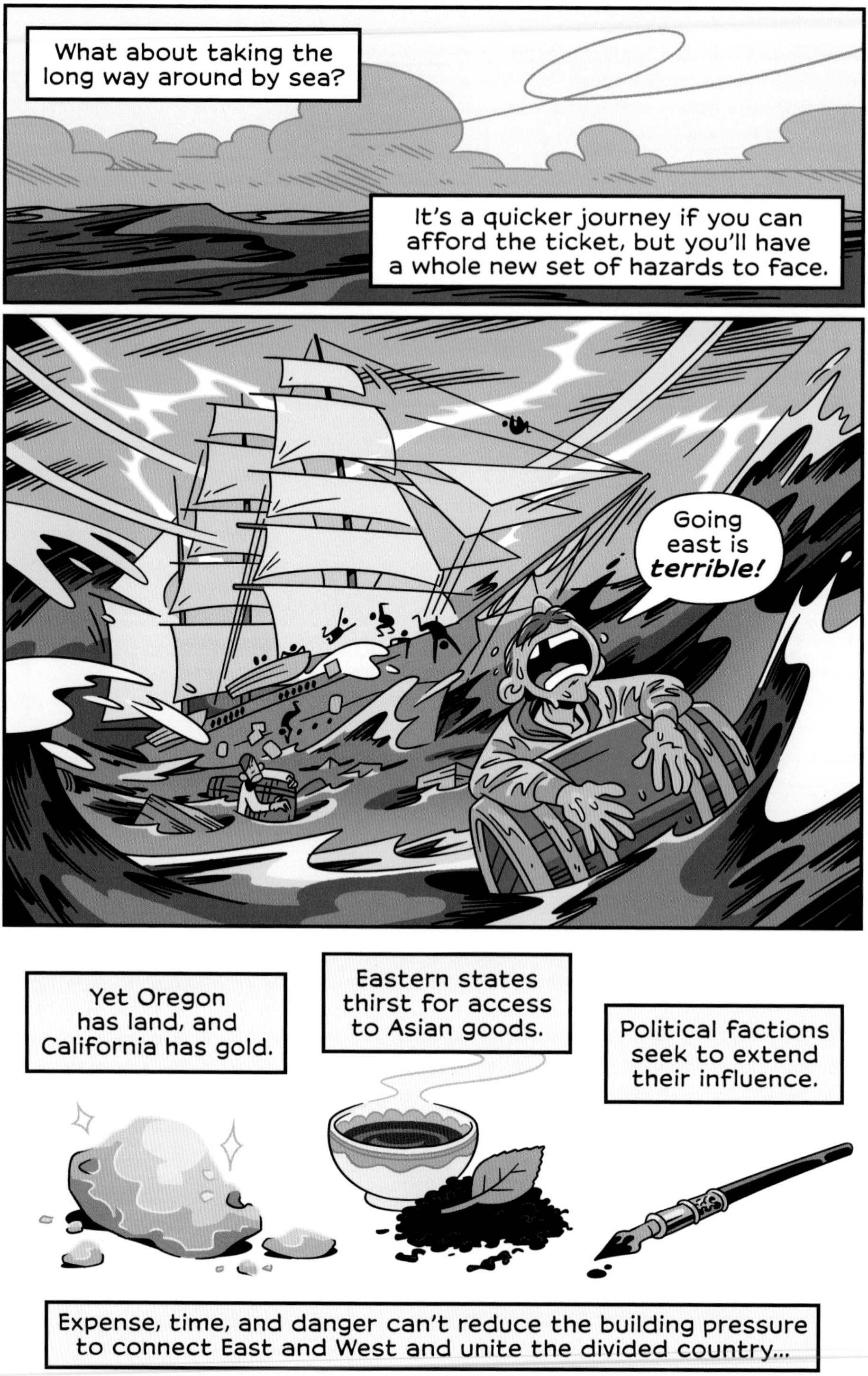
What about taking the long way around by sea?
It's a quicker journey if you can afford the ticket, but you'll have a whole new set of hazards to face.
Going east is *terrible!*
Yet Oregon has land, and California has gold.
Eastern states thirst for access to Asian goods.
Political factions seek to extend their influence.
Expense, time, and danger can't reduce the building pressure to connect East and West and unite the divided country...

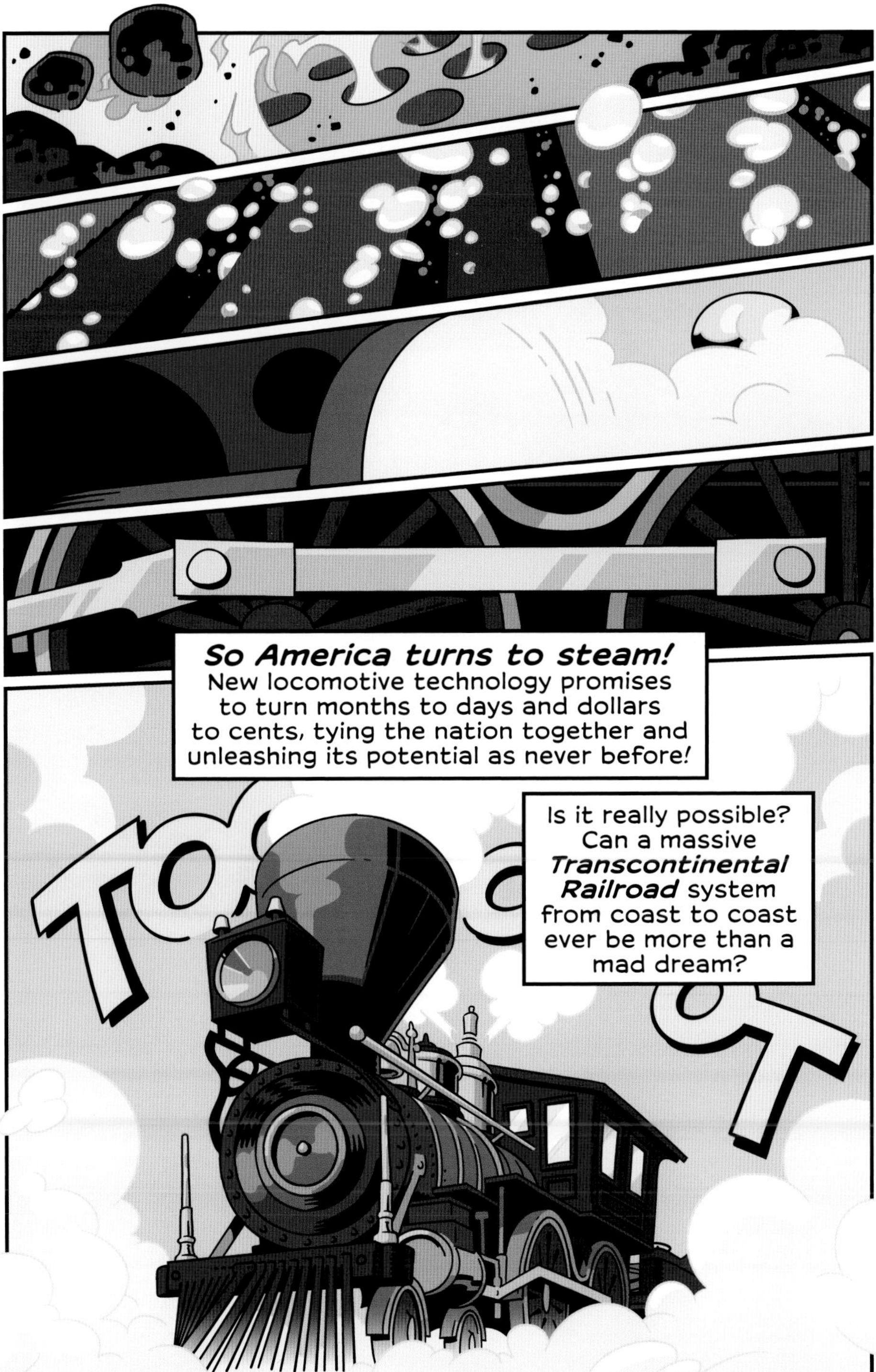

***So America turns to steam!***
New locomotive technology promises to turn months to days and dollars to cents, tying the nation together and unleashing its potential as never before!
Is it really possible? Can a massive ***Transcontinental Railroad*** system from coast to coast ever be more than a mad dream?

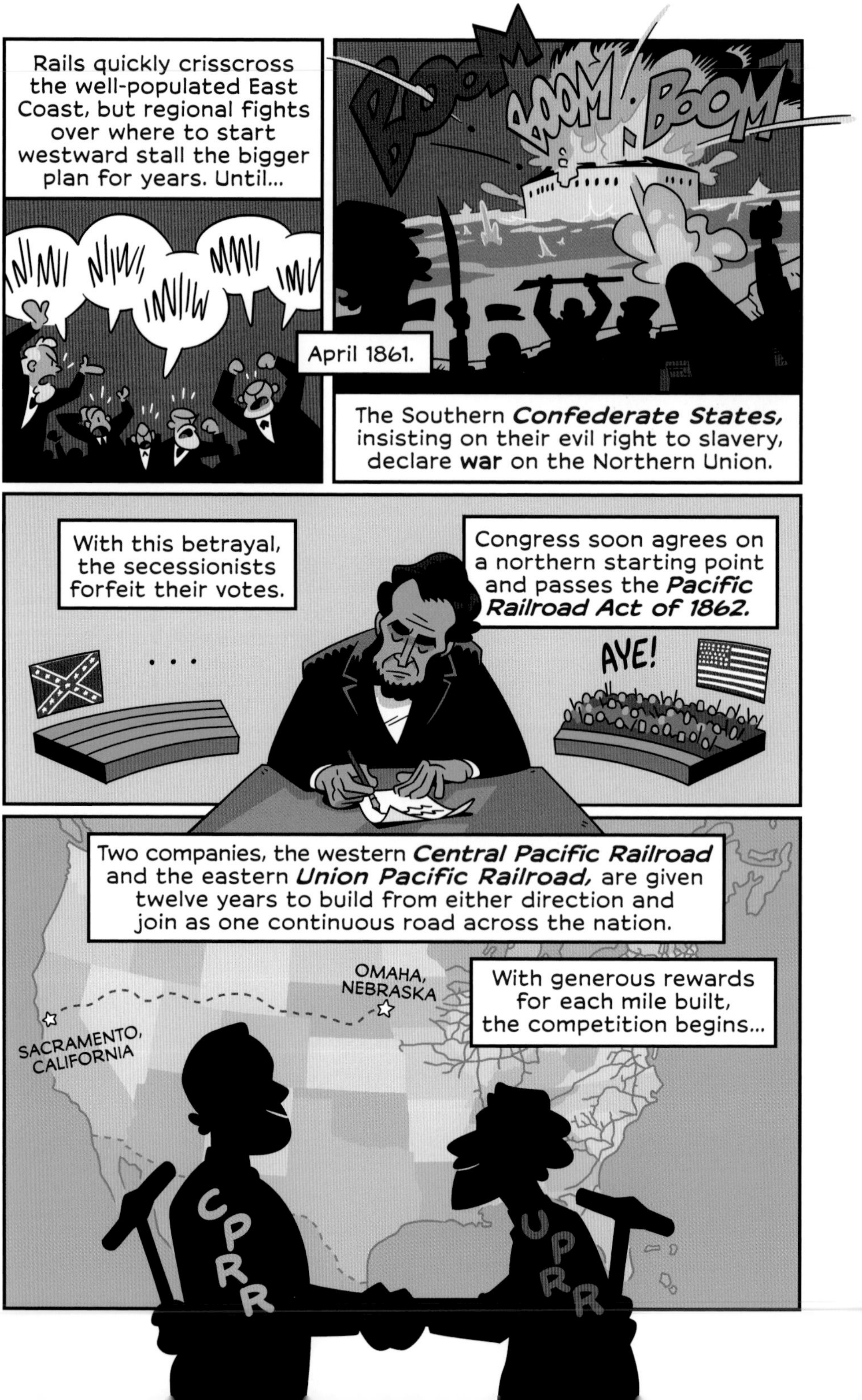
Rails quickly crisscross the well-populated East Coast, but regional fights over where to start westward stall the bigger plan for years. Until...
BOOM
BOOM
BOOM
April 1861.
The Southern *Confederate States,* insisting on their evil right to slavery, declare **war** on the Northern Union.
With this betrayal, the secessionists forfeit their votes.
Congress soon agrees on a northern starting point and passes the *Pacific Railroad Act of 1862.*
...
AYE!
Two companies, the western *Central Pacific Railroad* and the eastern *Union Pacific Railroad,* are given twelve years to build from either direction and join as one continuous road across the nation.
OMAHA, NEBRASKA
SACRAMENTO, CALIFORNIA
With generous rewards for each mile built, the competition begins...
CPRR
UPRR

EAST OF SACRAMENTO, CA
SUMMER 1864 • CPRR
The CPRR gets right to work. With few laborers and little initial funding, it slowly struggles up the foothills of the Sierra Nevada mountains...
CHOP
BOOM
CLANG
CREAK
shuff

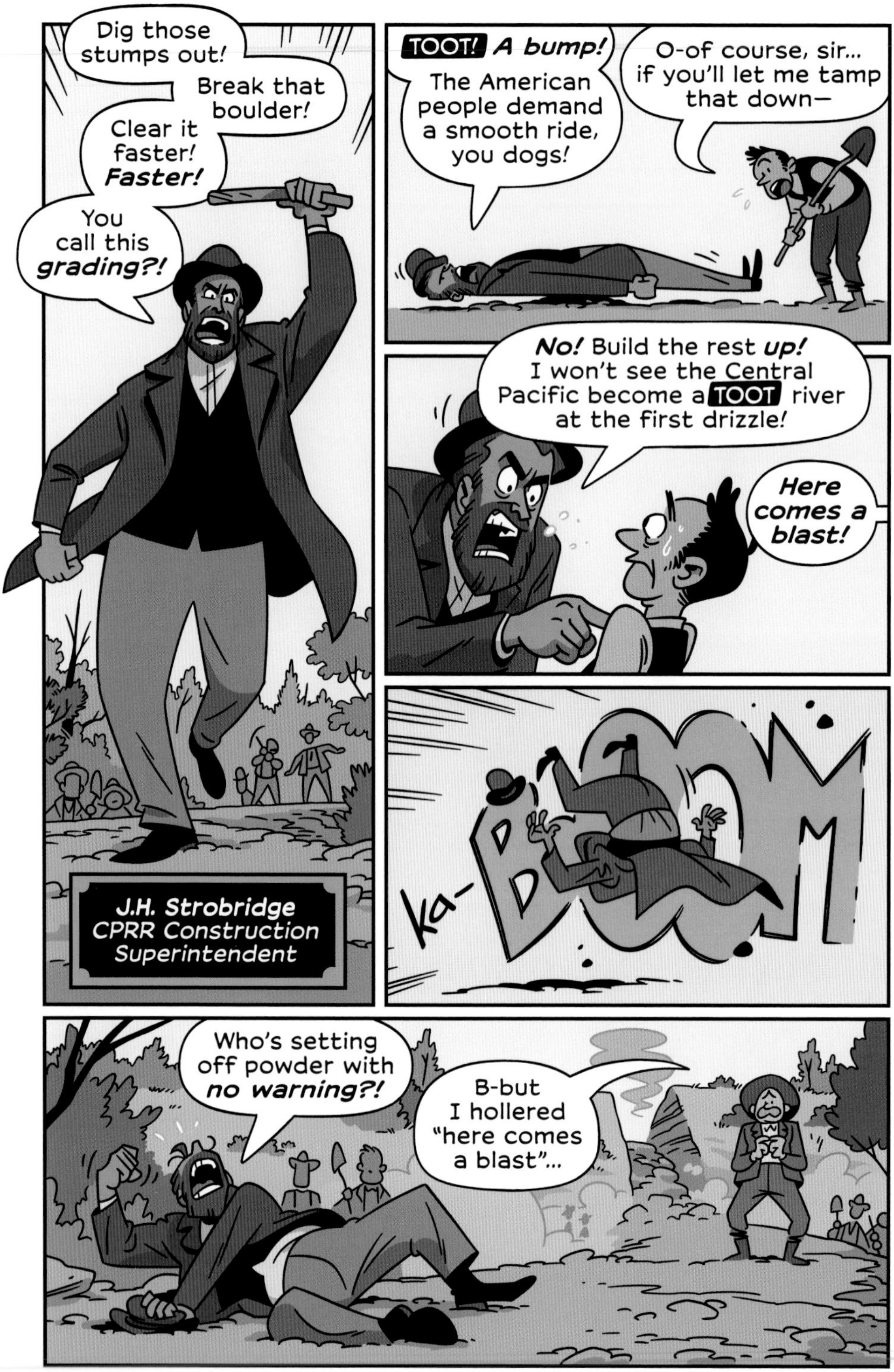
Dig those stumps out!
Break that boulder!
Clear it faster! Faster!
You call this grading?!
J.H. Strobridge
CPRR Construction Superintendent
TOOT! A bump! The American people demand a smooth ride, you dogs!
O-of course, sir... if you'll let me tamp that down—
No! Build the rest up! I won't see the Central Pacific become a TOOT river at the first drizzle!
Here comes a blast!
ka-BOOM
Who's setting off powder with no warning?!
B-but I hollered "here comes a blast"...

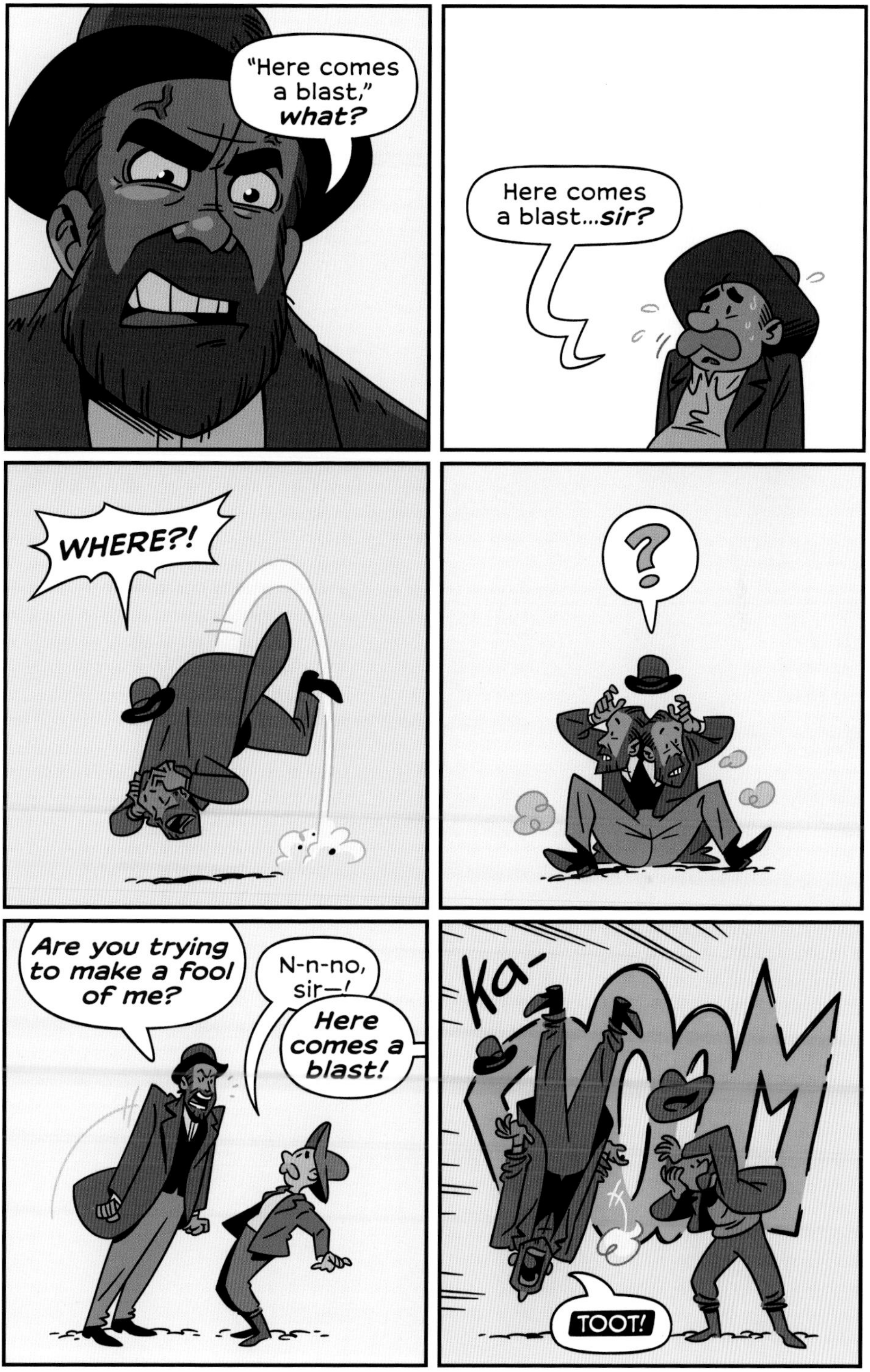
"Here comes a blast," *what?*
Here comes a blast...*sir?*
WHERE?!
?
*Are you trying to make a fool of me?*
N-n-no, sir—!
*Here comes a blast!*
Ka-
TOOT!

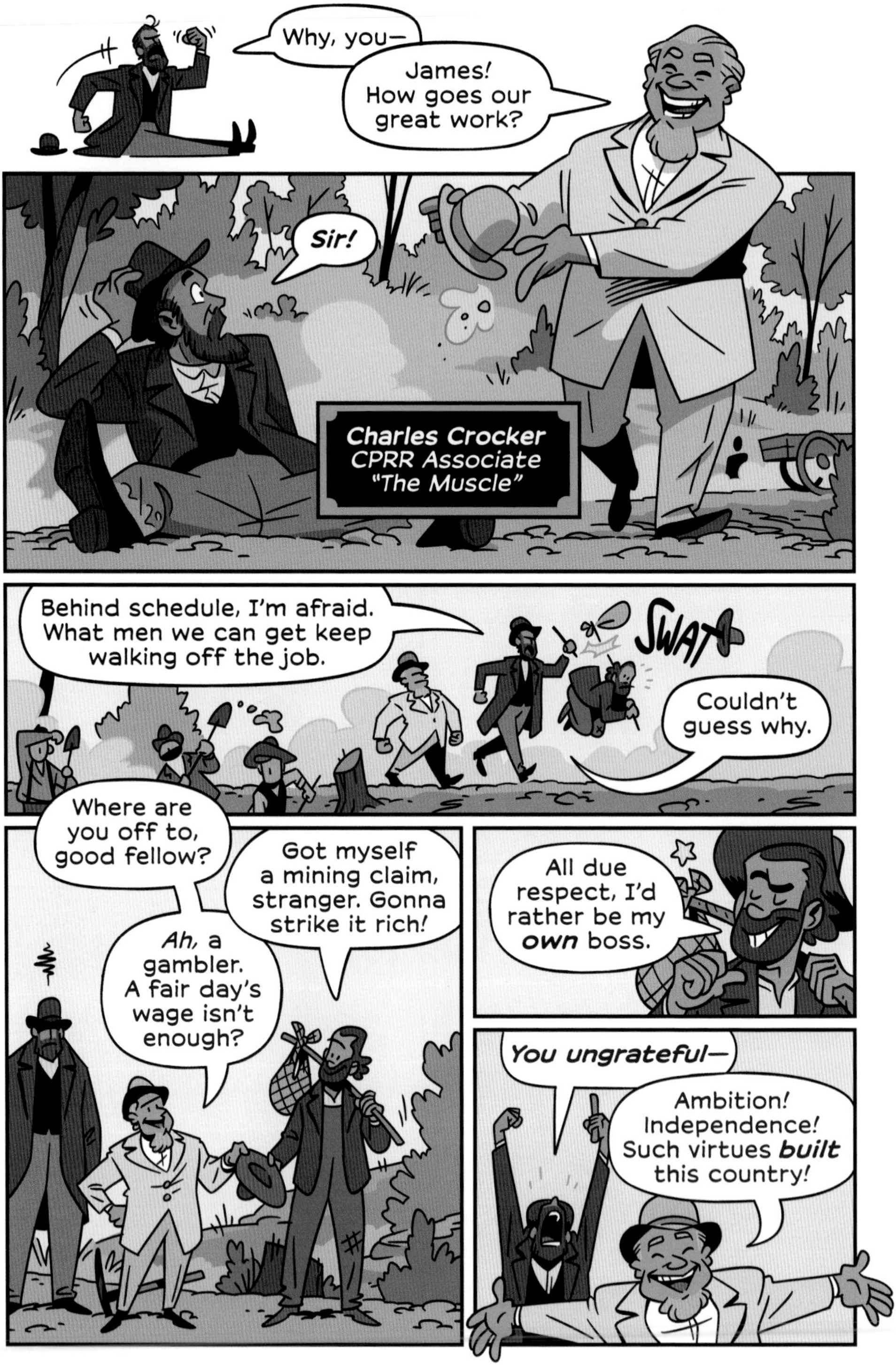

Why, you—
James! How goes our great work?
Sir!
Charles Crocker
CPRR Associate
"The Muscle"
Behind schedule, I'm afraid. What men we can get keep walking off the job.
SWAT
Couldn't guess why.
Where are you off to, good fellow?
Got myself a mining claim, stranger. Gonna strike it rich!
*Ah,* a gambler. A fair day's wage isn't enough?
All due respect, I'd rather be my ***own*** boss.
*You ungrateful—*
Ambition! Independence! Such virtues ***built*** this country!

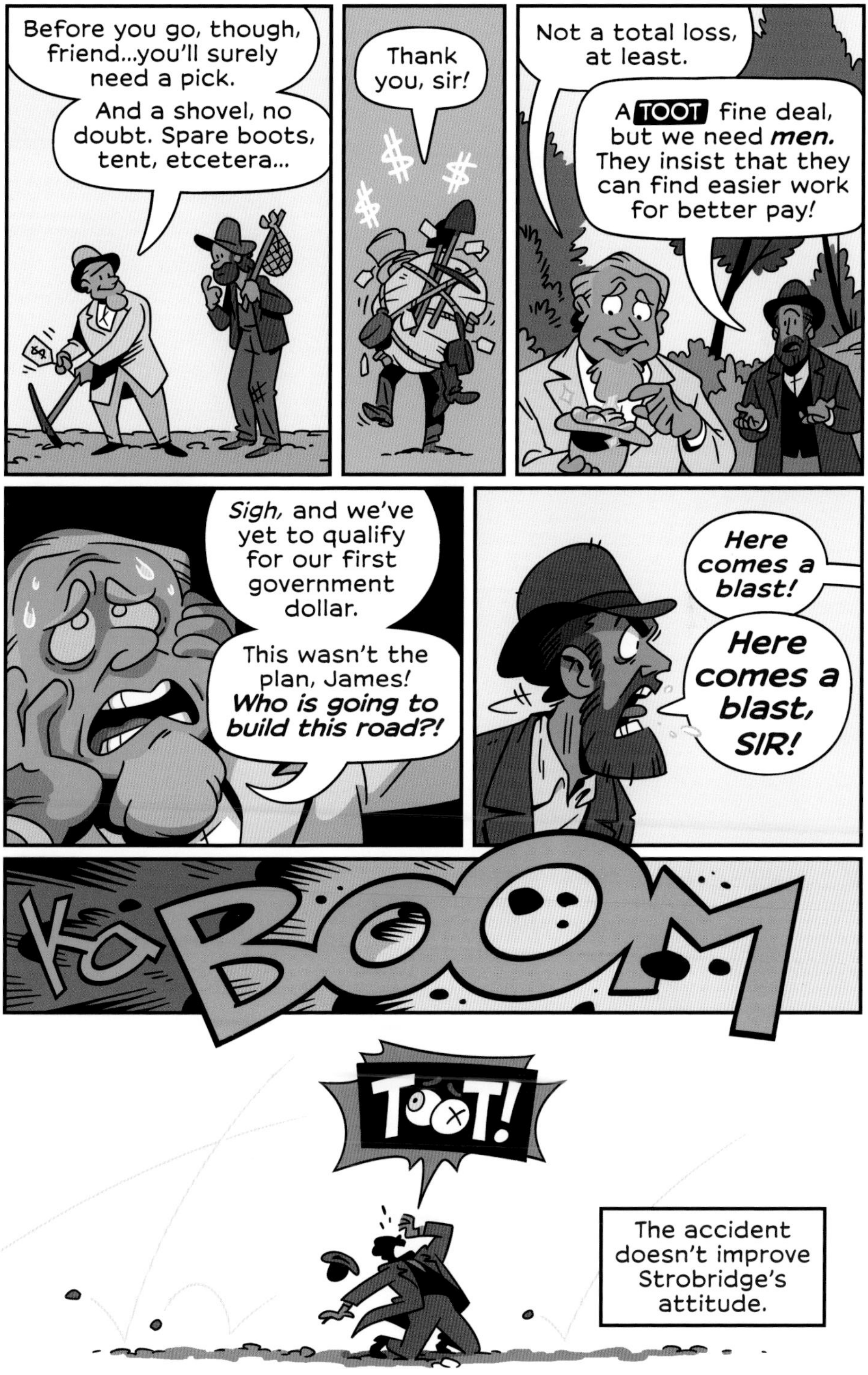
Before you go, though, friend...you'll surely need a pick.
And a shovel, no doubt. Spare boots, tent, etcetera...
Thank you, sir!
Not a total loss, at least.
A TOOT fine deal, but we need men. They insist that they can find easier work for better pay!
Sigh, and we've yet to qualify for our first government dollar.
This wasn't the plan, James! Who is going to build this road?!
Here comes a blast!
Here comes a blast, SIR!
KA-BOOM
TOOT!
The accident doesn't improve Strobridge's attitude.

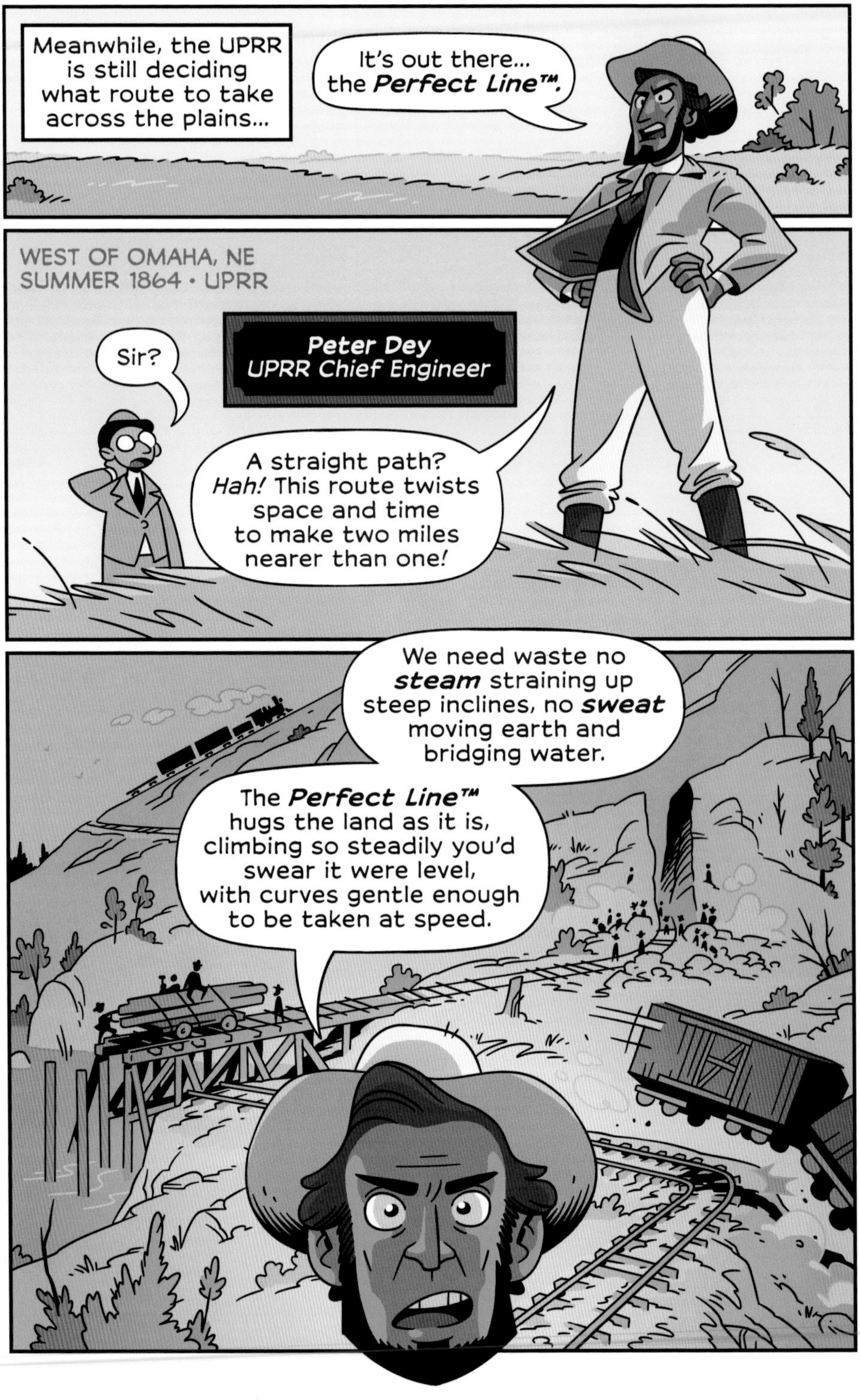
Meanwhile, the UPRR is still deciding what route to take across the plains...
It's out there... the *Perfect Line™*.
WEST OF OMAHA, NE
SUMMER 1864 • UPRR
Sir?
Peter Dey
UPRR Chief Engineer
A straight path? *Hah!* This route twists space and time to make two miles nearer than one!
We need waste no ***steam*** straining up steep inclines, no ***sweat*** moving earth and bridging water.
The *Perfect Line™* hugs the land as it is, climbing so steadily you'd swear it were level, with curves gentle enough to be taken at speed.

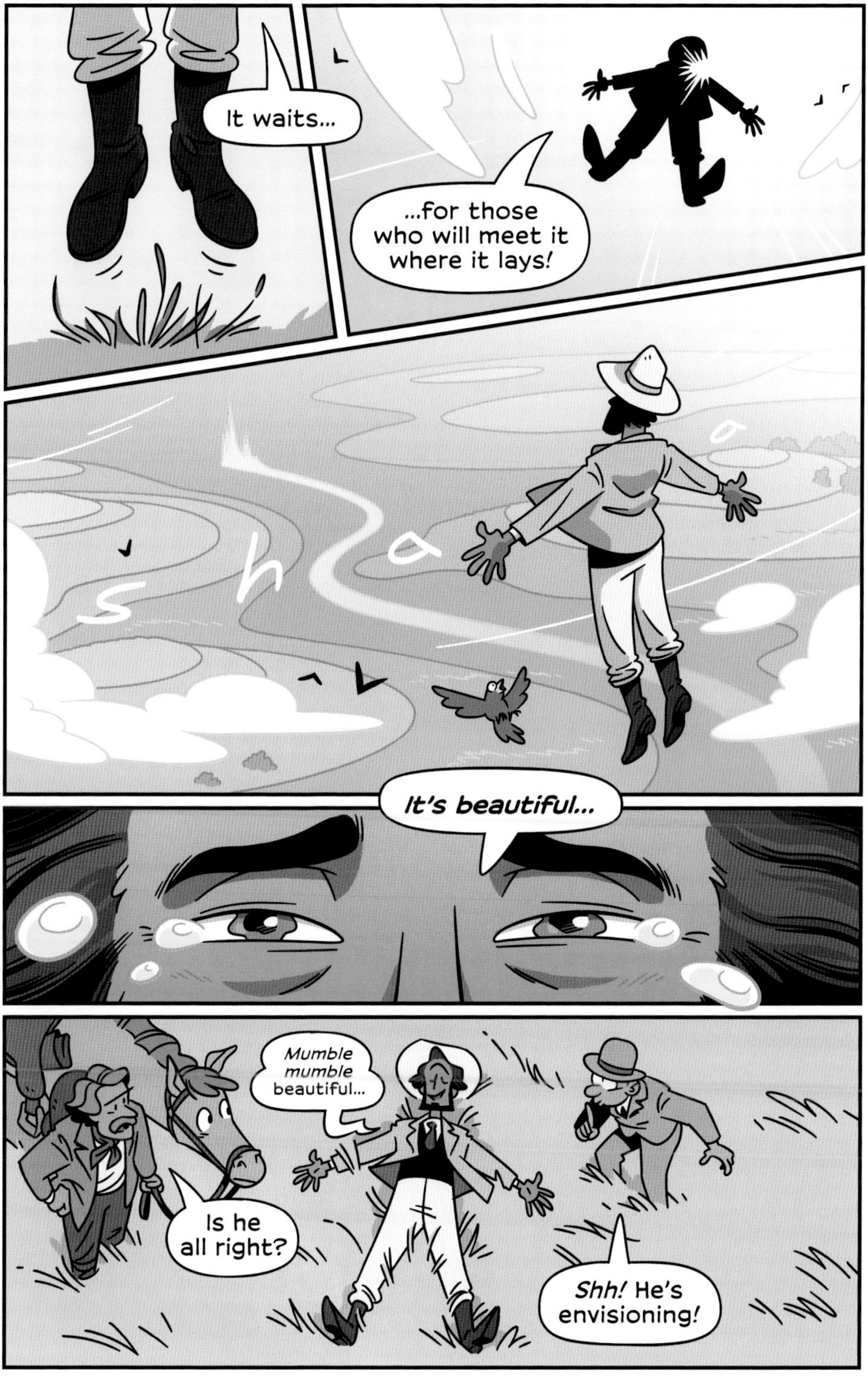
It waits...
...for those who will meet it where it lays!
s h a a
It's beautiful...
Mumble mumble beautiful...
Is he all right?
Shh! He's envisioning!

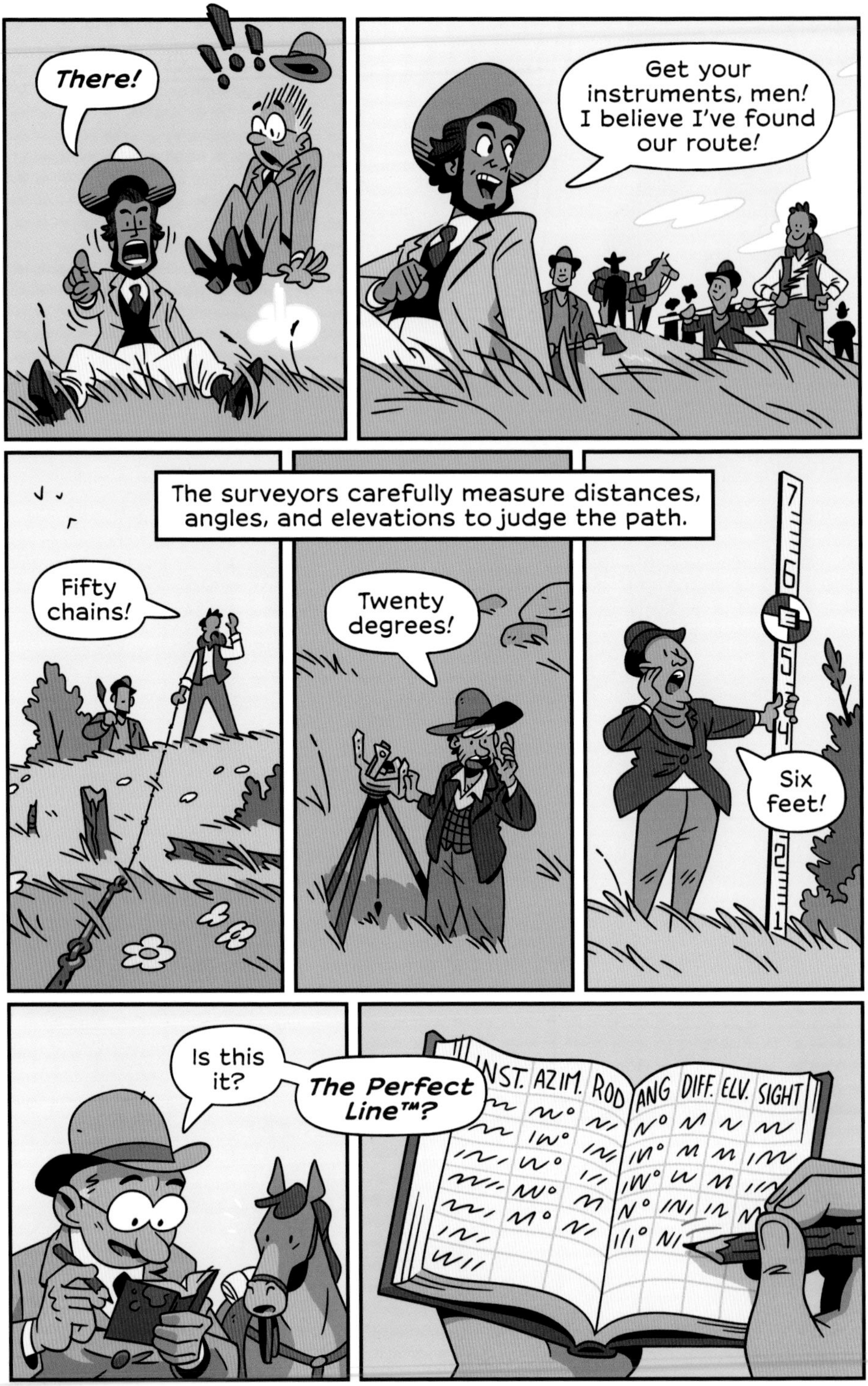
There!
Get your instruments, men! I believe I've found our route!
The surveyors carefully measure distances, angles, and elevations to judge the path.
Fifty chains!
Twenty degrees!
Six feet!
Is this it?
The Perfect Line™?
INST. AZIM. ROD ANG DIFF. ELV. SIGHT

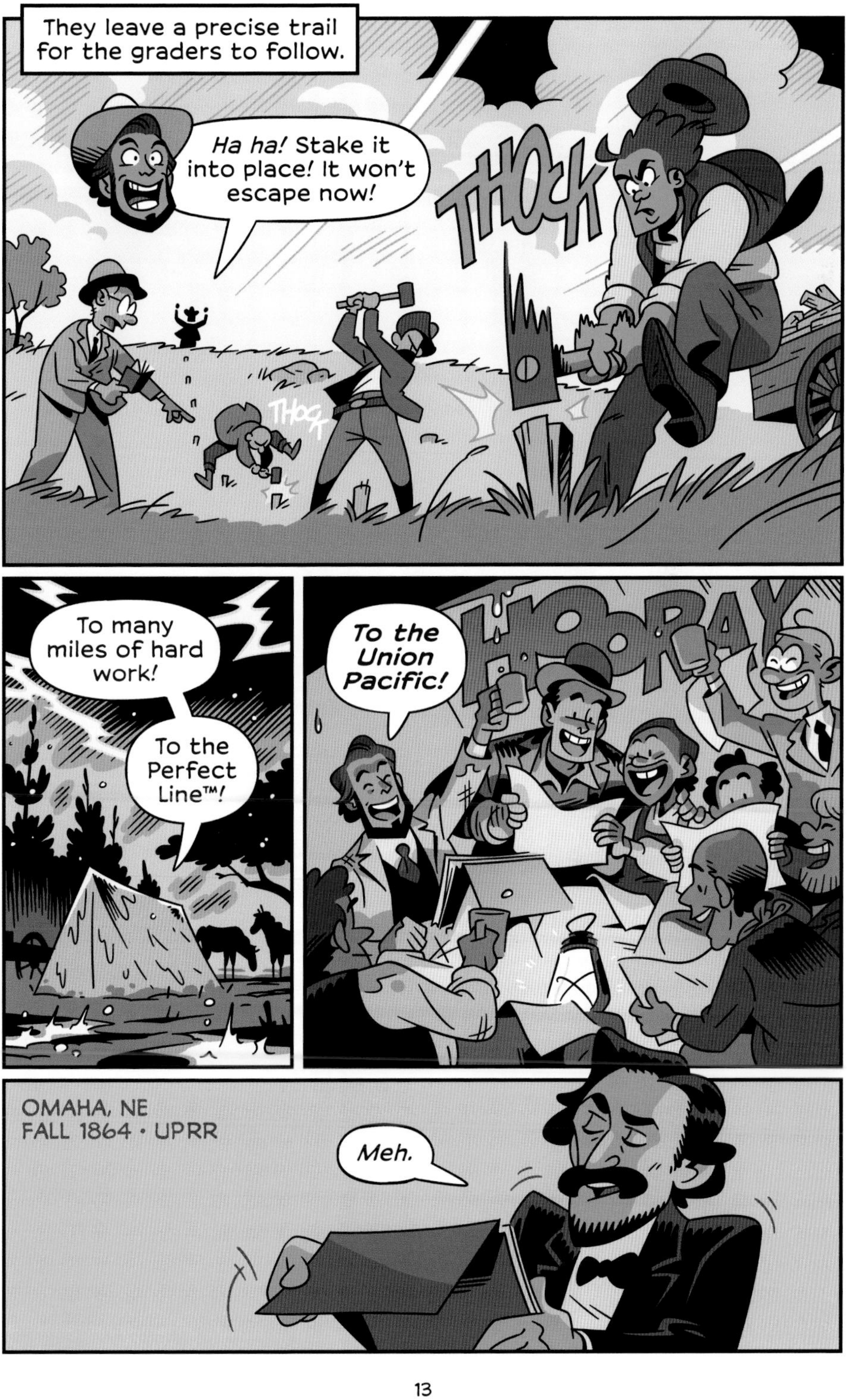
They leave a precise trail for the graders to follow.
*Ha ha!* Stake it into place! It won't escape now!
THOCK
THOCK
To many miles of hard work!
To the Perfect Line™!
**To the Union Pacific!**
HOORAY
OMAHA, NE
FALL 1864 • UPRR
*Meh.*

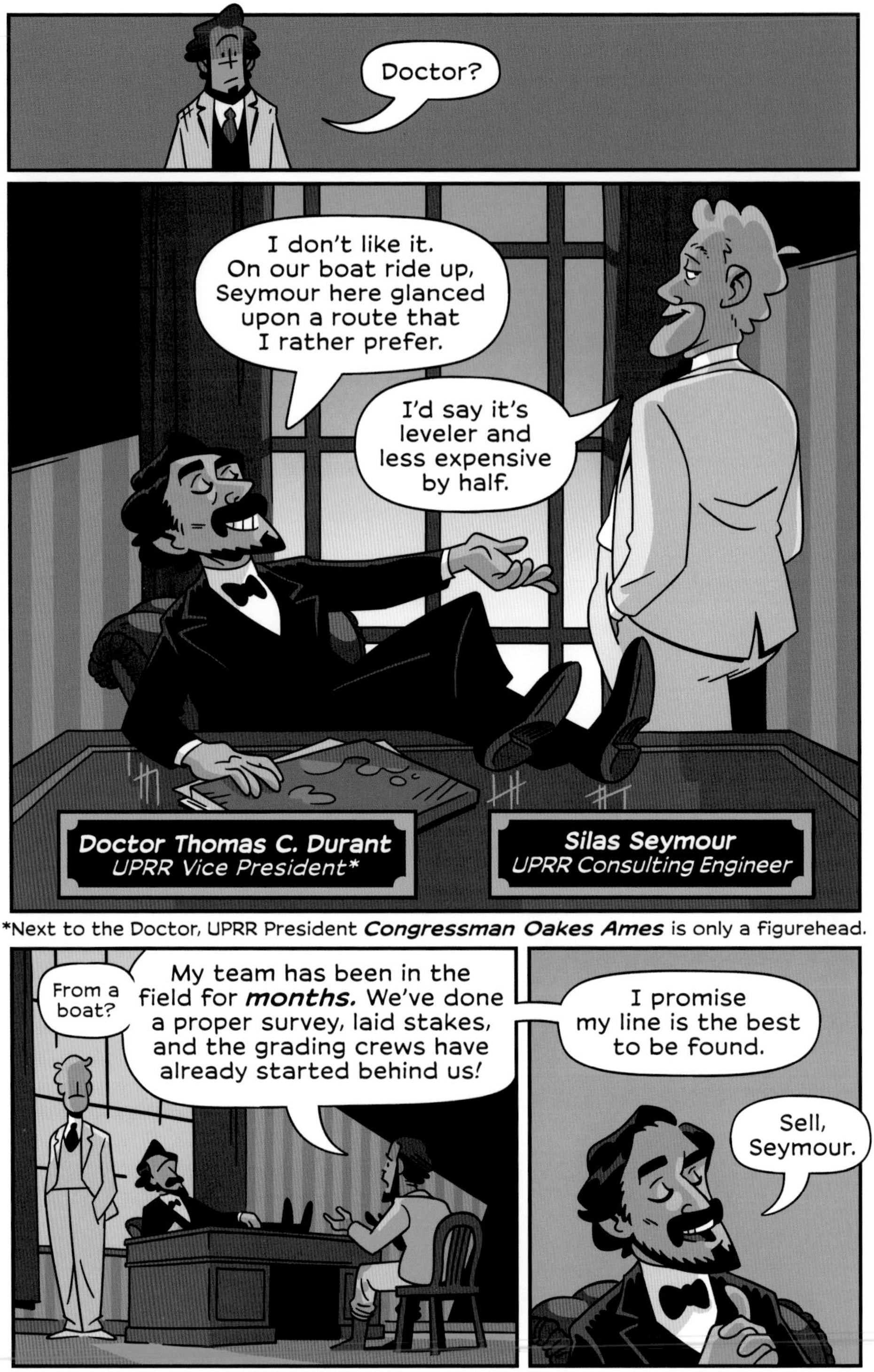
Doctor?
I don't like it. On our boat ride up, Seymour here glanced upon a route that I rather prefer.
I'd say it's leveler and less expensive by half.
Doctor Thomas C. Durant
UPRR Vice President*
Silas Seymour
UPRR Consulting Engineer
*Next to the Doctor, UPRR President Congressman Oakes Ames is only a figurehead.
From a boat?
My team has been in the field for months. We've done a proper survey, laid stakes, and the grading crews have already started behind us!
I promise my line is the best to be found.
Sell, Seymour.

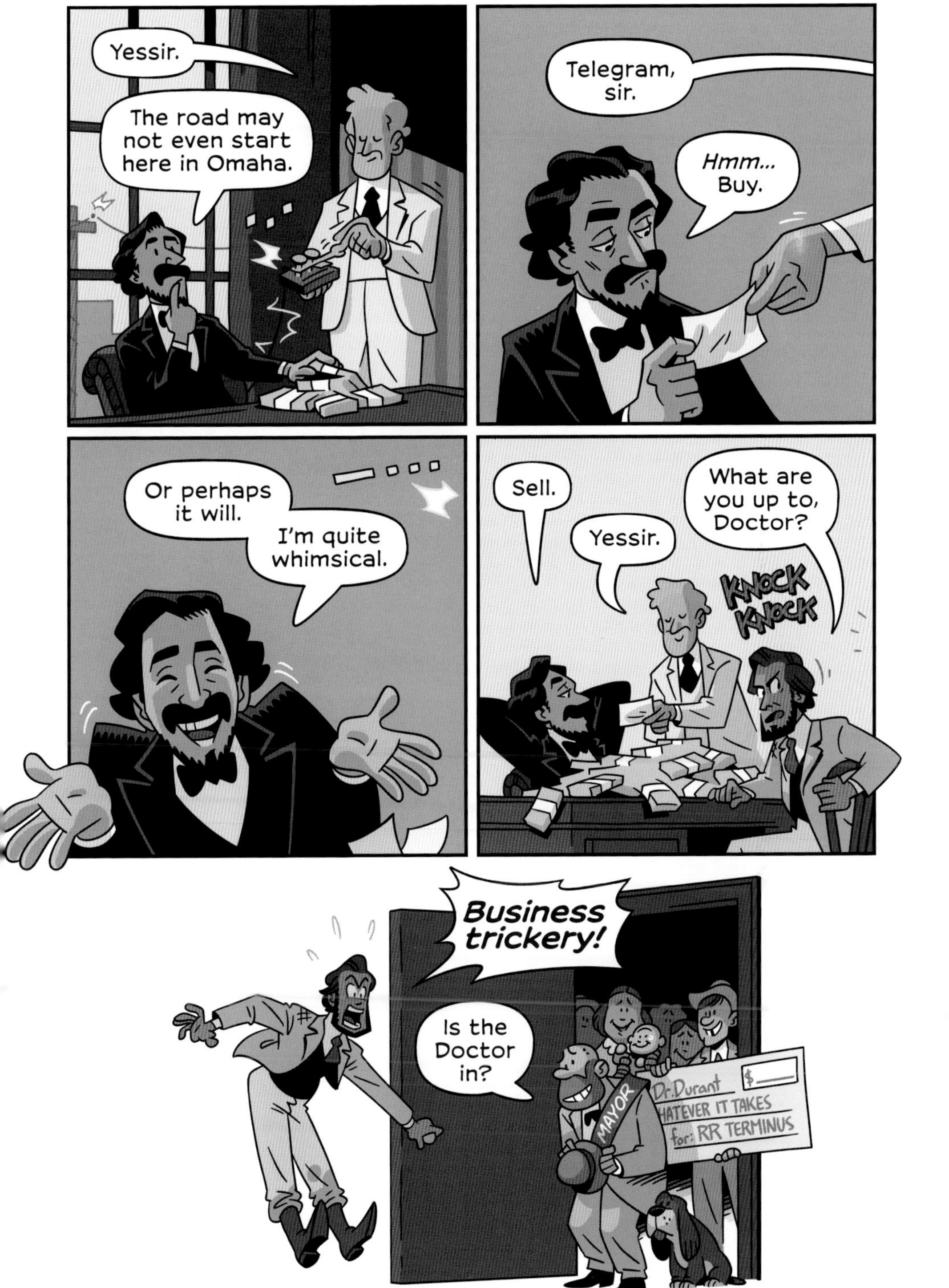
Yessir.
The road may not even start here in Omaha.
Telegram, sir.
Hmm... Buy.
Or perhaps it will.
I'm quite whimsical.
Sell.
Yessir.
What are you up to, Doctor?
KNOCK KNOCK
Business trickery!
Is the Doctor in?
MAYOR
Dr. Durant
$
HATEVER IT TAKES
for: RR TERMINUS

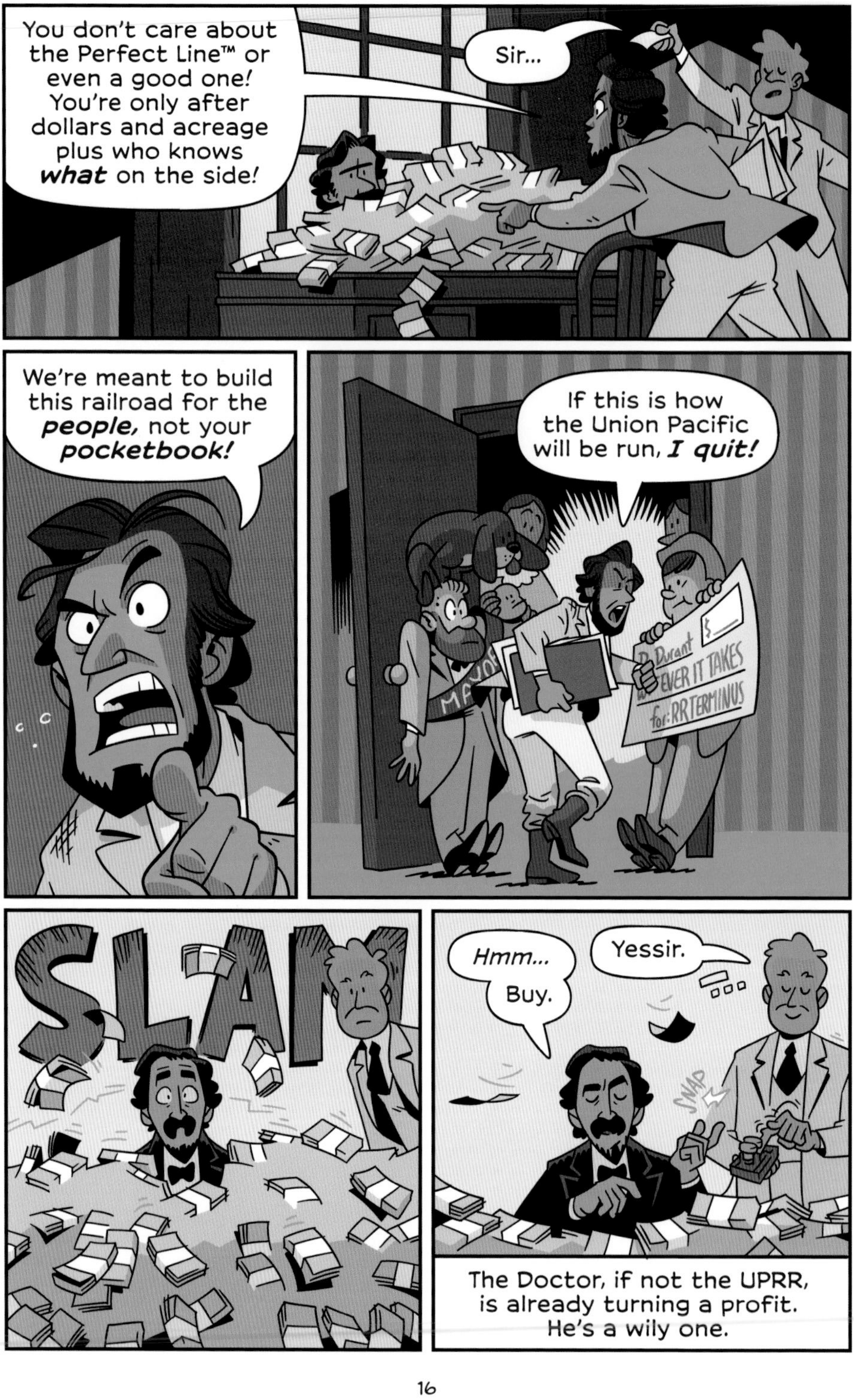

You don't care about the Perfect Line™ or even a good one! You're only after dollars and acreage plus who knows *what* on the side!
Sir...
We're meant to build this railroad for the *people,* not your *pocketbook!*
If this is how the Union Pacific will be run, ***I quit!***
Durant
EVER IT TAKES
for: RR TERMINUS
SLAM
Hmm...
Buy.
Yessir.
SNAP
The Doctor, if not the UPRR, is already turning a profit. He's a wily one.

Can his competition out-sneak him?

*Huntington,* you brilliant *sneak!* How did you do it?

SACRAMENTO, CA
FALL 1864 · CPRR

They'll certainly try.

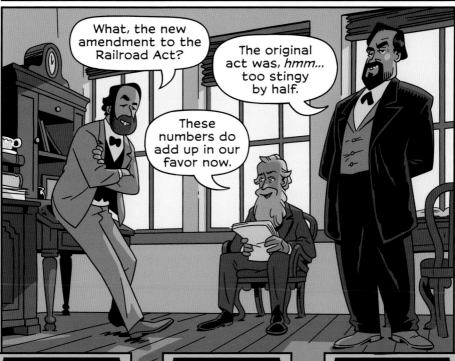

What, the new amendment to the Railroad Act?

The original act was, *hmm...* too stingy by half.

These numbers do add up in our favor now.

**Collis Huntington**
*CPRR Associate*
*"The Fixer"*

**Mark Hopkins**
*CPRR Associate*
*"The Brains"*

**Leland Stanford**
*CPRR Associate*
*"The Face"*

Meet the rest of the Central Pacific bosses, AKA "The Associates," AKA "The Big Four," AKA "Misters Monopoly."

Isn't it natural to support a company you own a piece of? Congressmen think the same as you or I do.

A *small gift* here and there smooths our path considerably.

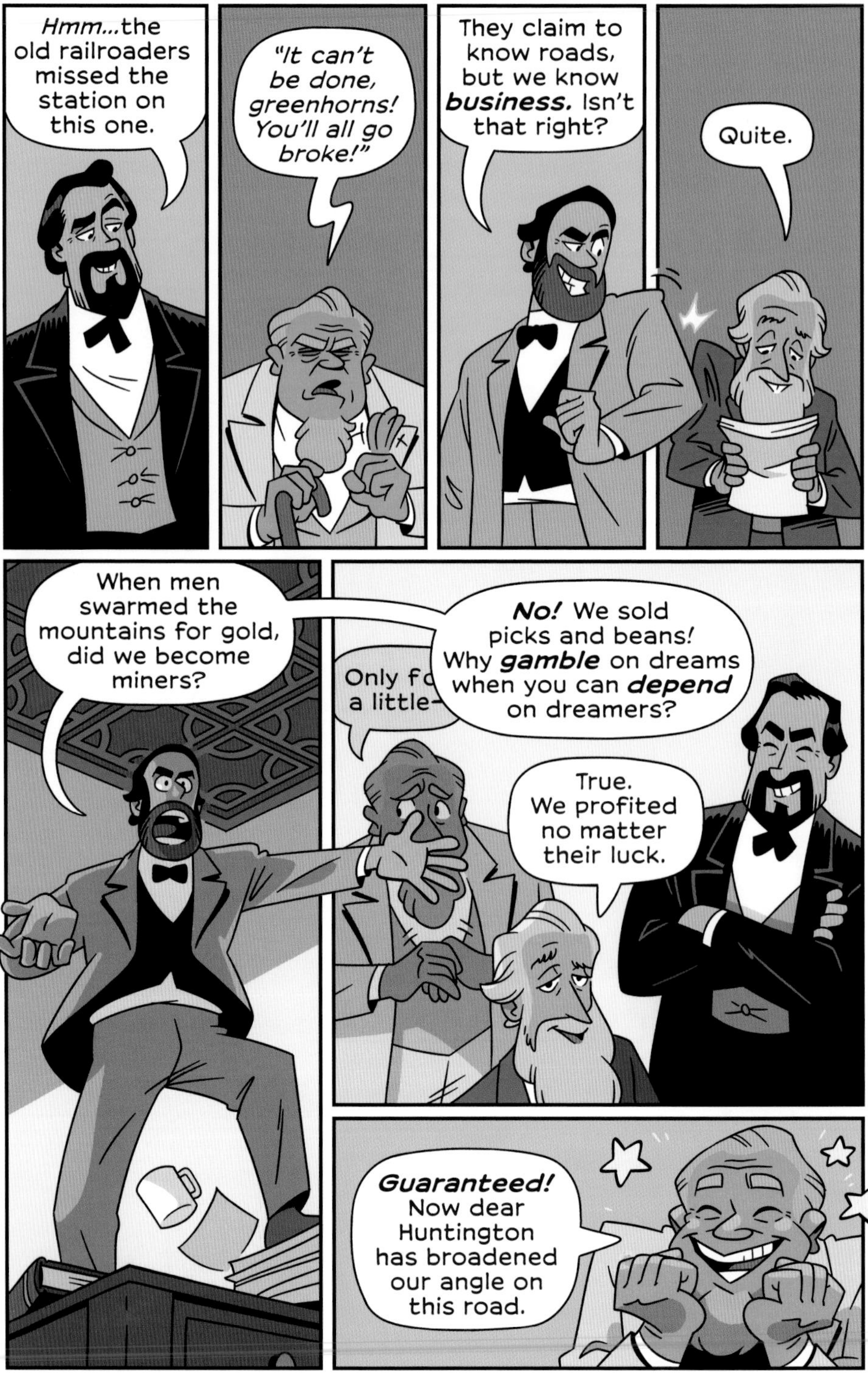

*Hmm...*the old railroaders missed the station on this one.
*"It can't be done, greenhorns! You'll all go broke!"*
They claim to know roads, but we know ***business.*** Isn't that right?
Quite.
When men swarmed the mountains for gold, did we become miners?
Only fo a little-
***No!*** We sold picks and beans! Why ***gamble*** on dreams when you can ***depend*** on dreamers?
True. We profited no matter their luck.
***Guaranteed!*** Now dear Huntington has broadened our angle on this road.

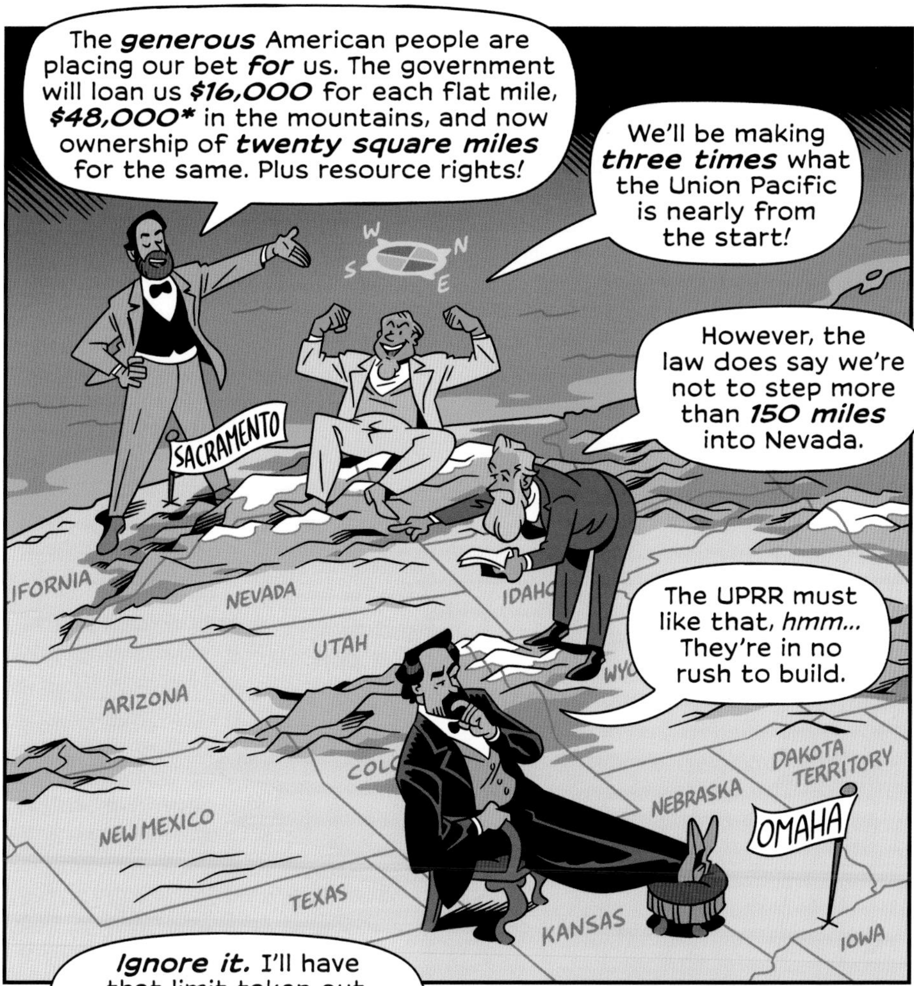
The *generous* American people are placing our bet *for* us. The government will loan us *$16,000* for each flat mile, *$48,000** in the mountains, and now ownership of *twenty square miles* for the same. Plus resource rights!
We'll be making *three times* what the Union Pacific is nearly from the start!
W
N
S
E
However, the law does say we're not to step more than *150 miles* into Nevada.
SACRAMENTO
IFORNIA
NEVADA
IDAH
UTAH
WYO
ARIZONA
The UPRR must like that, *hmm...* They're in no rush to build.
COLO
DAKOTA TERRITORY
NEBRASKA
OMAHA
NEW MEXICO
TEXAS
KANSAS
IOWA

*Worth many times more today

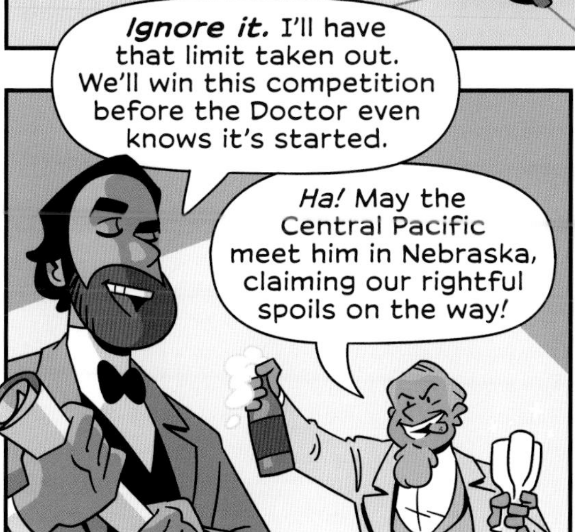
*Ignore it.* I'll have that limit taken out. We'll win this competition before the Doctor even knows it's started.
*Ha!* May the Central Pacific meet him in Nebraska, claiming our rightful spoils on the way!

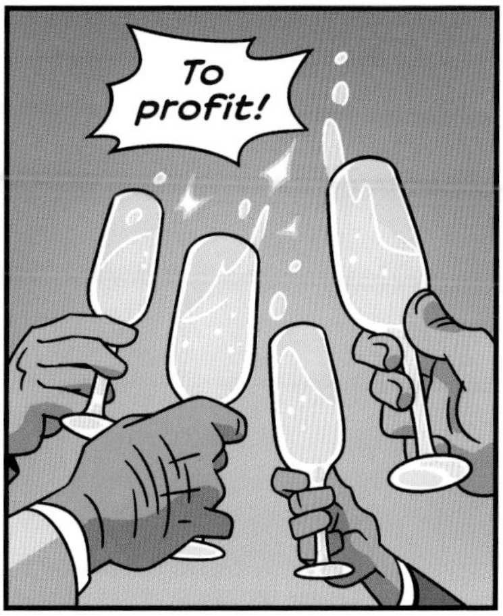
*To profit!*

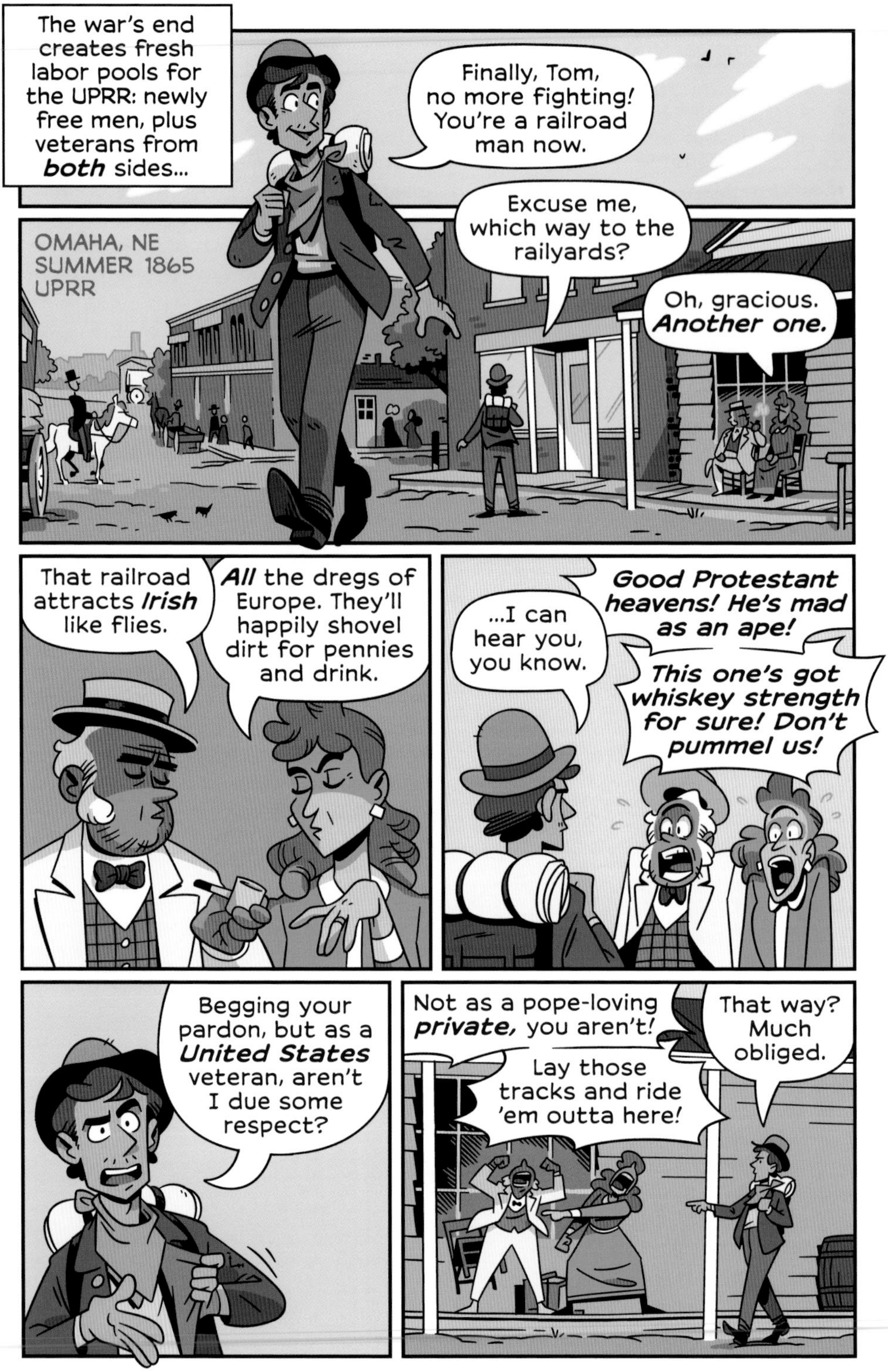
The war's end creates fresh labor pools for the UPRR: newly free men, plus veterans from **both** sides...
Finally, Tom, no more fighting! You're a railroad man now.
OMAHA, NE
SUMMER 1865
UPRR
Excuse me, which way to the railyards?
Oh, gracious. ***Another one.***
That railroad attracts *Irish* like flies.
***All*** the dregs of Europe. They'll happily shovel dirt for pennies and drink.
...I can hear you, you know.
***Good Protestant heavens! He's mad as an ape!***
***This one's got whiskey strength for sure! Don't pummel us!***
Begging your pardon, but as a ***United States*** veteran, aren't I due some respect?
Not as a pope-loving ***private,*** you aren't!
Lay those tracks and ride 'em outta here!
That way? Much obliged.

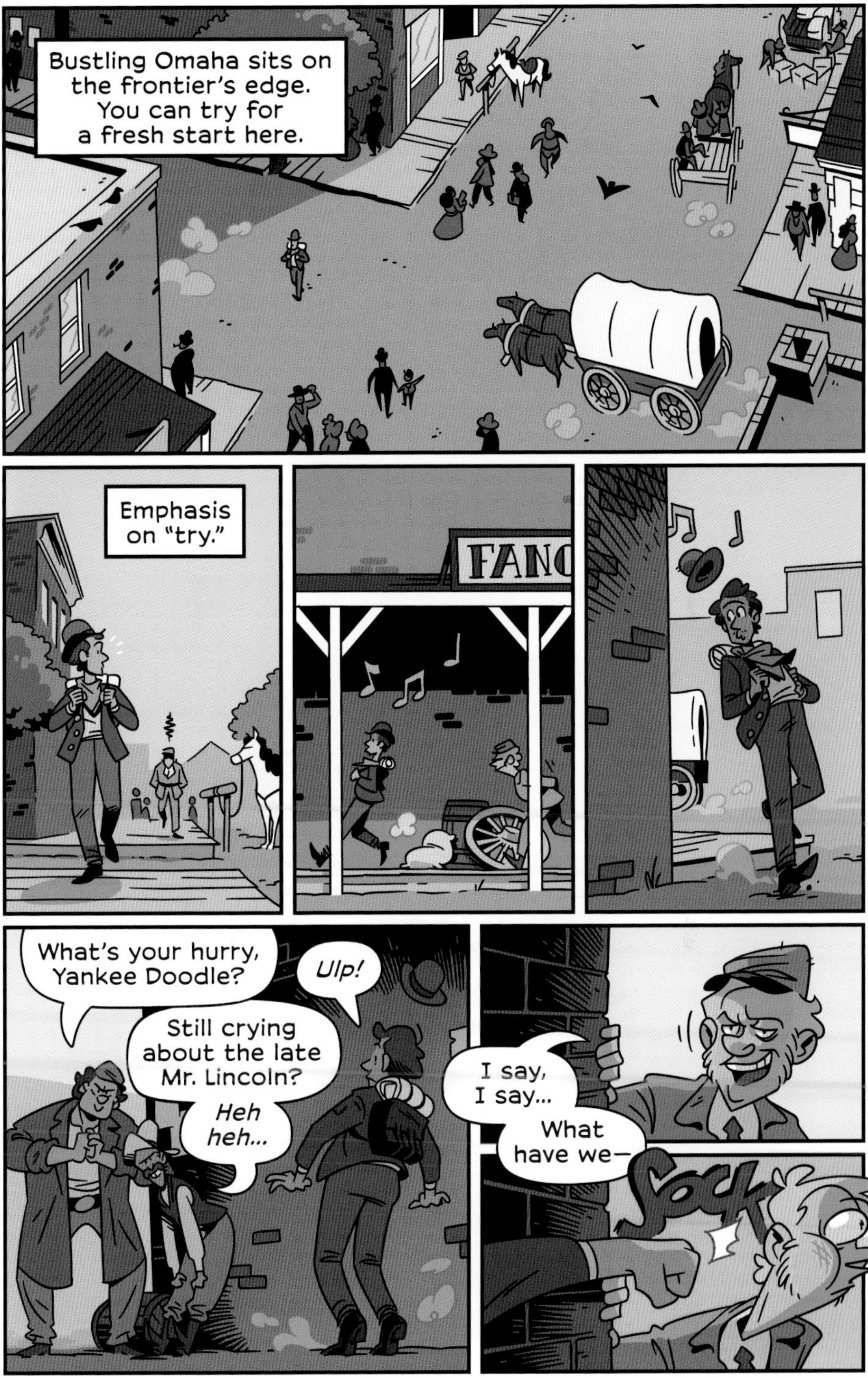
Bustling Omaha sits on the frontier's edge. You can try for a fresh start here.
Emphasis on "try."
FANC
What's your hurry, Yankee Doodle?
Ulp!
Still crying about the late Mr. Lincoln?
Heh heh...
I say, I say...
What have we—
SOCK

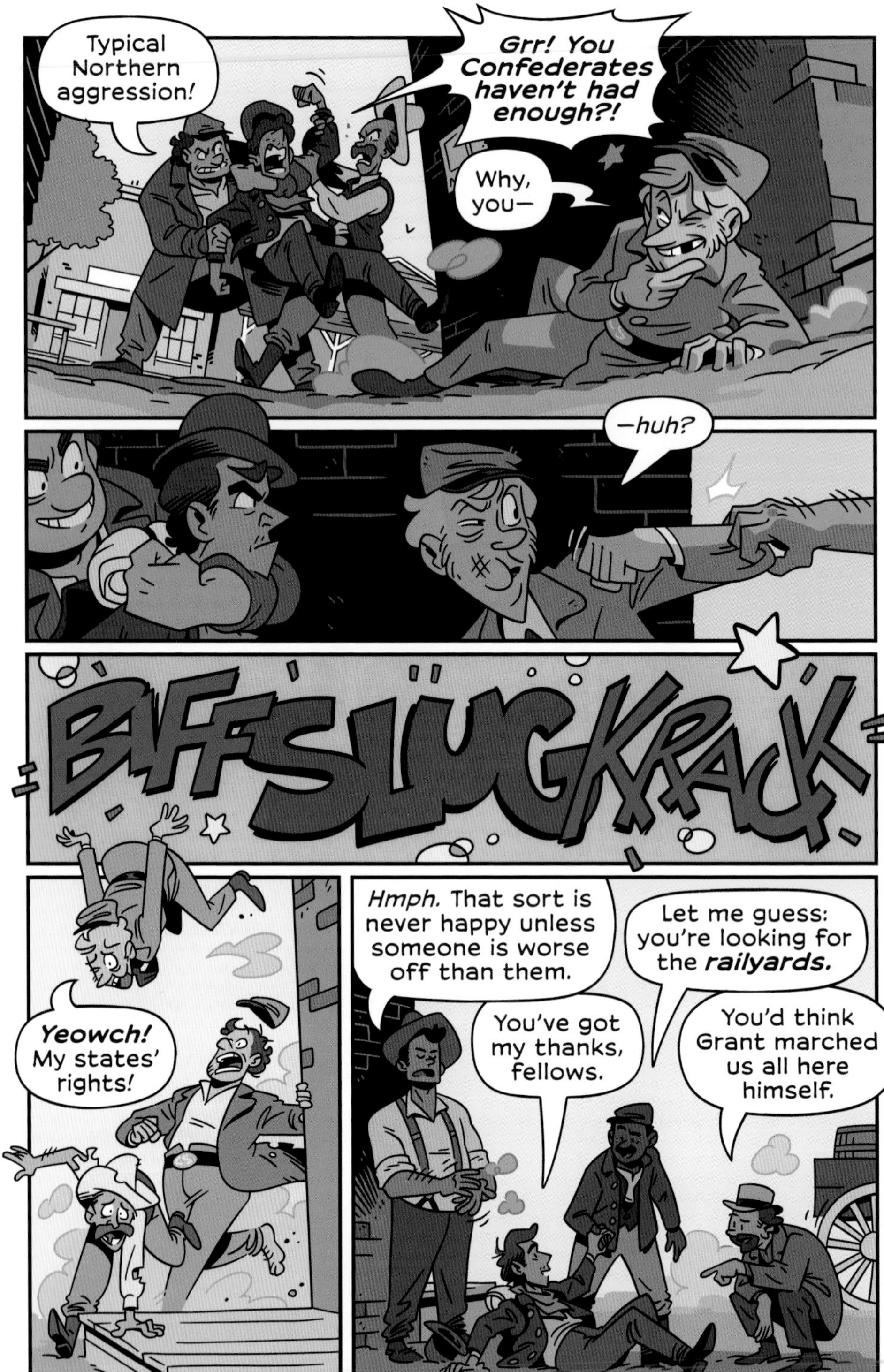
Typical Northern aggression!
Grr! You Confederates haven't had enough?!
Why, you—
—huh?
BAFF SLUG KRACK
Yeowch! My states' rights!
Hmph. That sort is never happy unless someone is worse off than them.
You've got my thanks, fellows.
Let me guess: you're looking for the railyards.
You'd think Grant marched us all here himself.

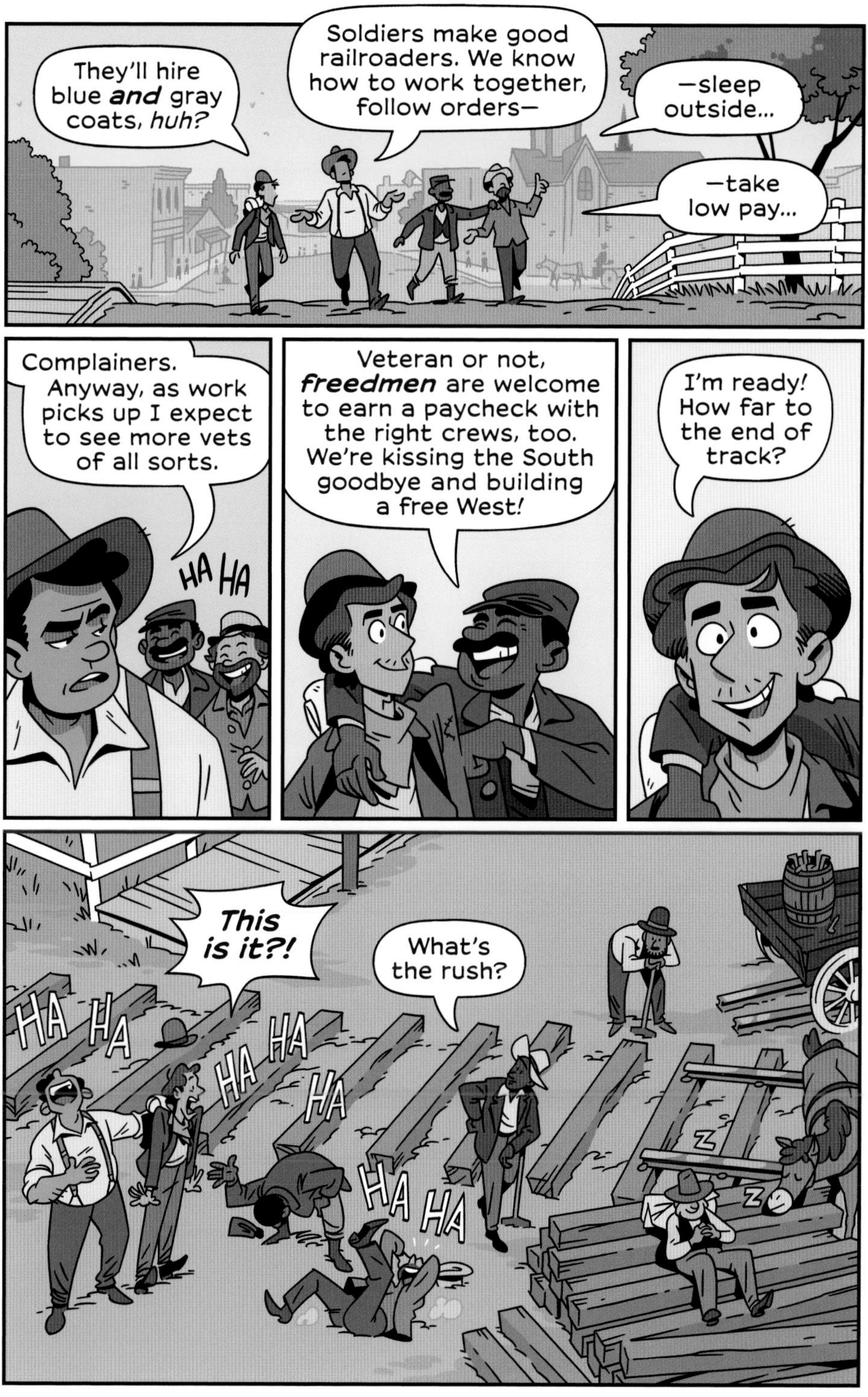

They'll hire blue *and* gray coats, *huh?*
Soldiers make good railroaders. We know how to work together, follow orders—
—sleep outside...
—take low pay...
Complainers. Anyway, as work picks up I expect to see more vets of all sorts.
HA HA
Veteran or not, *freedmen* are welcome to earn a paycheck with the right crews, too. We're kissing the South goodbye and building a free West!
I'm ready! How far to the end of track?
*This is it?!*
What's the rush?
HA HA
HA HA
HA
HA HA
Z
Z

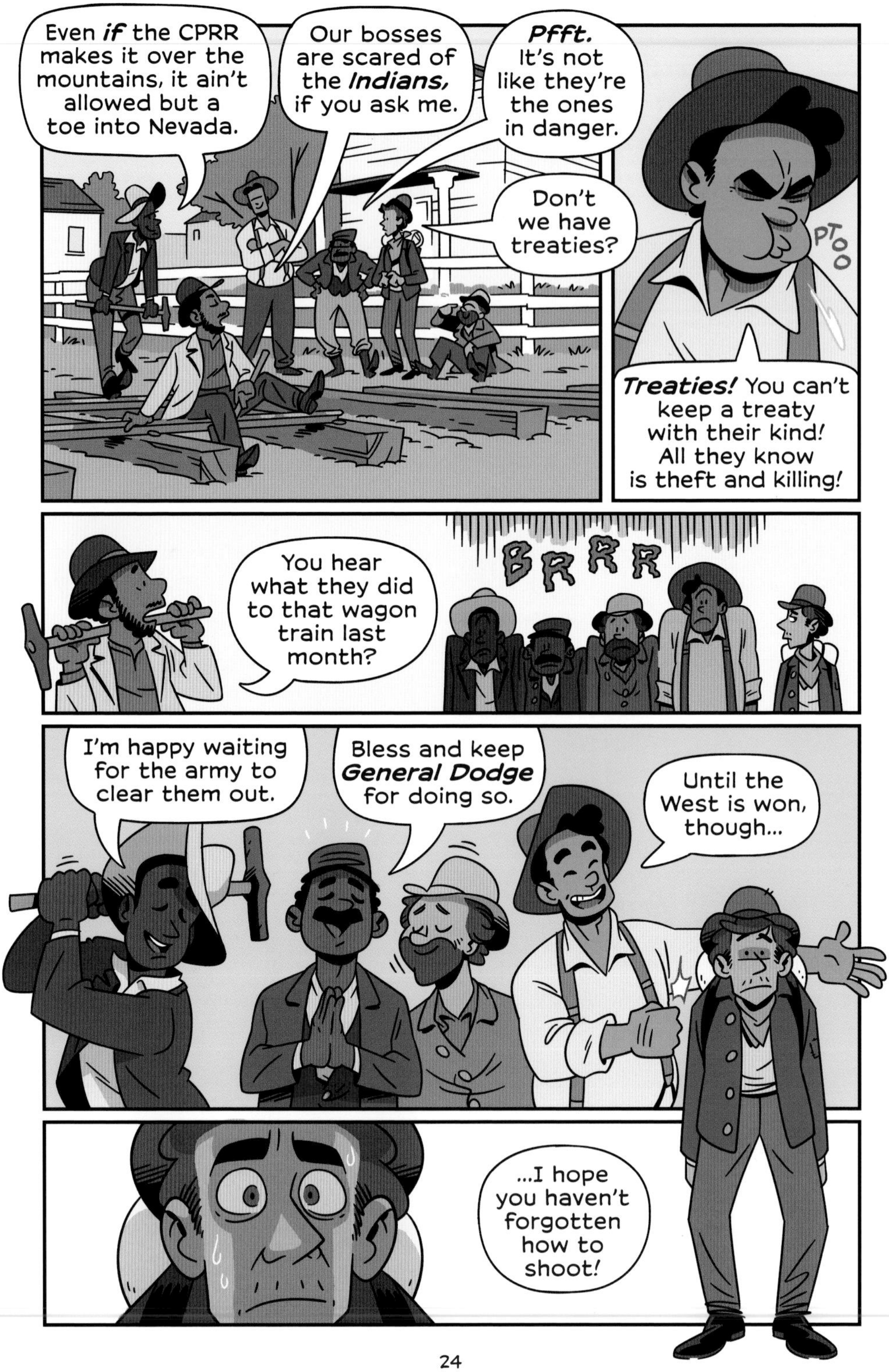
Even *if* the CPRR makes it over the mountains, it ain't allowed but a toe into Nevada.
Our bosses are scared of the *Indians,* if you ask me.
*Pfft.* It's not like they're the ones in danger.
Don't we have treaties?
PTOO
*Treaties!* You can't keep a treaty with their kind! All they know is theft and killing!
You hear what they did to that wagon train last month?
BRRR
I'm happy waiting for the army to clear them out.
Bless and keep *General Dodge* for doing so.
Until the West is won, though...
...I hope you haven't forgotten how to shoot!

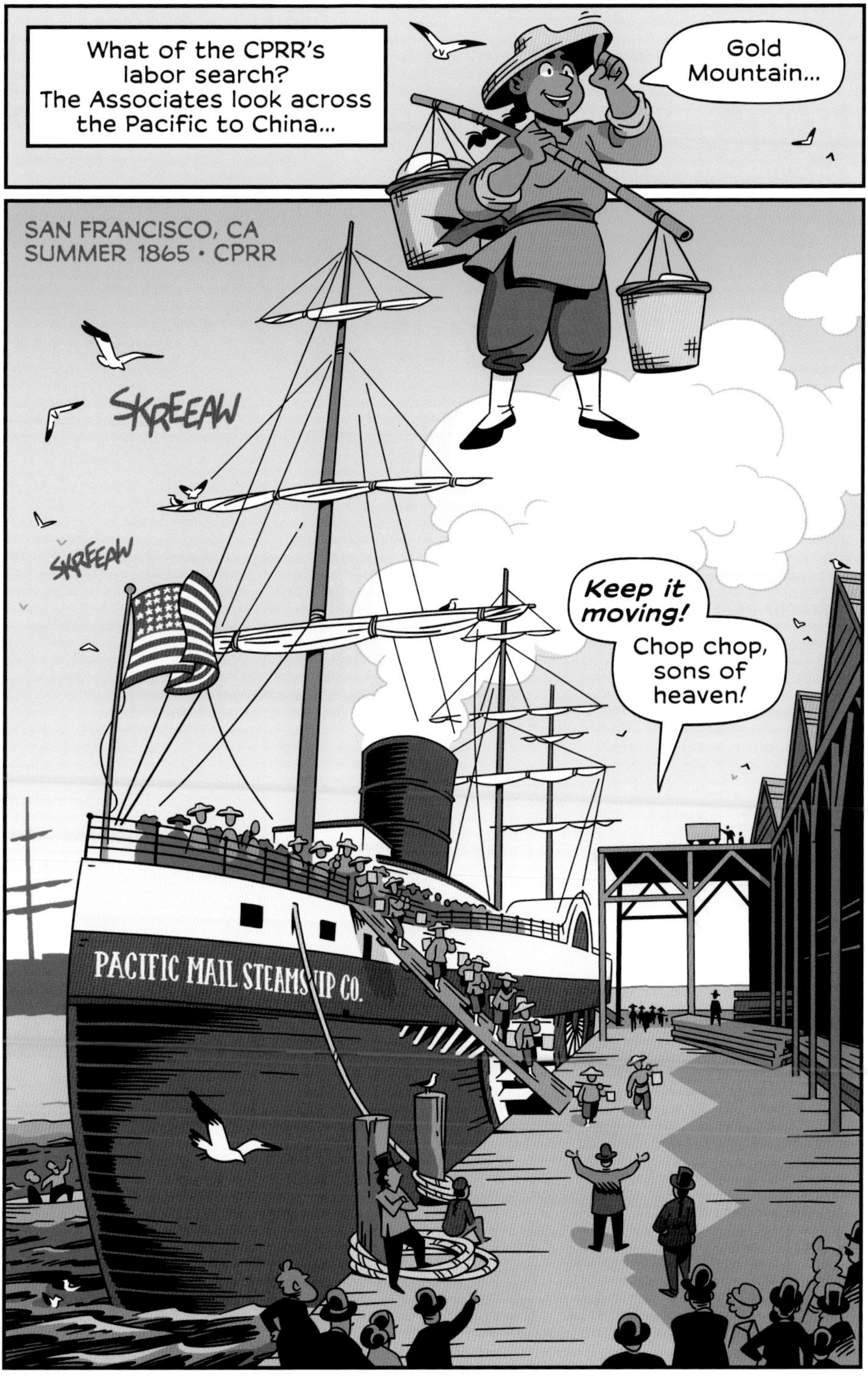
What of the CPRR's labor search? The Associates look across the Pacific to China...
Gold Mountain...
SAN FRANCISCO, CA
SUMMER 1865 • CPRR
SKREEAW
SKREEAW
Keep it moving!
Chop chop, sons of heaven!
PACIFIC MAIL STEAMSHIP CO.

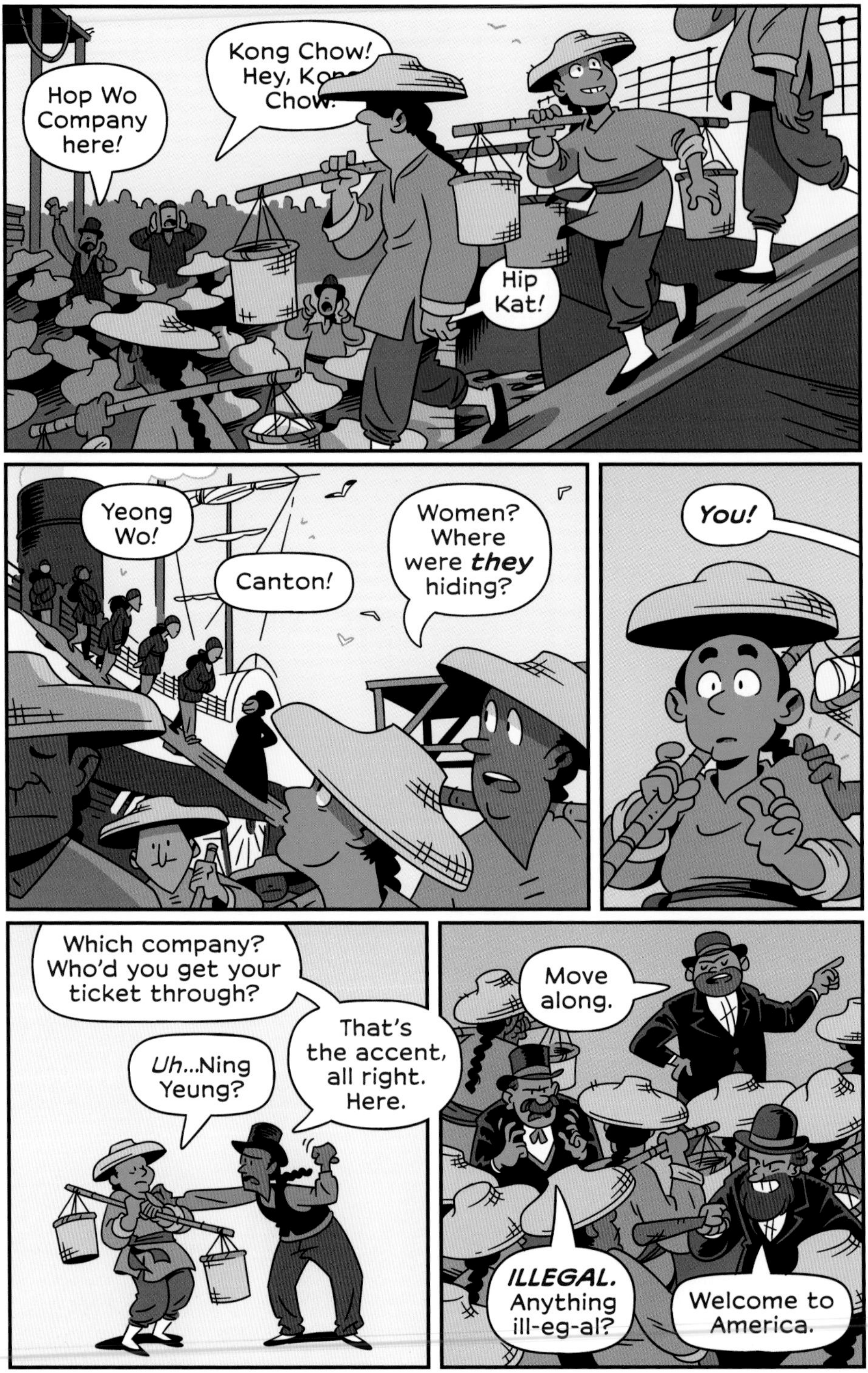
Hop Wo Company here!
Kong Chow! Hey, Kong Chow!
Hip Kat!
Yeong Wo!
Canton!
Women? Where were *they* hiding?
*You!*
Which company? Who'd you get your ticket through?
*Uh*...Ning Yeung?
That's the accent, all right. Here.
Move along.
*ILLEGAL.* Anything ill-eg-al?
Welcome to America.

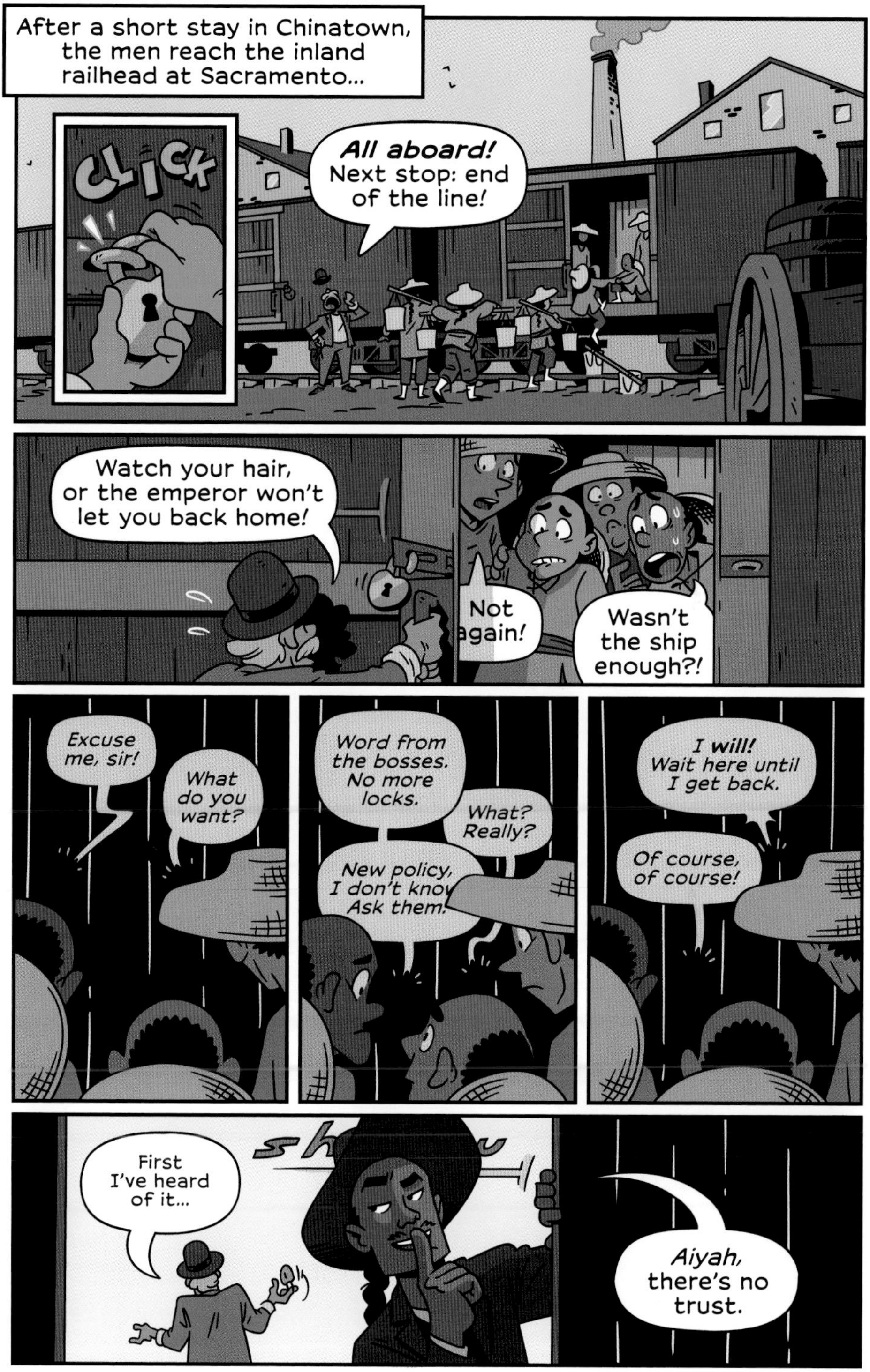
After a short stay in Chinatown, the men reach the inland railhead at Sacramento...
CLICK
All aboard! Next stop: end of the line!
Watch your hair, or the emperor won't let you back home!
Not again!
Wasn't the ship enough?!
Excuse me, sir!
What do you want?
Word from the bosses. No more locks.
What? Really?
New policy, I don't know. Ask them.
I will! Wait here until I get back.
Of course, of course!
First I've heard of it...
Aiyah, there's no trust.

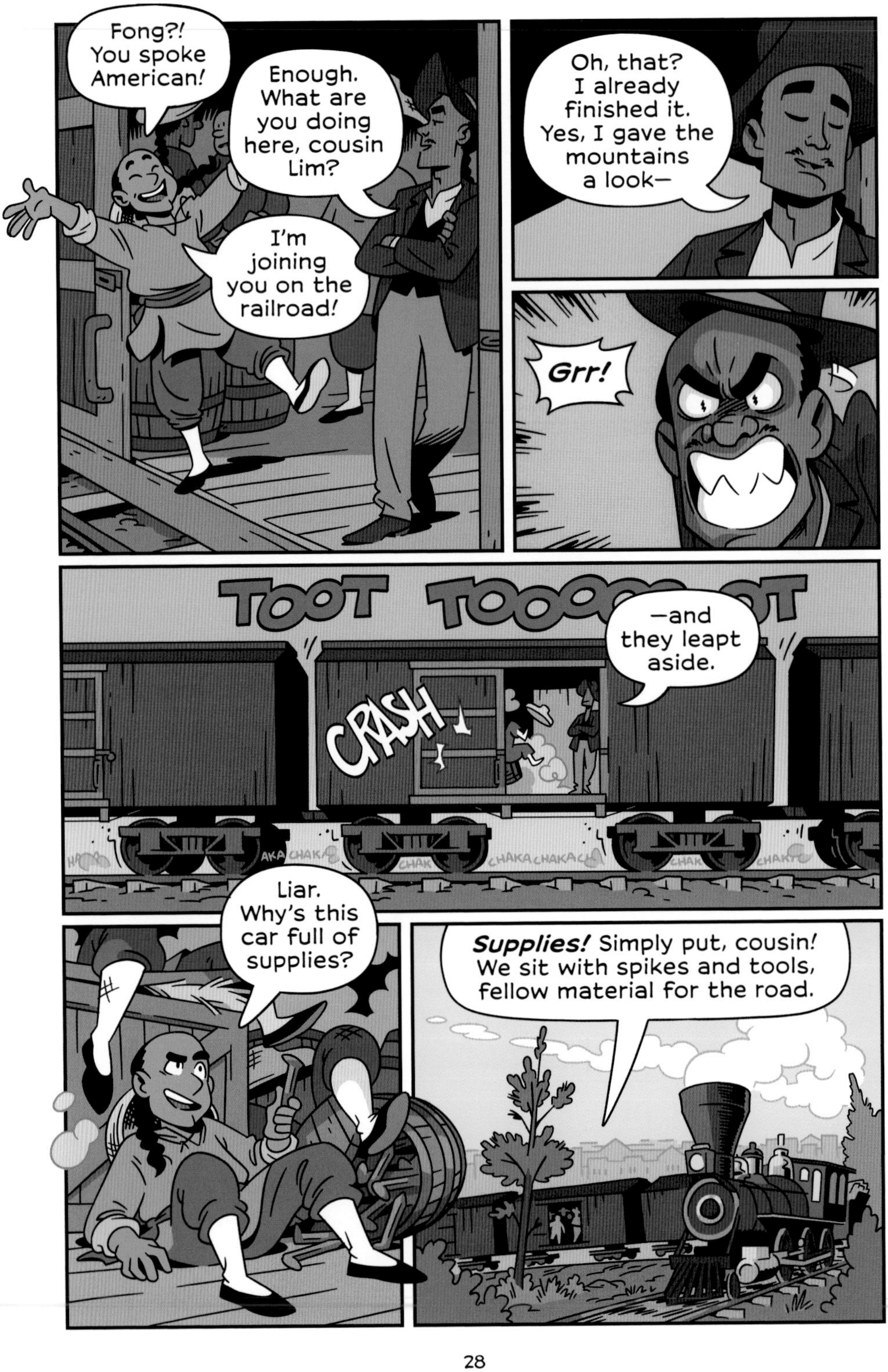
Fong?! You spoke American!
Enough. What are you doing here, cousin Lim?
I'm joining you on the railroad!
Oh, that? I already finished it. Yes, I gave the mountains a look—
Grr!
TOOT TOOOO OT
—and they leapt aside.
CRASH
Liar. Why's this car full of supplies?
*Supplies!* Simply put, cousin! We sit with spikes and tools, fellow material for the road.

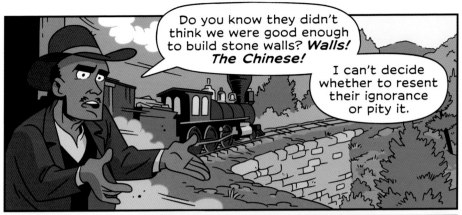

Do you know they didn't think we were good enough to build stone walls? **Walls!** **The Chinese!**

I can't decide whether to resent their ignorance or pity it.

*Hmm,* why not both?

What does he mean?

Should we have come?

Stop your negativity! This is *Gold Mountain,* where fortunes are made!

Hey, hey! I'm here, aren't I?

But understand: at home you all sold your crops or crafts, yes?

During the Gold Rush years, I sold flakes and nuggets.

This is different. *New.* We sell the railroad our *labor.*

SKWEEEE

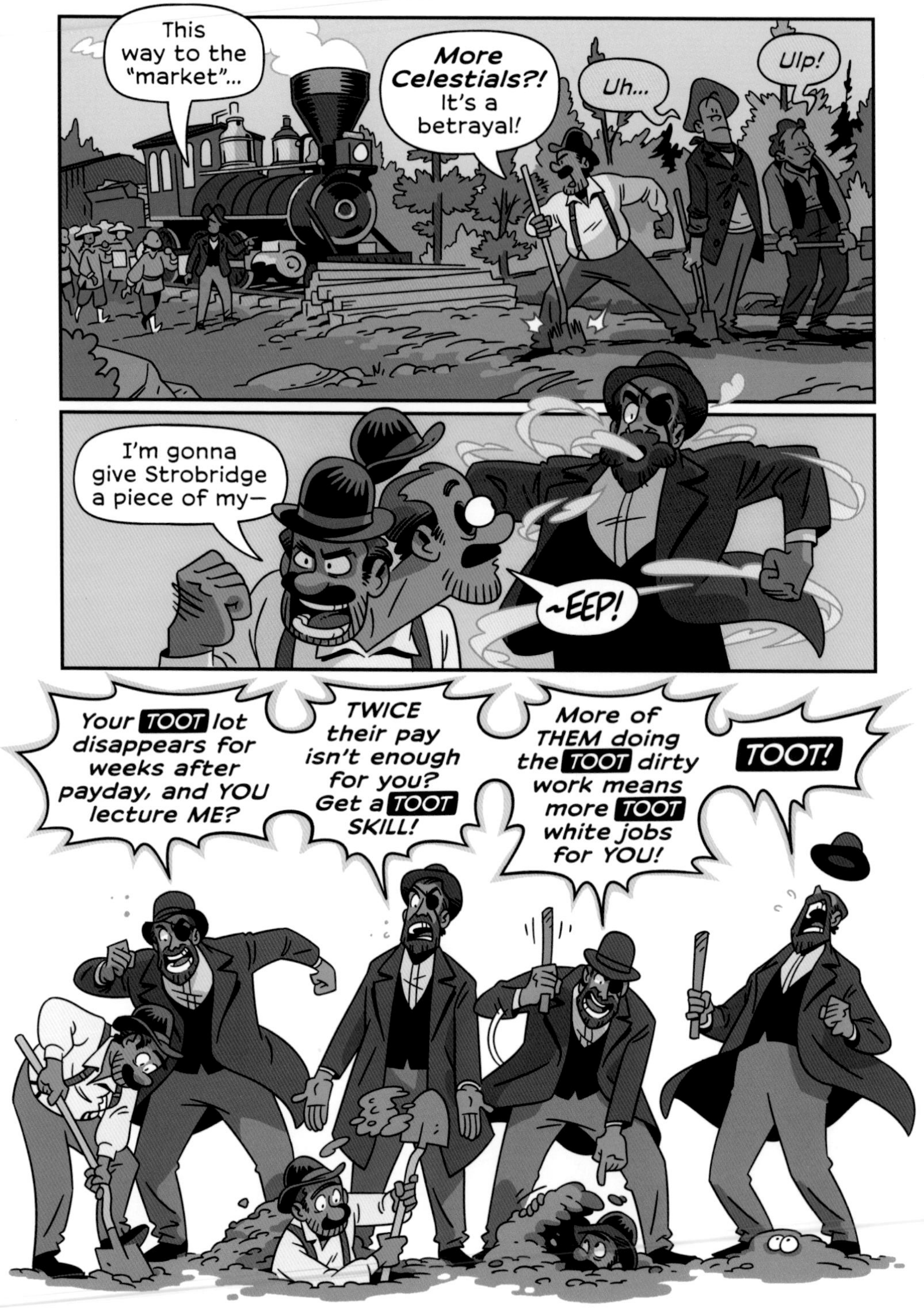
This way to the "market"...
*More Celestials?!* It's a betrayal!
Uh...
Ulp!
I'm gonna give Strobridge a piece of my—
~EEP!
Your TOOT lot disappears for weeks after payday, and YOU lecture ME?
TWICE their pay isn't enough for you? Get a TOOT SKILL!
More of THEM doing the TOOT dirty work means more TOOT white jobs for YOU!
TOOT!

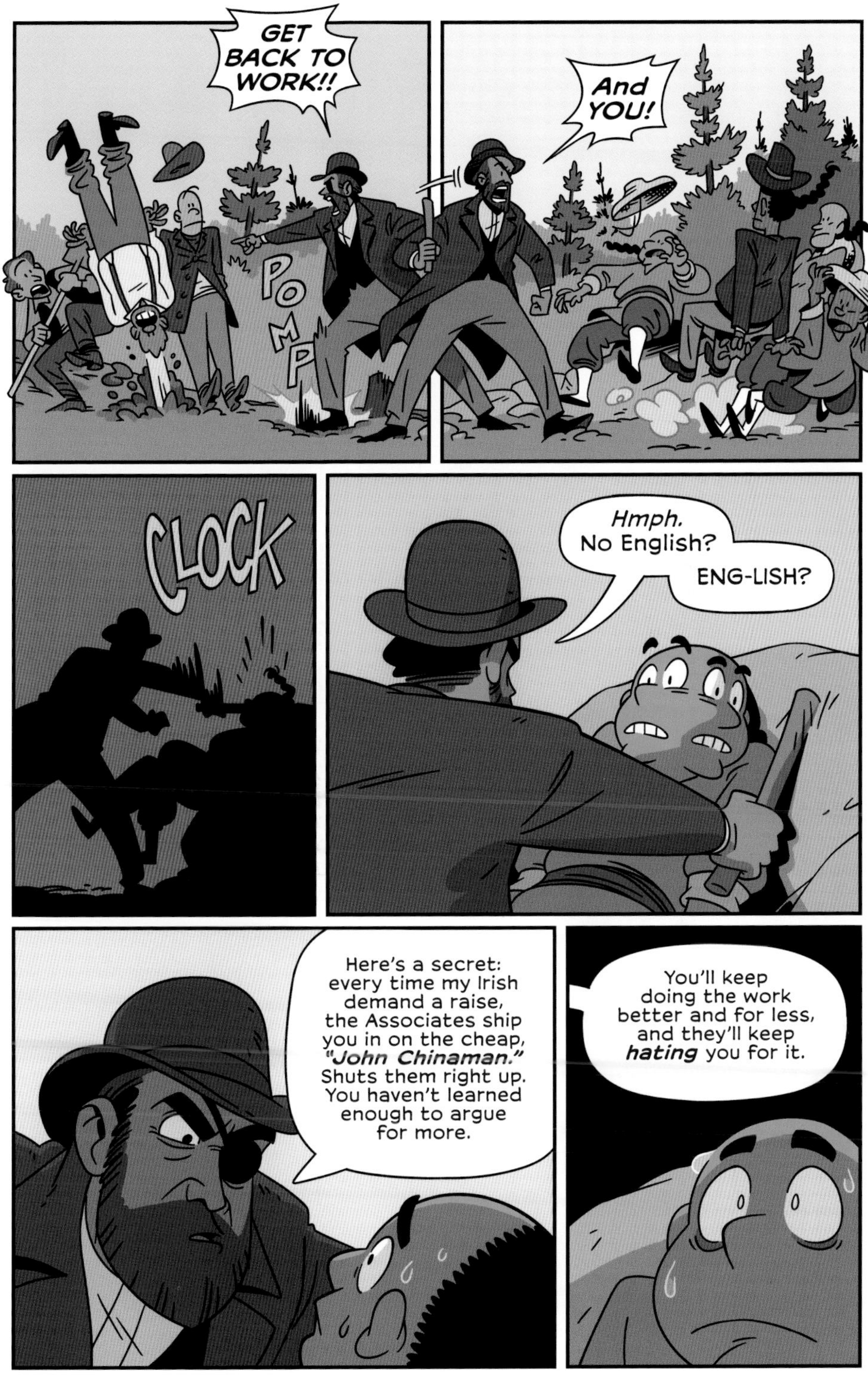
GET BACK TO WORK!!
POMP
And YOU!
CLOCK
Hmph. No English?
ENG-LISH?
Here's a secret: every time my Irish demand a raise, the Associates ship you in on the cheap, *"John Chinaman."* Shuts them right up. You haven't learned enough to argue for more.
You'll keep doing the work better and for less, and they'll keep *hating* you for it.

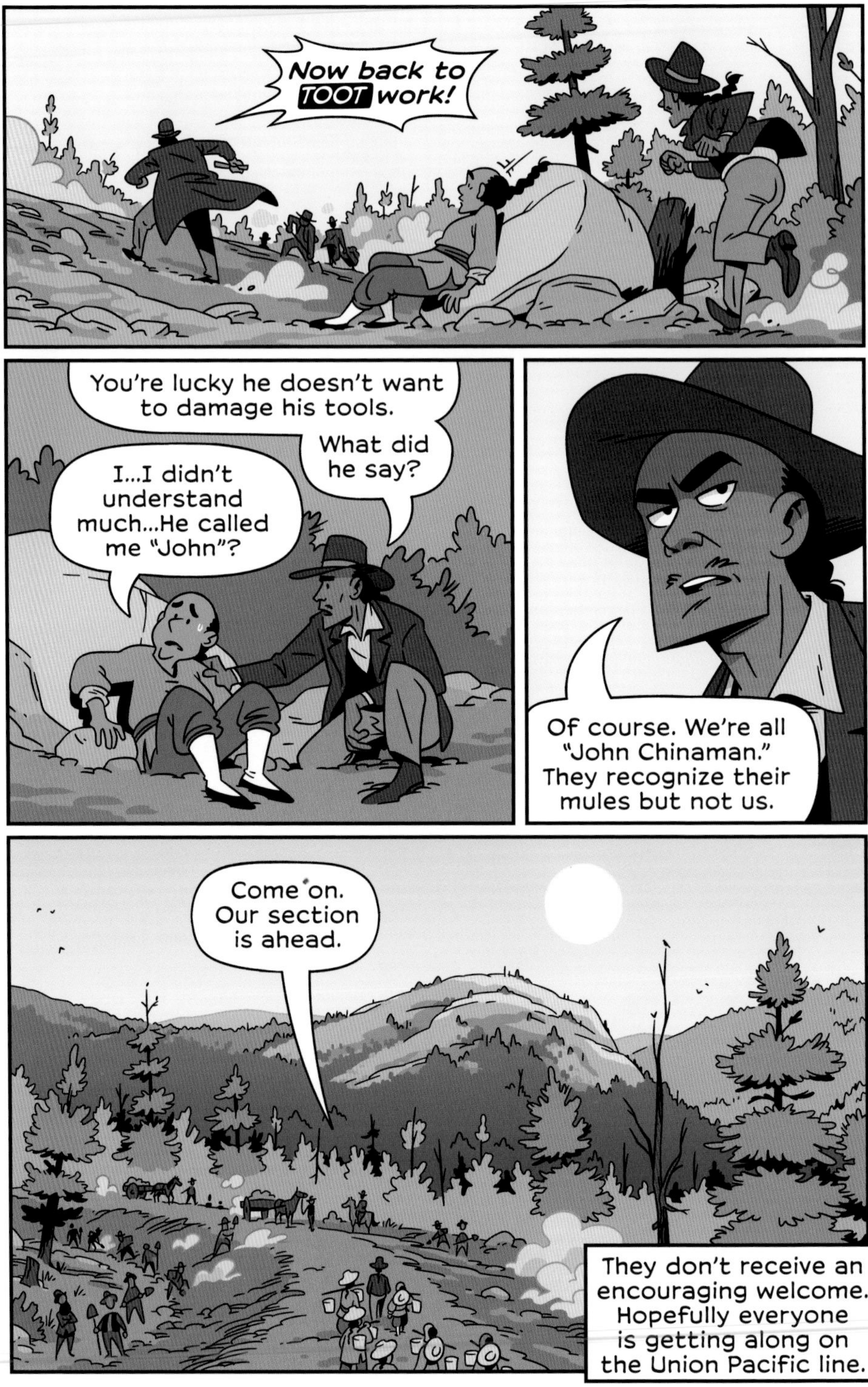
Now back to TOOT work!
You're lucky he doesn't want to damage his tools.
I...I didn't understand much...He called me "John"?
What did he say?
Of course. We're all "John Chinaman." They recognize their mules but not us.
Come on. Our section is ahead.
They don't receive an encouraging welcome. Hopefully everyone is getting along on the Union Pacific line.

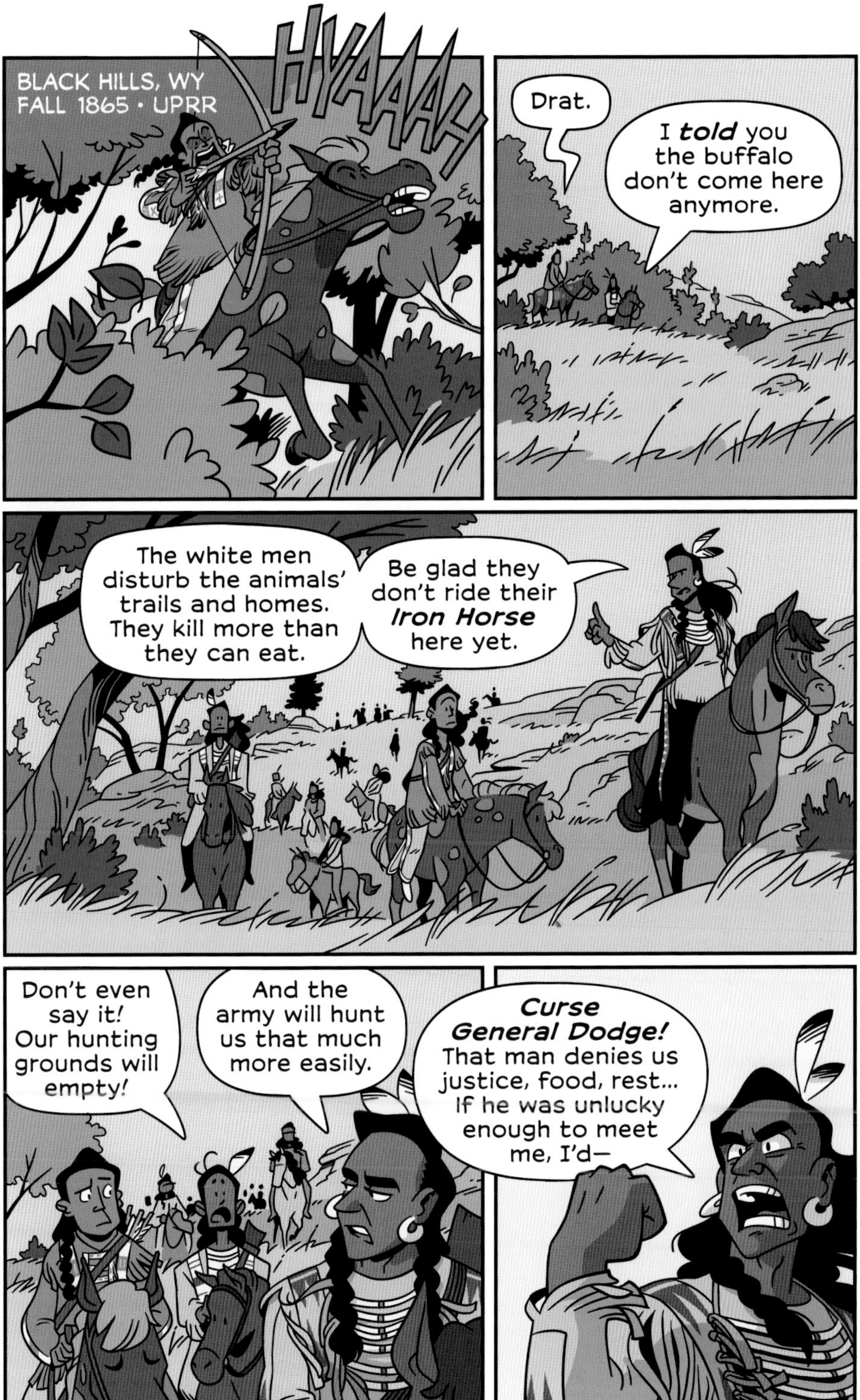
BLACK HILLS, WY
FALL 1865 • UPRR
HYAAAH
Drat.
I *told* you the buffalo don't come here anymore.
The white men disturb the animals' trails and homes. They kill more than they can eat.
Be glad they don't ride their *Iron Horse* here yet.
Don't even say it! Our hunting grounds will empty!
And the army will hunt us that much more easily.
*Curse General Dodge!* That man denies us justice, food, rest... If he was unlucky enough to meet me, I'd—

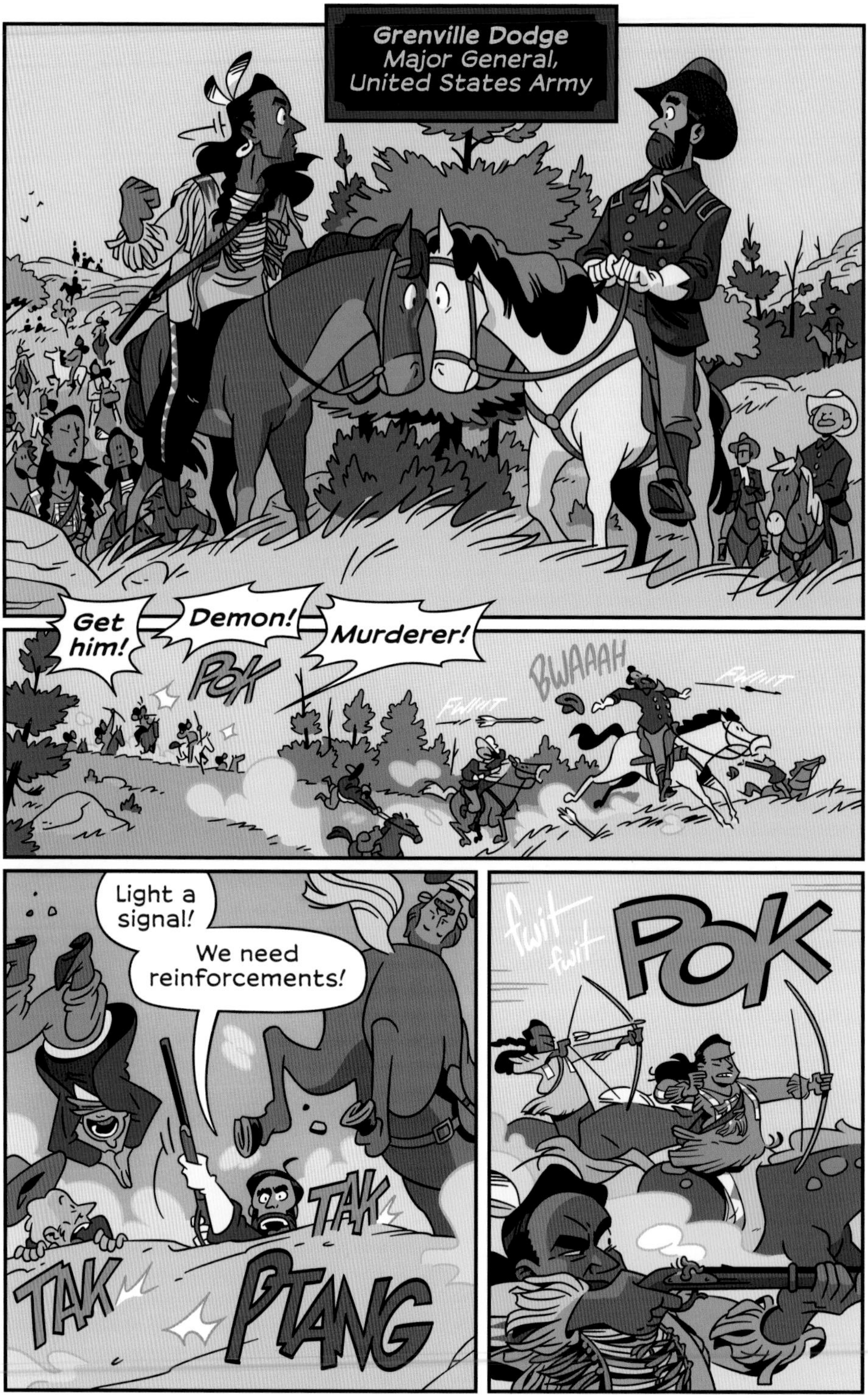

Grenville Dodge
Major General,
United States Army
Get him!
Demon!
Murderer!
POK
BWAAAH
FWIIT
FWIIT
Light a signal!
We need reinforcements!
TAK
TAK
PTANG
fwit
fwit
POK

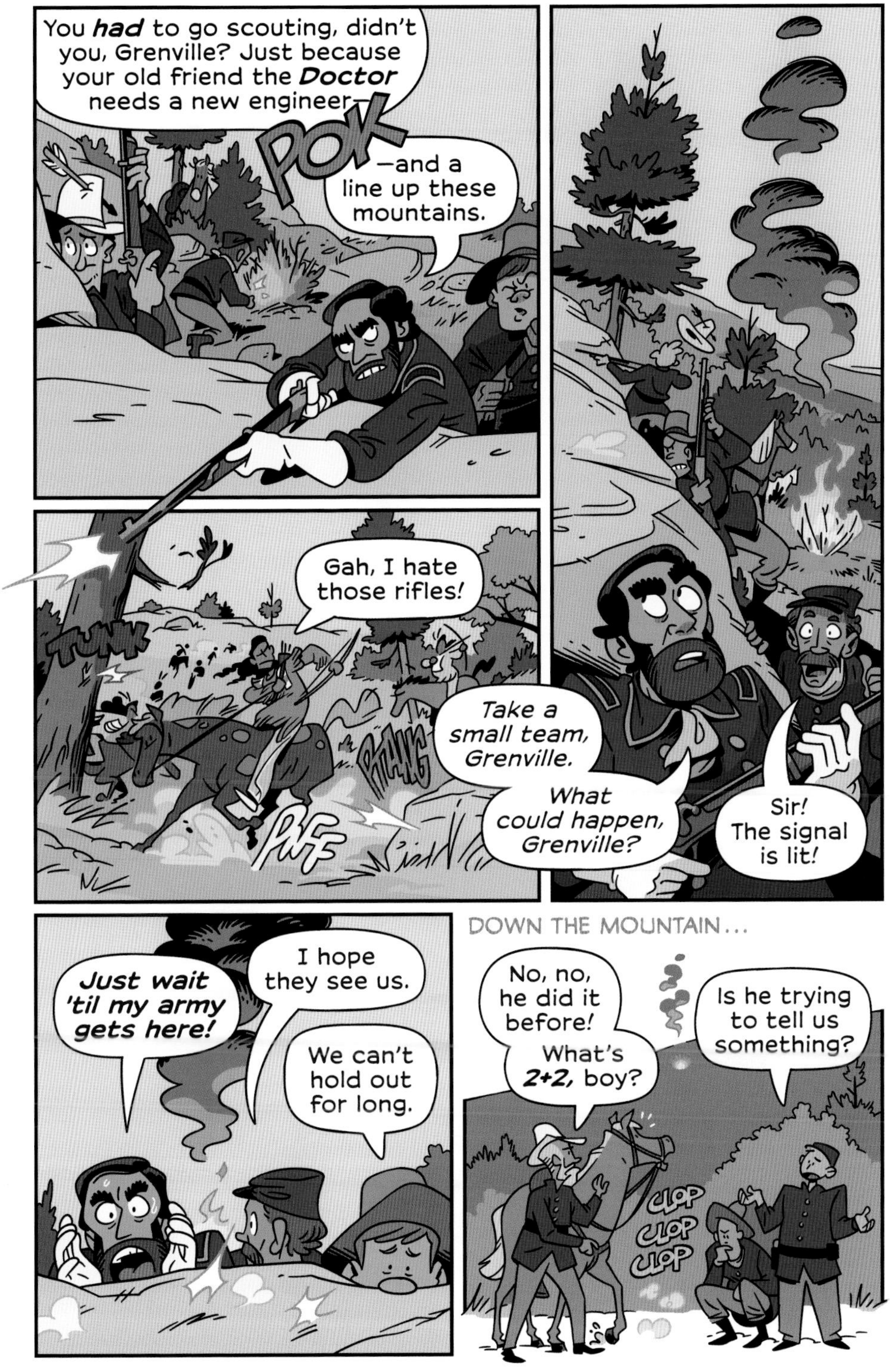
You *had* to go scouting, didn't you, Grenville? Just because your old friend the *Doctor* needs a new engineer—
POK
—and a line up these mountains.
Gah, I hate those rifles!
TUNK
PTANG
PWF
Take a small team, Grenville.
What could happen, Grenville?
Sir! The signal is lit!
Just wait 'til my army gets here!
I hope they see us.
We can't hold out for long.
DOWN THE MOUNTAIN...
No, no, he did it before!
What's 2+2, boy?
Is he trying to tell us something?
CLOP
CLOP
CLOP

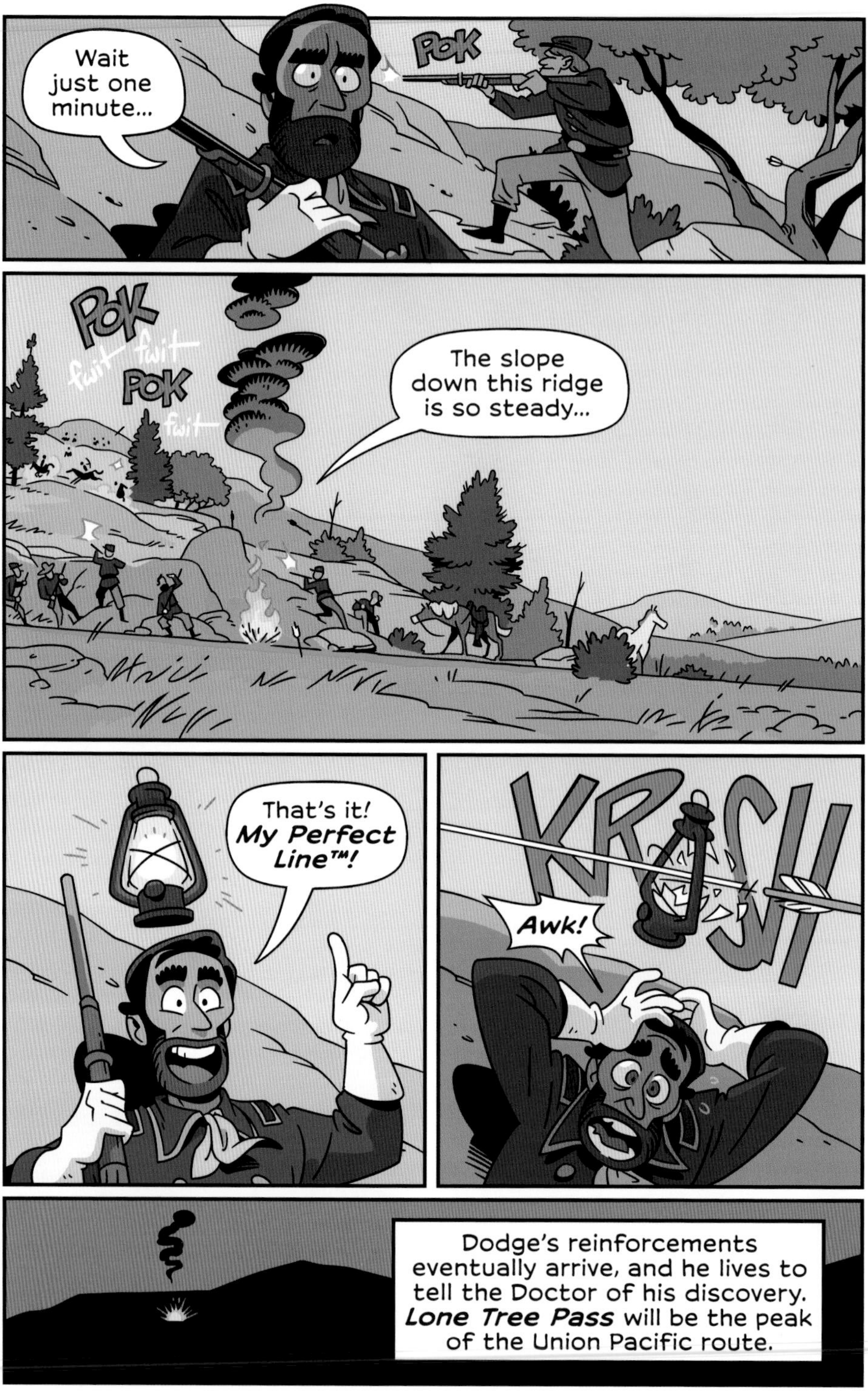
Wait just one minute...
POK
POK
fwit fwit
POK
fwit
The slope down this ridge is so steady...
That's it! *My Perfect Line™!*
KRASH
Awk!
Dodge's reinforcements eventually arrive, and he lives to tell the Doctor of his discovery. *Lone Tree Pass* will be the peak of the Union Pacific route.

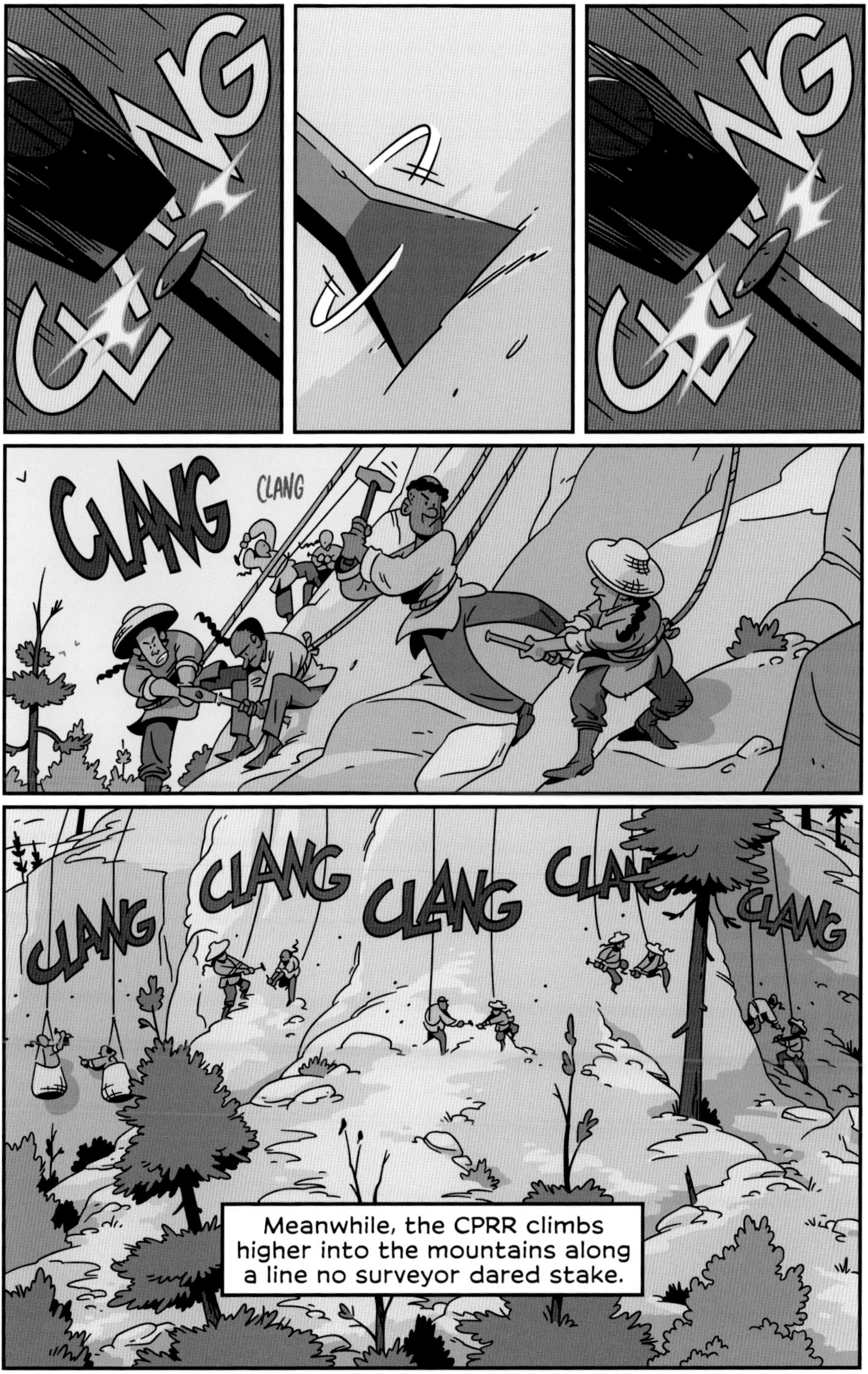
CLANG
CLANG
CLANG
CLANG
CLANG
CLANG
CLANG
CLANG
CLANG
Meanwhile, the CPRR climbs higher into the mountains along a line no surveyor dared stake.

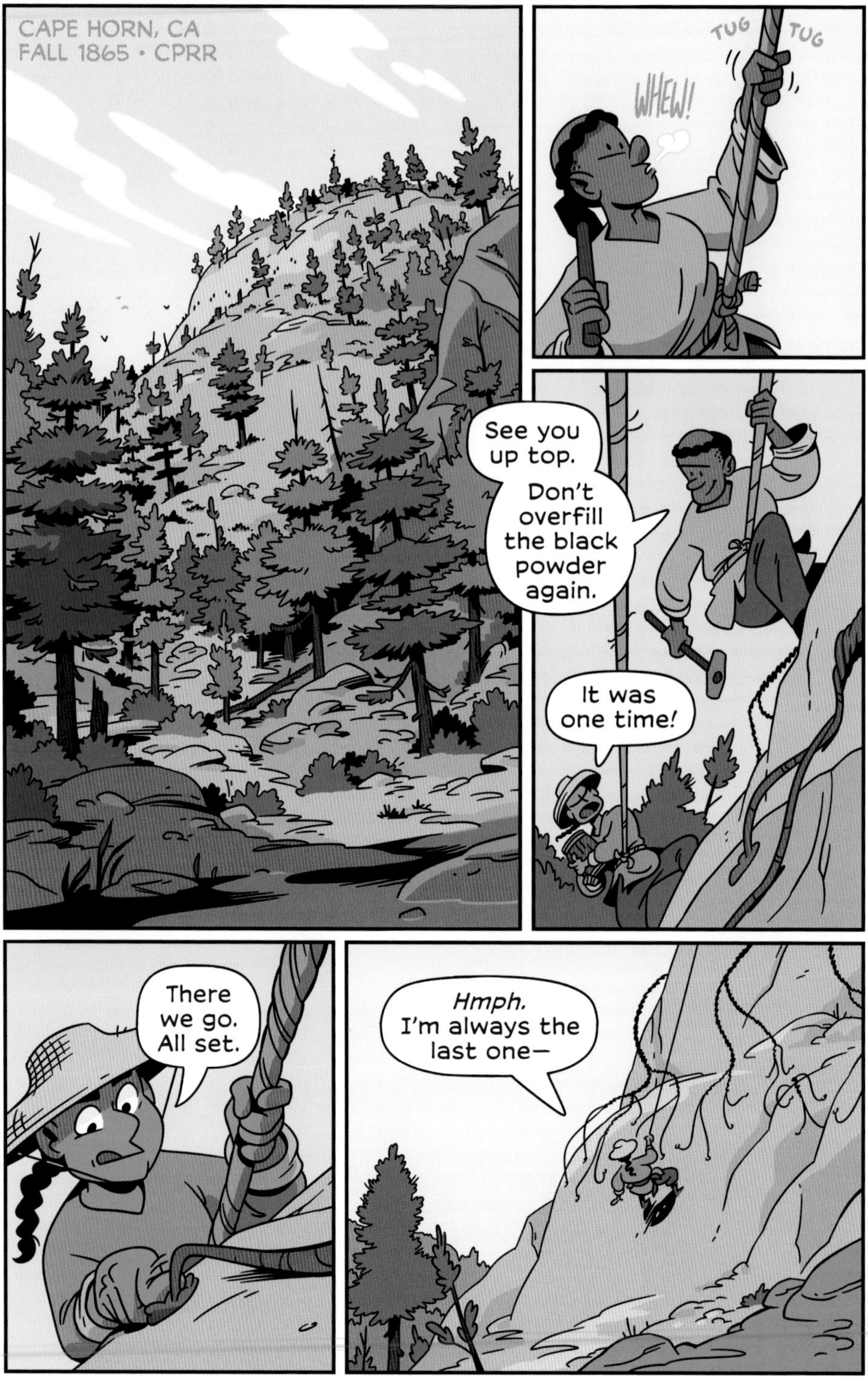
CAPE HORN, CA
FALL 1865 • CPRR
TUG TUG
WHEW!
See you up top.
Don't overfill the black powder again.
It was one time!
There we go. All set.
*Hmph.* I'm always the last one—

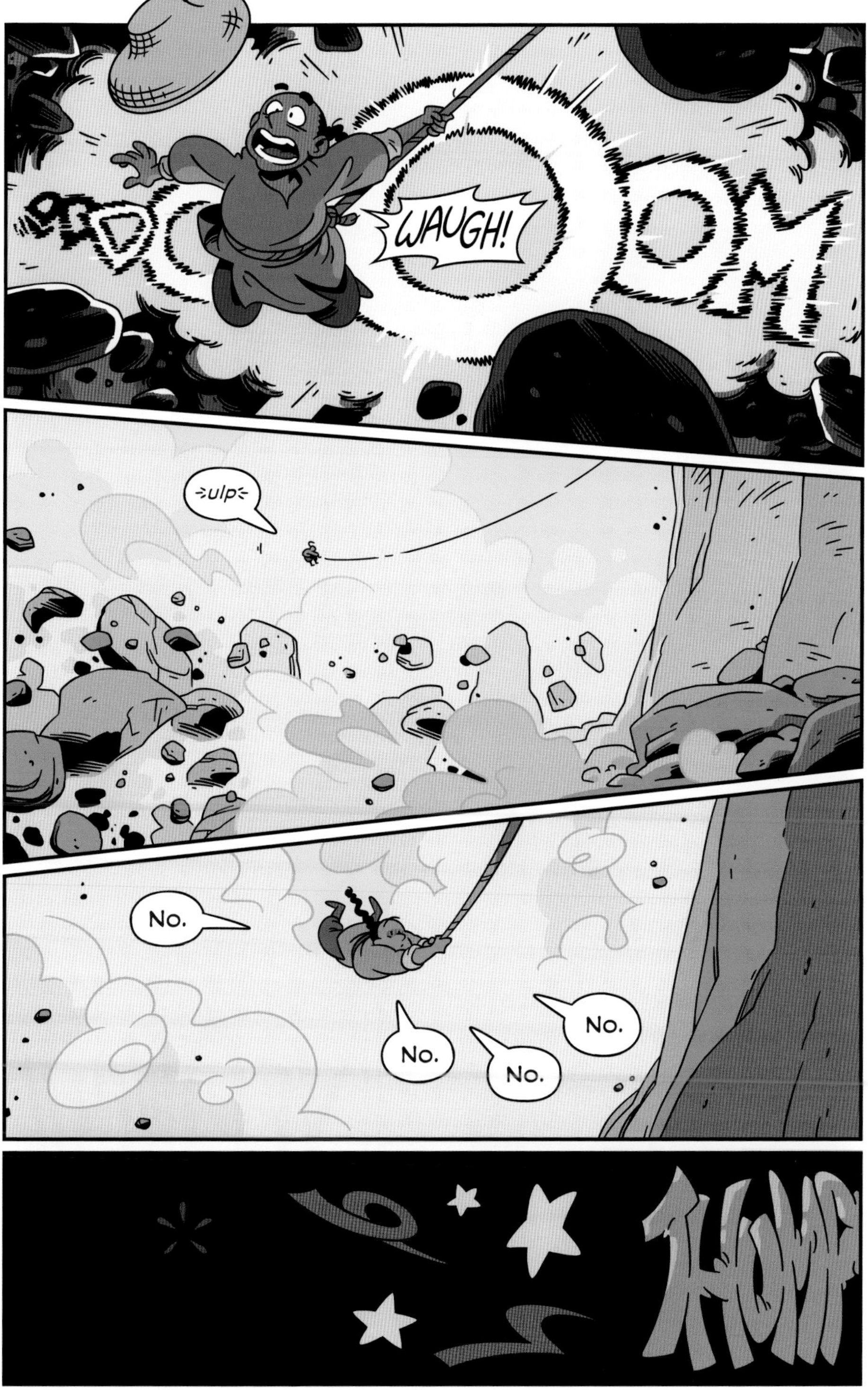
WAUGH!
ulp
No.
No.
No.
No.

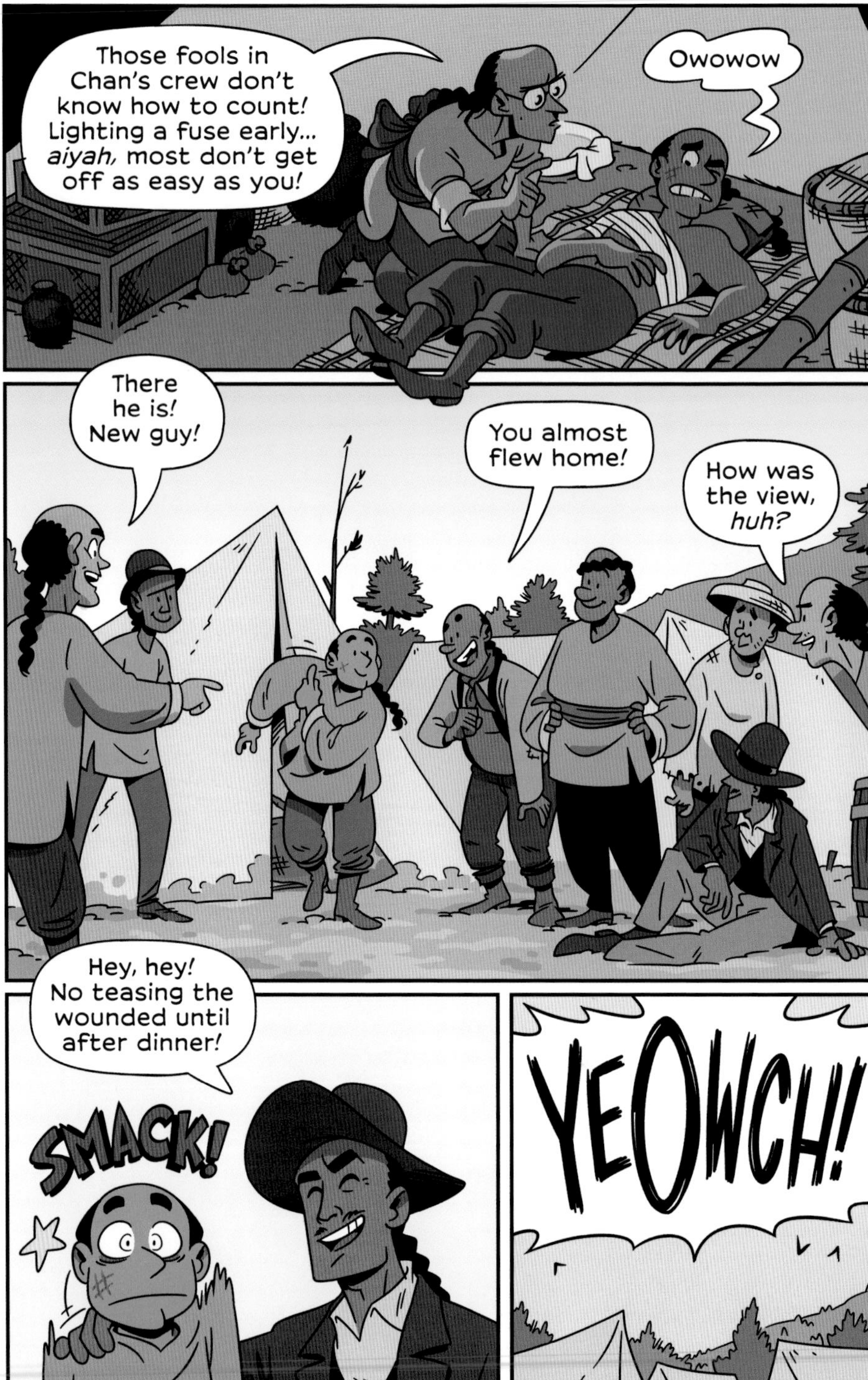
Those fools in Chan's crew don't know how to count! Lighting a fuse early... *aiyah,* most don't get off as easy as you!
Owowow
There he is! New guy!
You almost flew home!
How was the view, *huh?*
Hey, hey! No teasing the wounded until after dinner!
SMACK!
YEOWCH!

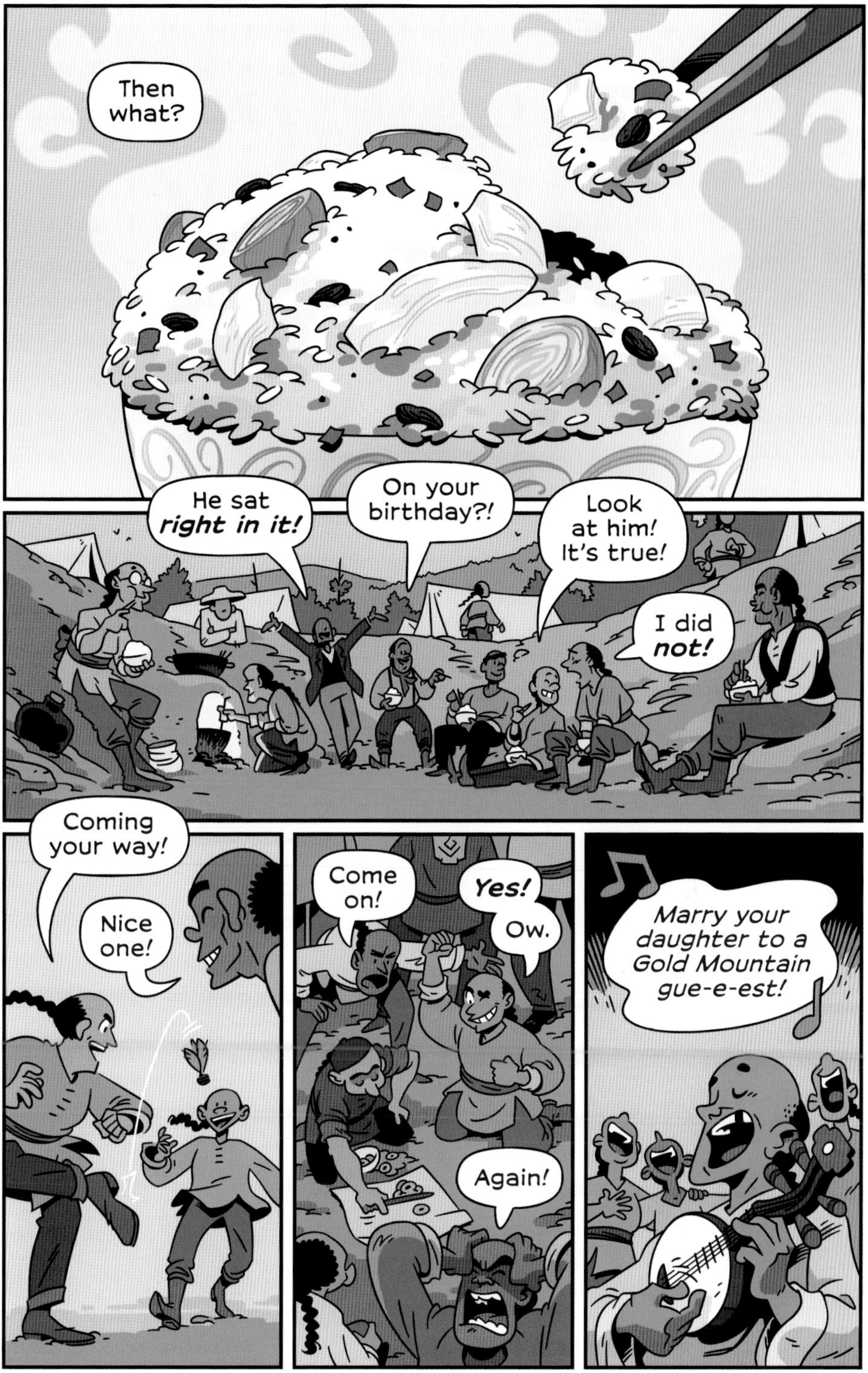
Then what?
He sat *right in it!*
On your birthday?!
Look at him! It's true!
I did *not!*
Coming your way!
Nice one!
Come on!
*Yes!*
Ow.
Again!
*Marry your daughter to a Gold Mountain gue-e-est!*

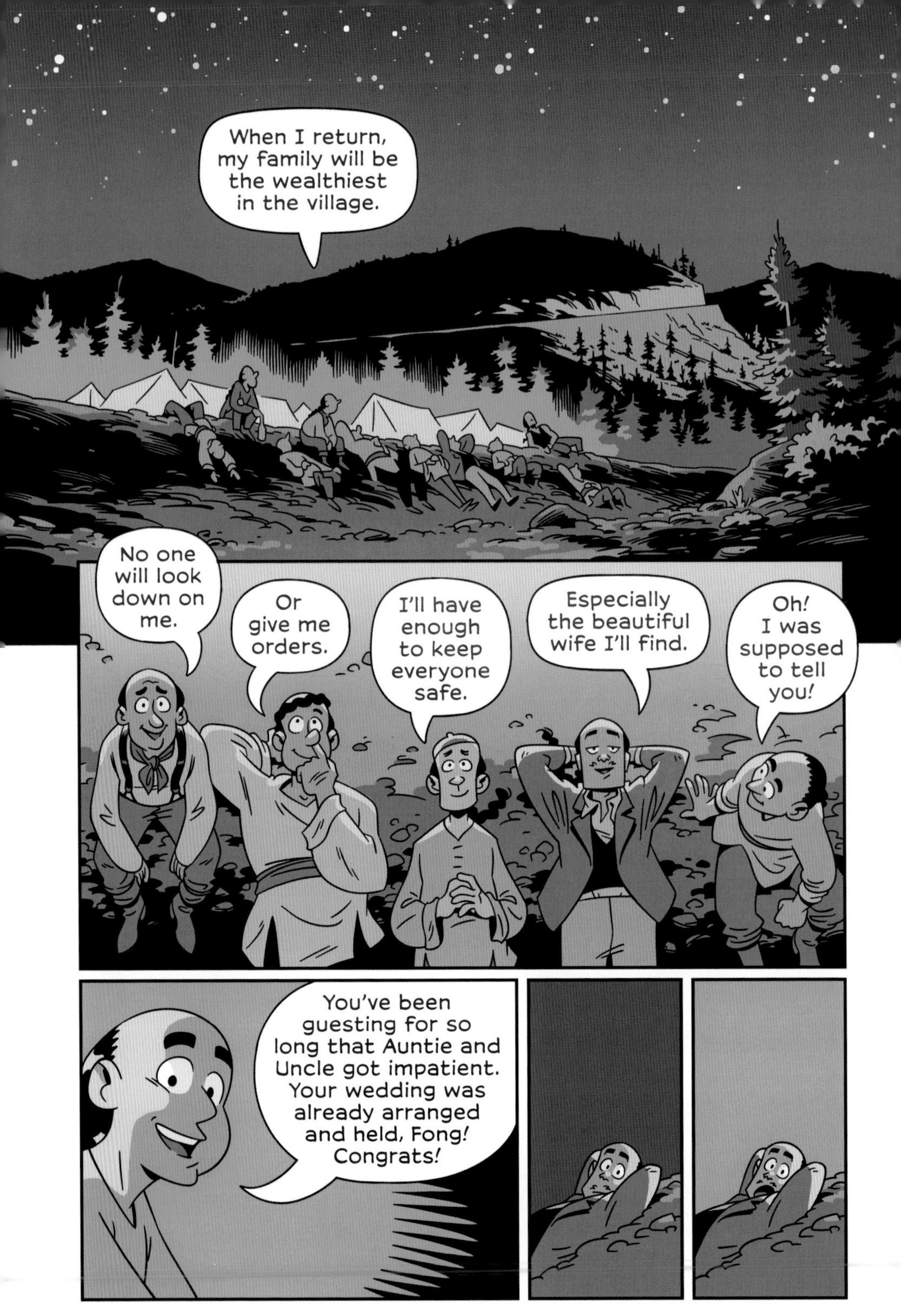
When I return, my family will be the wealthiest in the village.
No one will look down on me.
Or give me orders.
I'll have enough to keep everyone safe.
Especially the beautiful wife I'll find.
Oh! I was supposed to tell you!
You've been guesting for so long that Auntie and Uncle got impatient. Your wedding was already arranged and held, Fong! Congrats!

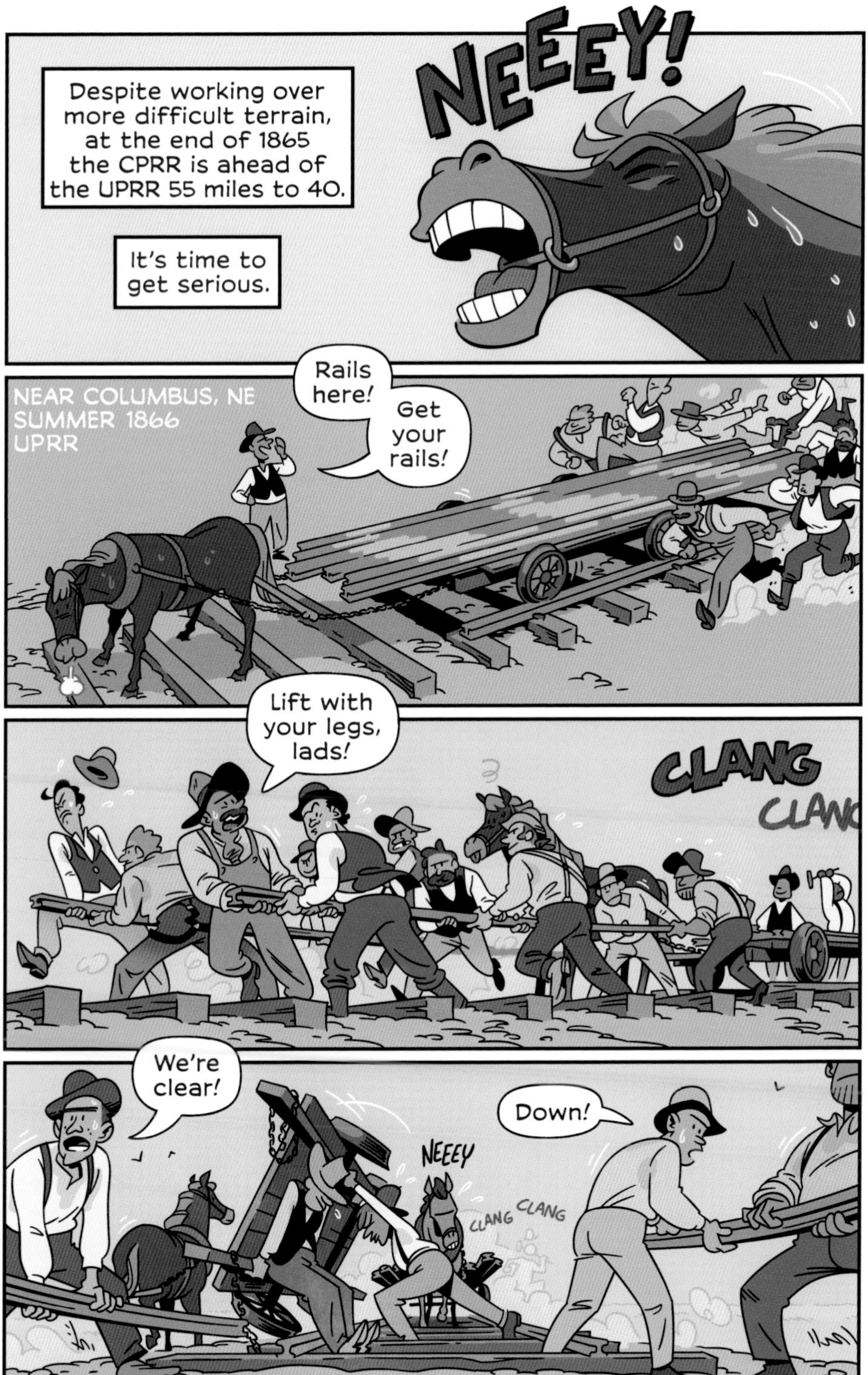
Despite working over more difficult terrain, at the end of 1865 the CPRR is ahead of the UPRR 55 miles to 40.
It's time to get serious.
NEEEY!
NEAR COLUMBUS, NE
SUMMER 1866
UPRR
Rails here!
Get your rails!
Lift with your legs, lads!
CLANG
CLANG
We're clear!
Down!
NEEEY
CLANG
CLANG

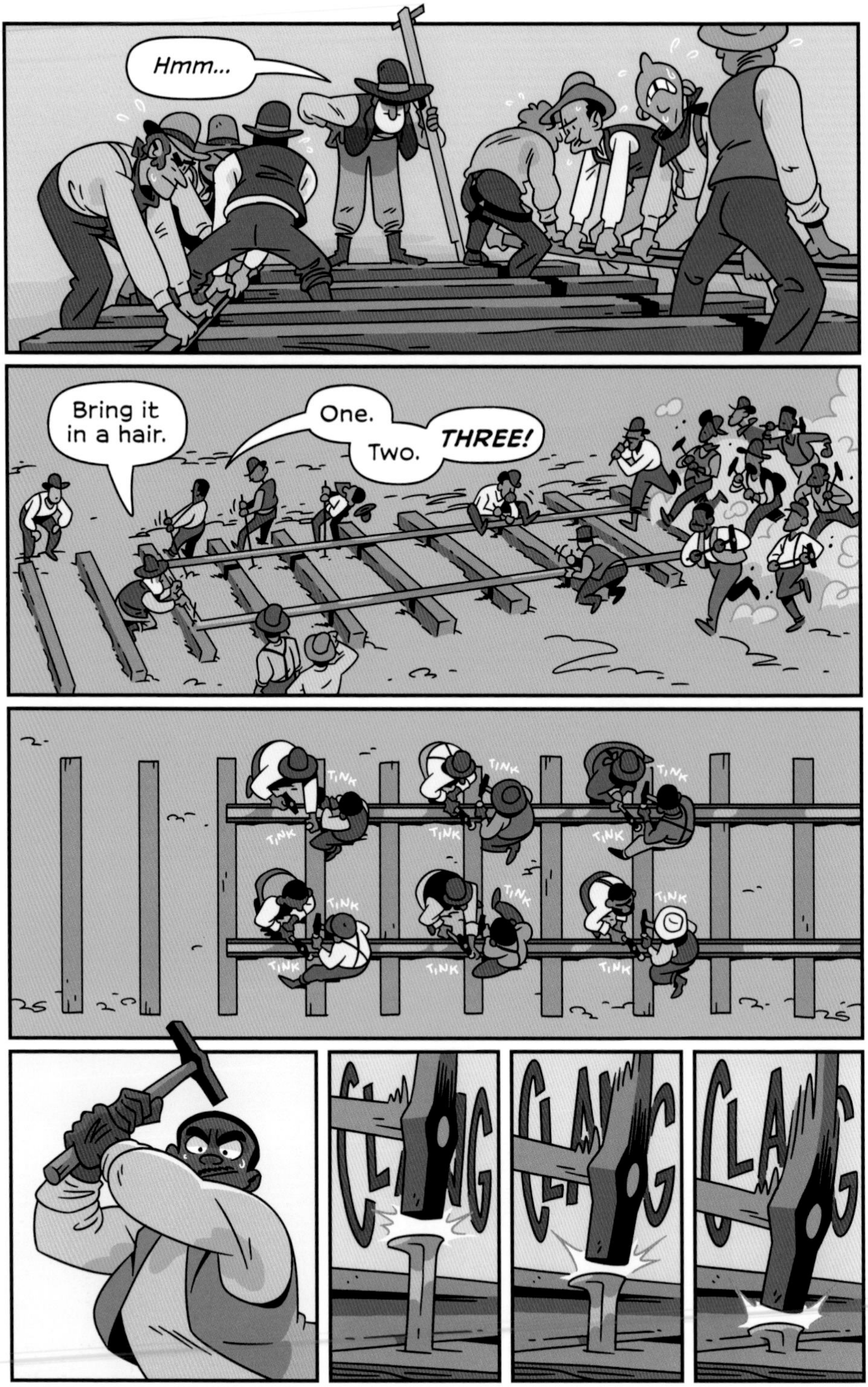
Hmm...
Bring it in a hair.
One.
Two.
THREE!
TINK
TINK
TINK
TINK
TINK
TINK
TINK
TINK
TINK
TINK
TINK
TINK
CLANG
CLANG
CLANG

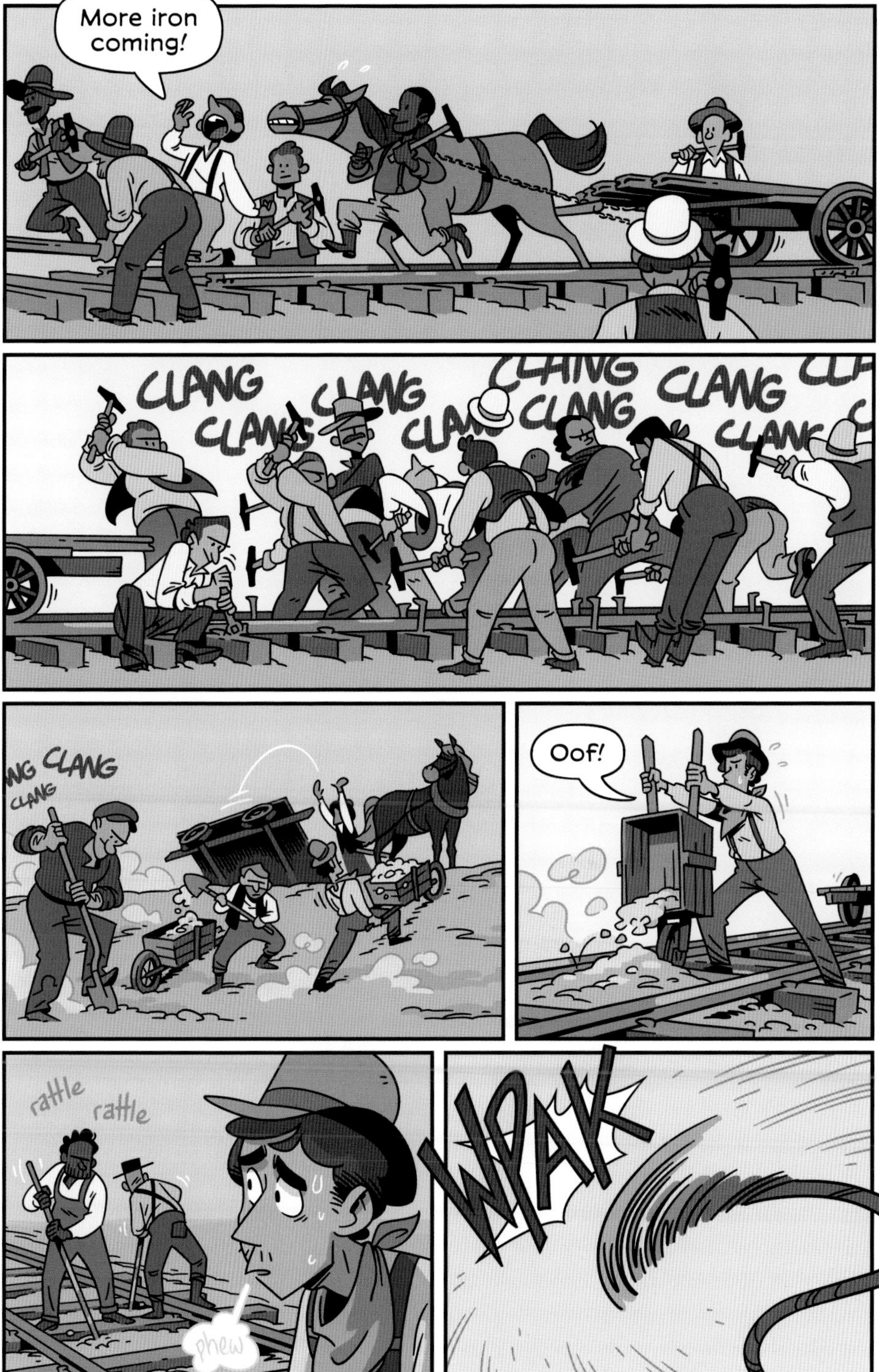
More iron coming!
CLANG CLANG CLANG CLANG CLANG CLANG CLANG CLANG CLANG
CLANG
CLANG
Oof!
rattle rattle
phew
WPAK

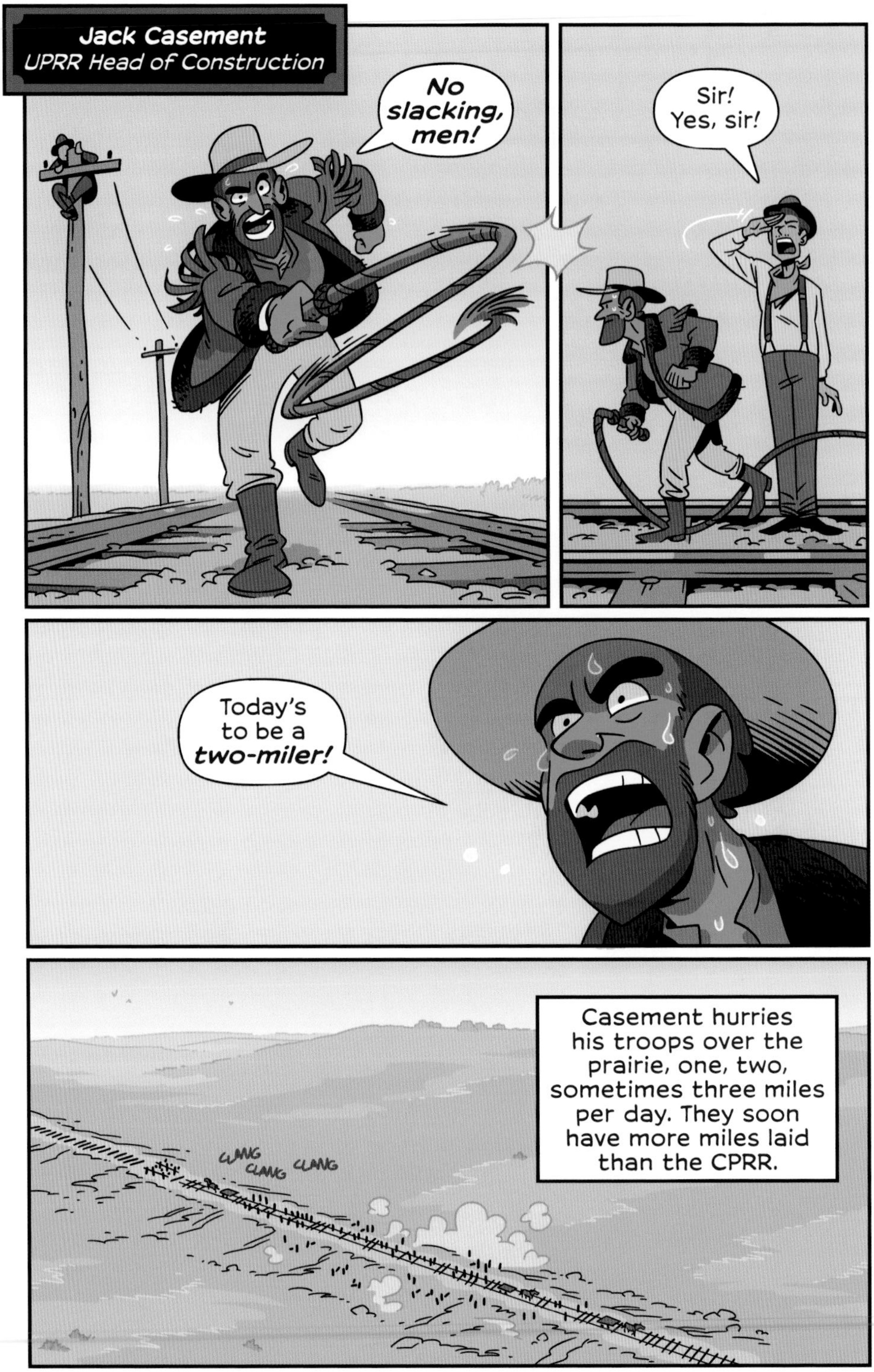
Jack Casement
UPRR Head of Construction
No slacking, men!
Sir! Yes, sir!
Today's to be a two-miler!
Casement hurries his troops over the prairie, one, two, sometimes three miles per day. They soon have more miles laid than the CPRR.
CLANG CLANG CLANG

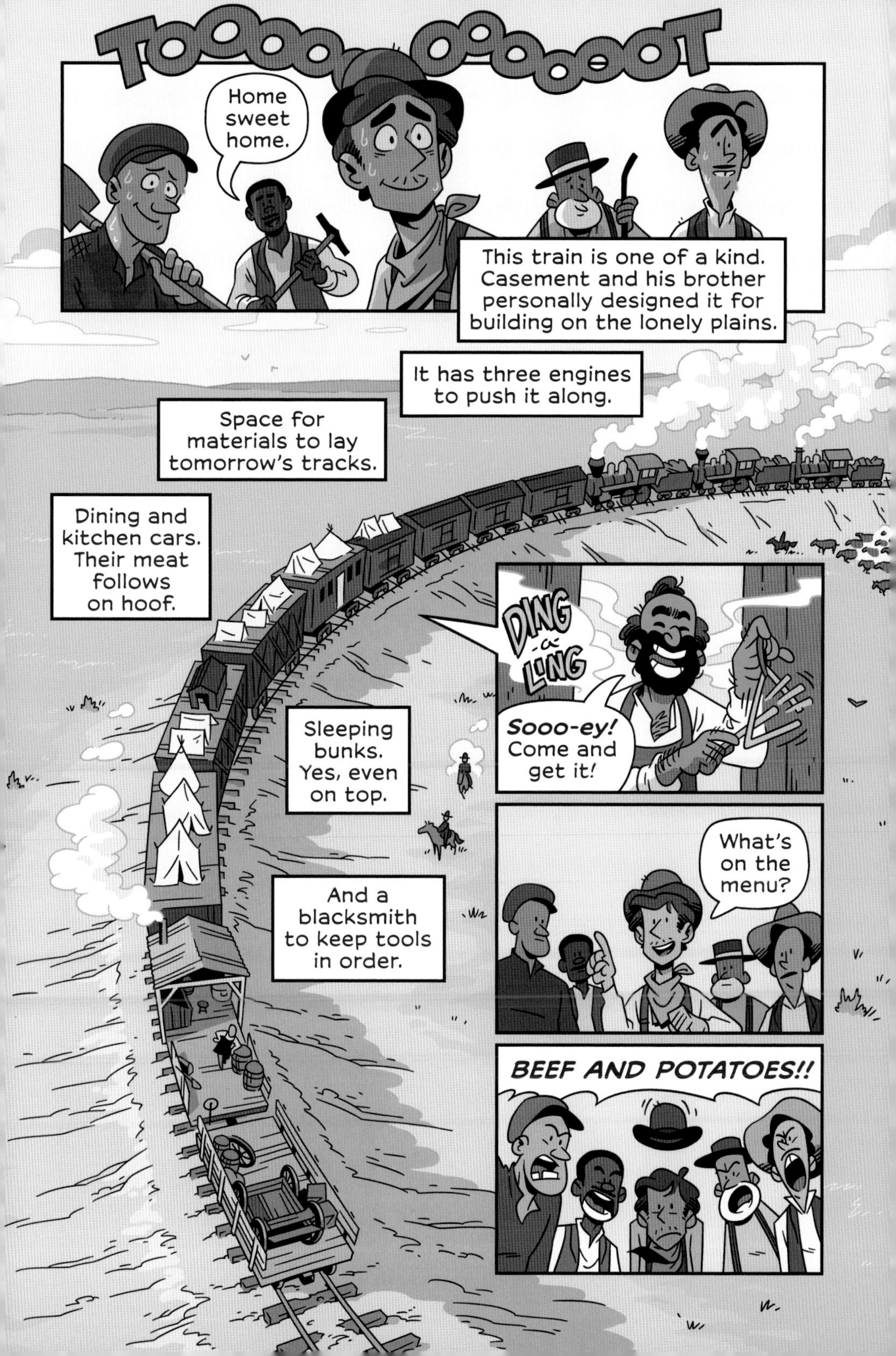
TOOOOOOOOOOOOOT
Home sweet home.
This train is one of a kind. Casement and his brother personally designed it for building on the lonely plains.
It has three engines to push it along.
Space for materials to lay tomorrow's tracks.
Dining and kitchen cars. Their meat follows on hoof.
DING -a- LING
*Sooo-ey!* Come and get it!
Sleeping bunks. Yes, even on top.
And a blacksmith to keep tools in order.
What's on the menu?
*BEEF AND POTATOES!!*

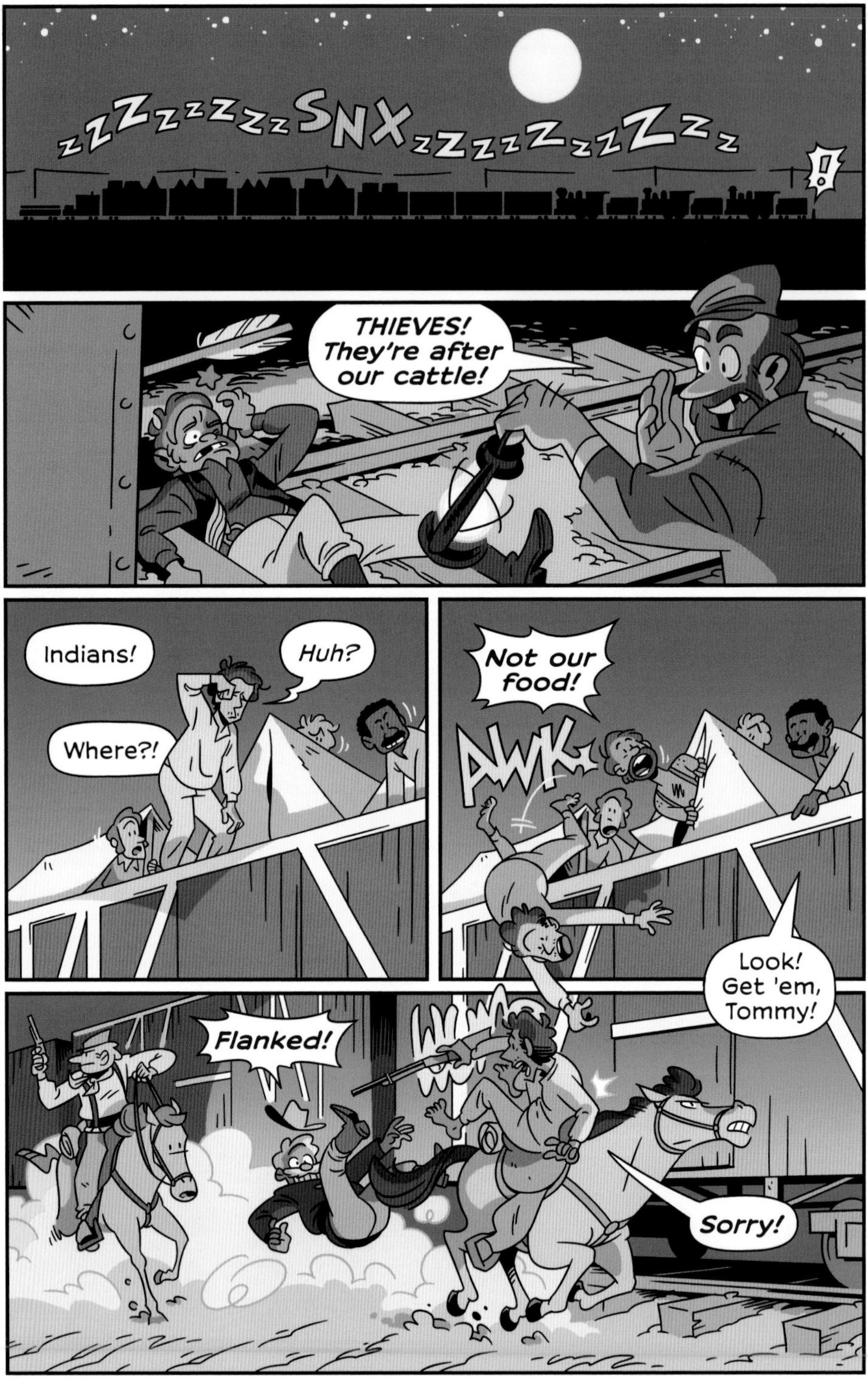
zZZzzZzzzSNXzZZzzZzzZZz
!
THIEVES! They're after our cattle!
Indians!
Huh?
Where?!
Not our food!
AWK
Look! Get 'em, Tommy!
Flanked!
Sorry!

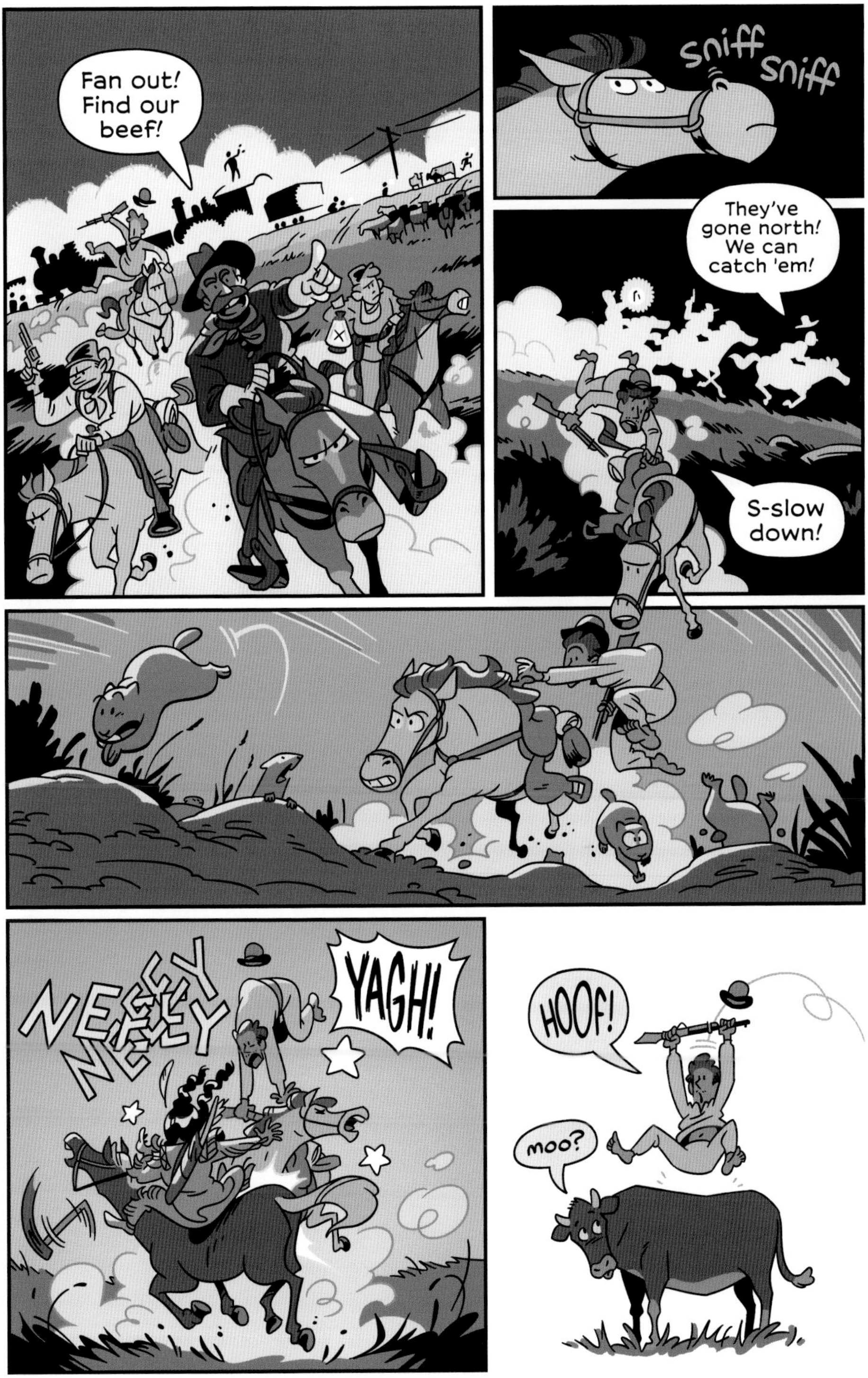

Fan out! Find our beef!
sniff sniff
They've gone north! We can catch 'em!
S-slow down!
NEEEY NEEEY
YAGH!
HOOF!
moo?

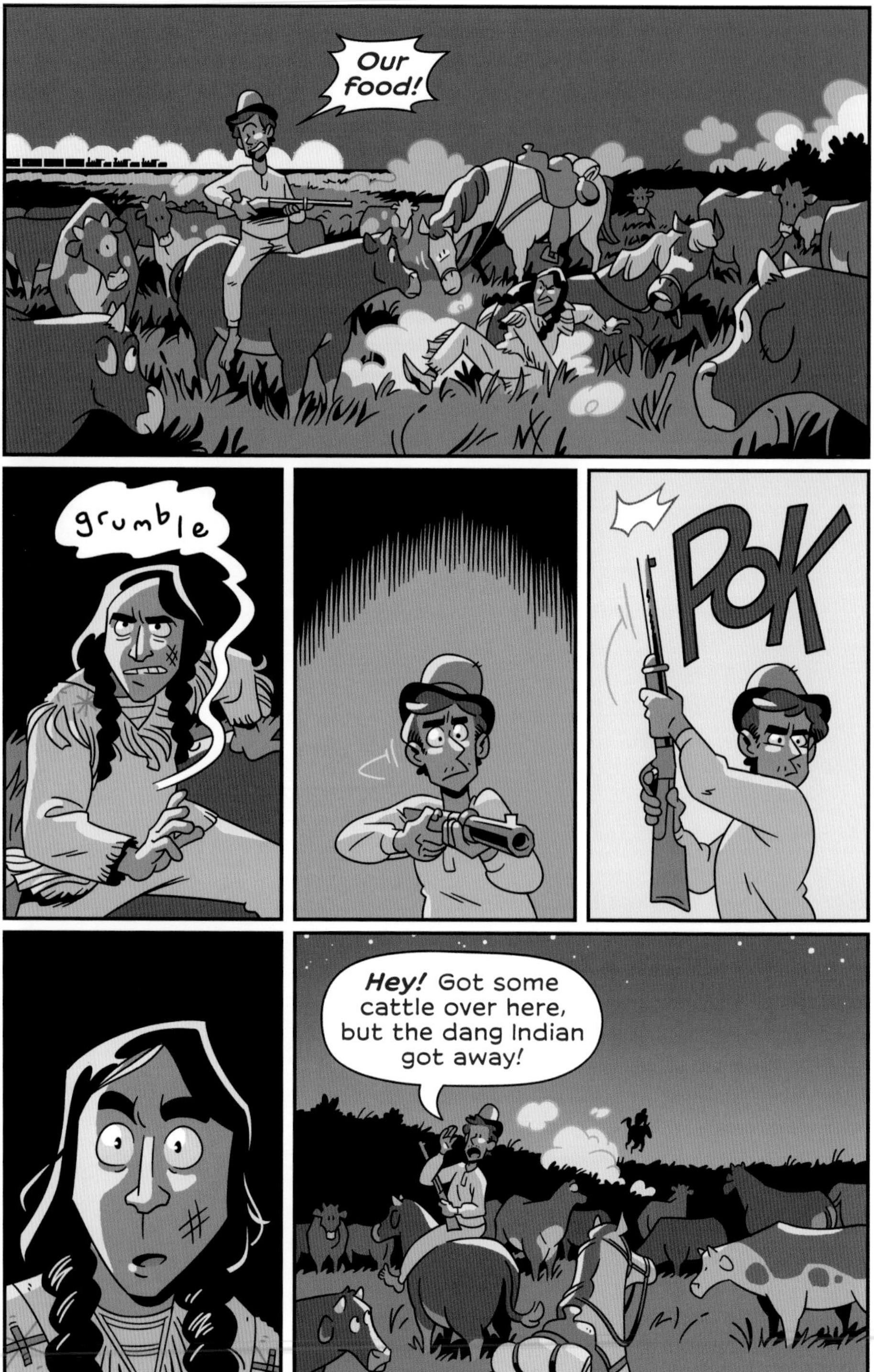
Our food!
grumble
POK
Hey! Got some cattle over here, but the dang Indian got away!

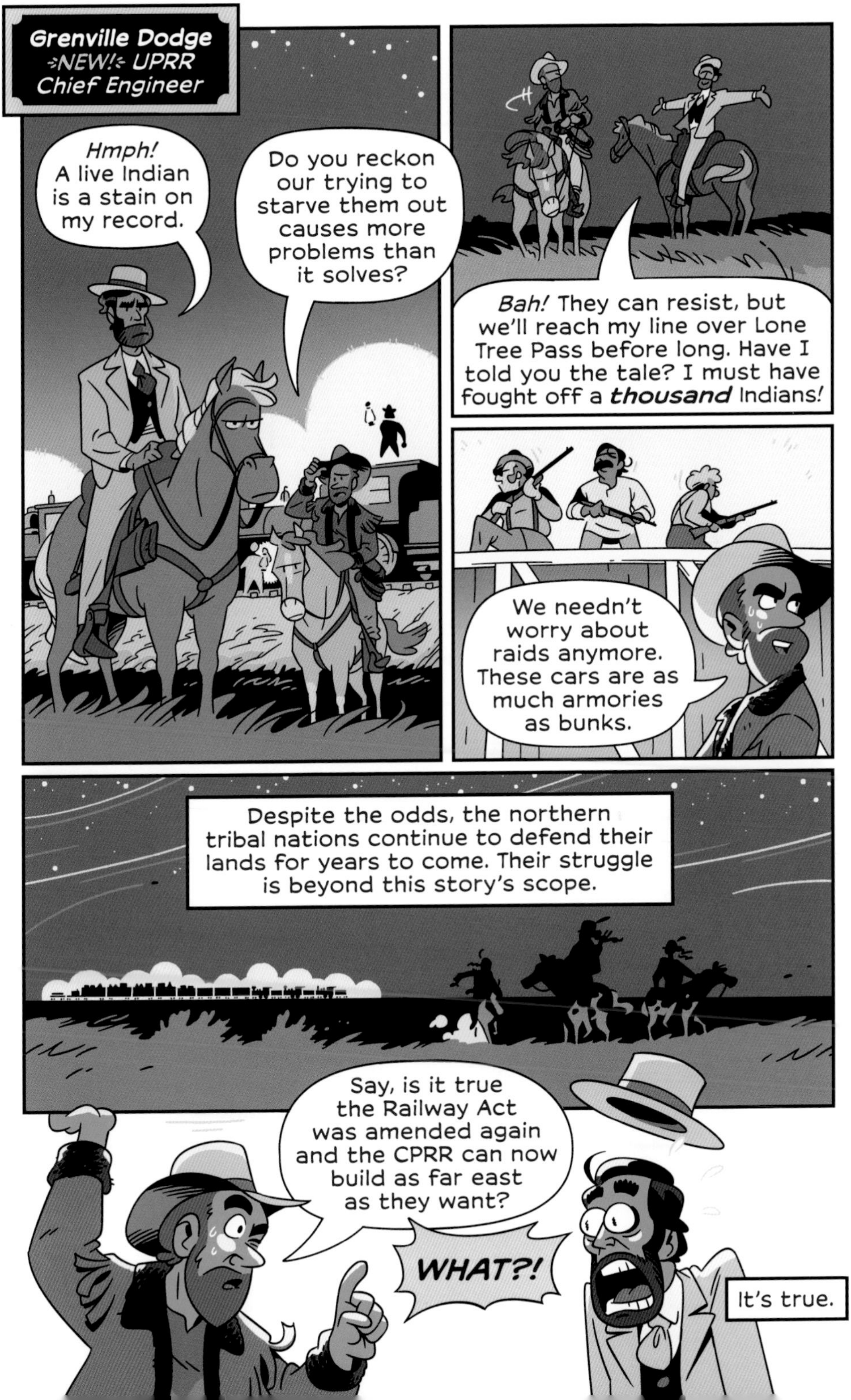

Grenville Dodge
NEW! UPRR
Chief Engineer
*Hmph!* A live Indian is a stain on my record.
Do you reckon our trying to starve them out causes more problems than it solves?
*Bah!* They can resist, but we'll reach my line over Lone Tree Pass before long. Have I told you the tale? I must have fought off a ***thousand*** Indians!
We needn't worry about raids anymore. These cars are as much armories as bunks.
Despite the odds, the northern tribal nations continue to defend their lands for years to come. Their struggle is beyond this story's scope.
Say, is it true the Railway Act was amended again and the CPRR can now build as far east as they want?
WHAT?!
It's true.

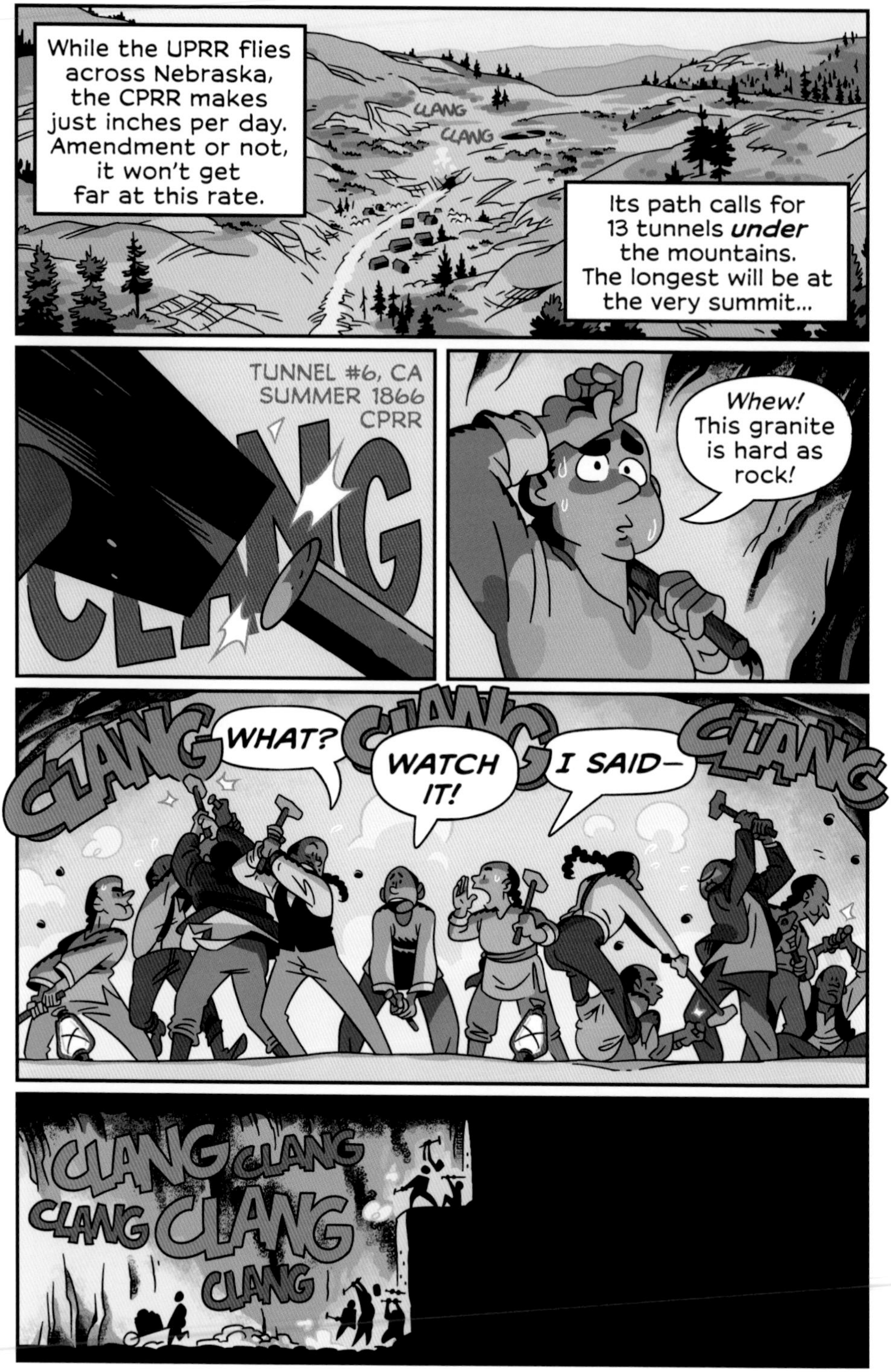
While the UPRR flies across Nebraska, the CPRR makes just inches per day. Amendment or not, it won't get far at this rate.
CLANG
CLANG
Its path calls for 13 tunnels *under* the mountains. The longest will be at the very summit...
TUNNEL #6, CA SUMMER 1866 CPRR
CLANG
*Whew!* This granite is hard as rock!
CLANG
WHAT?
CLANG
WATCH IT!
I SAID—
CLANG
CLANG CLANG
CLANG CLANG
CLANG

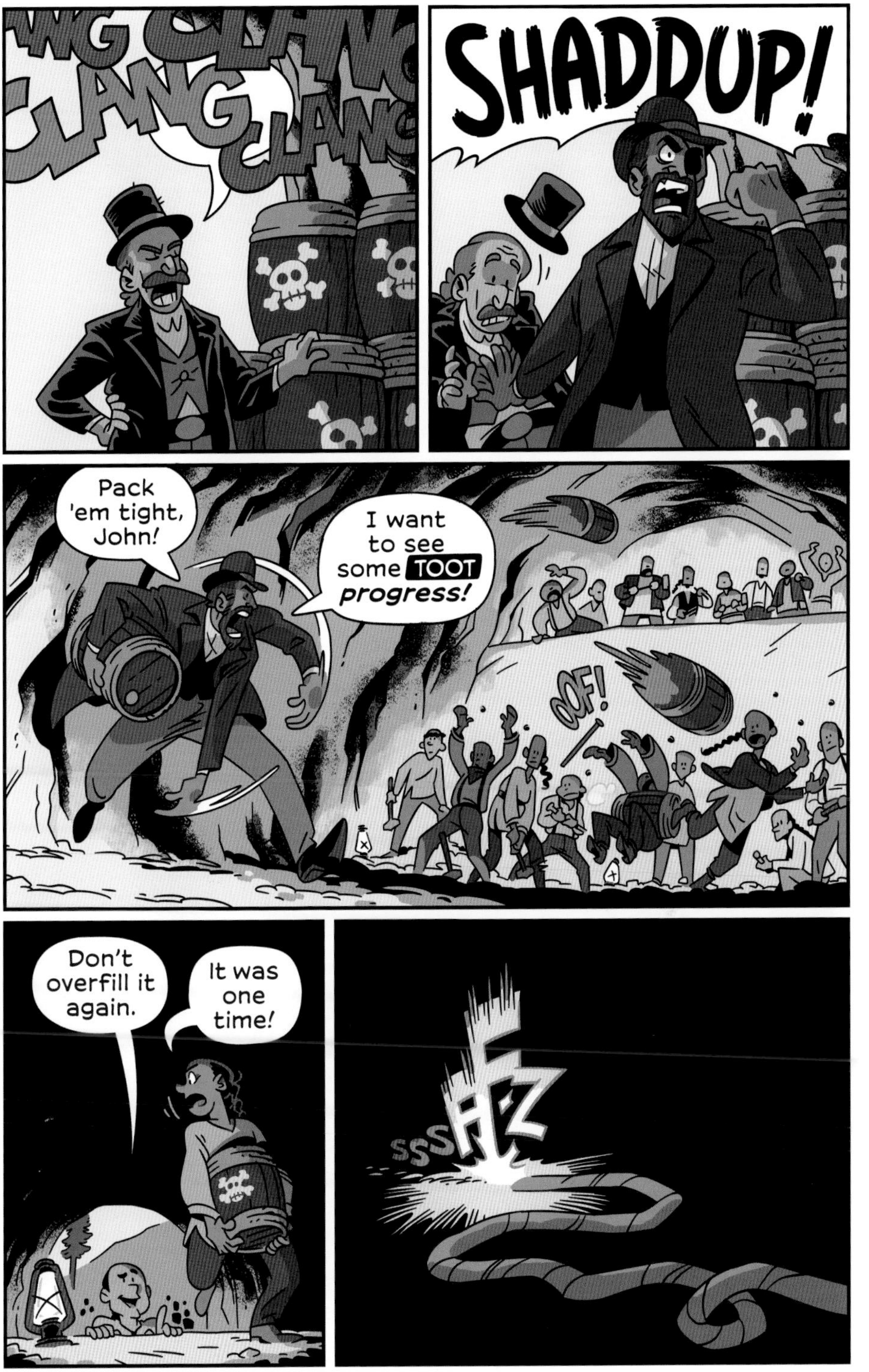

CLANG CLANG
CLANG CLANG
SHADDUP!
Pack 'em tight, John!
I want to see some TOOT progress!
OOF!
Don't overfill it again.
It was one time!
SSSFFZ

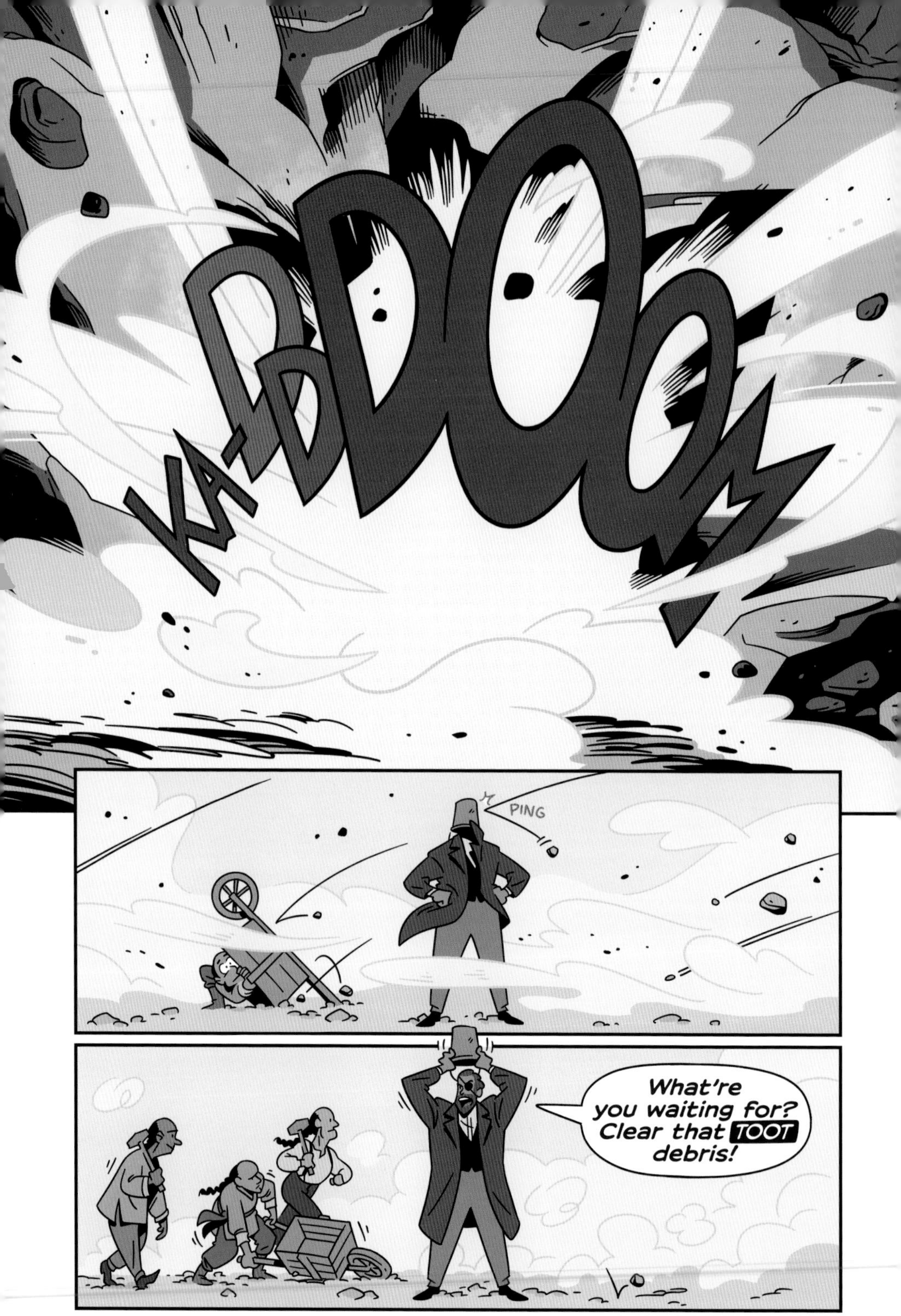
KA-BOOM
PING
What're you waiting for? Clear that TOOT debris!

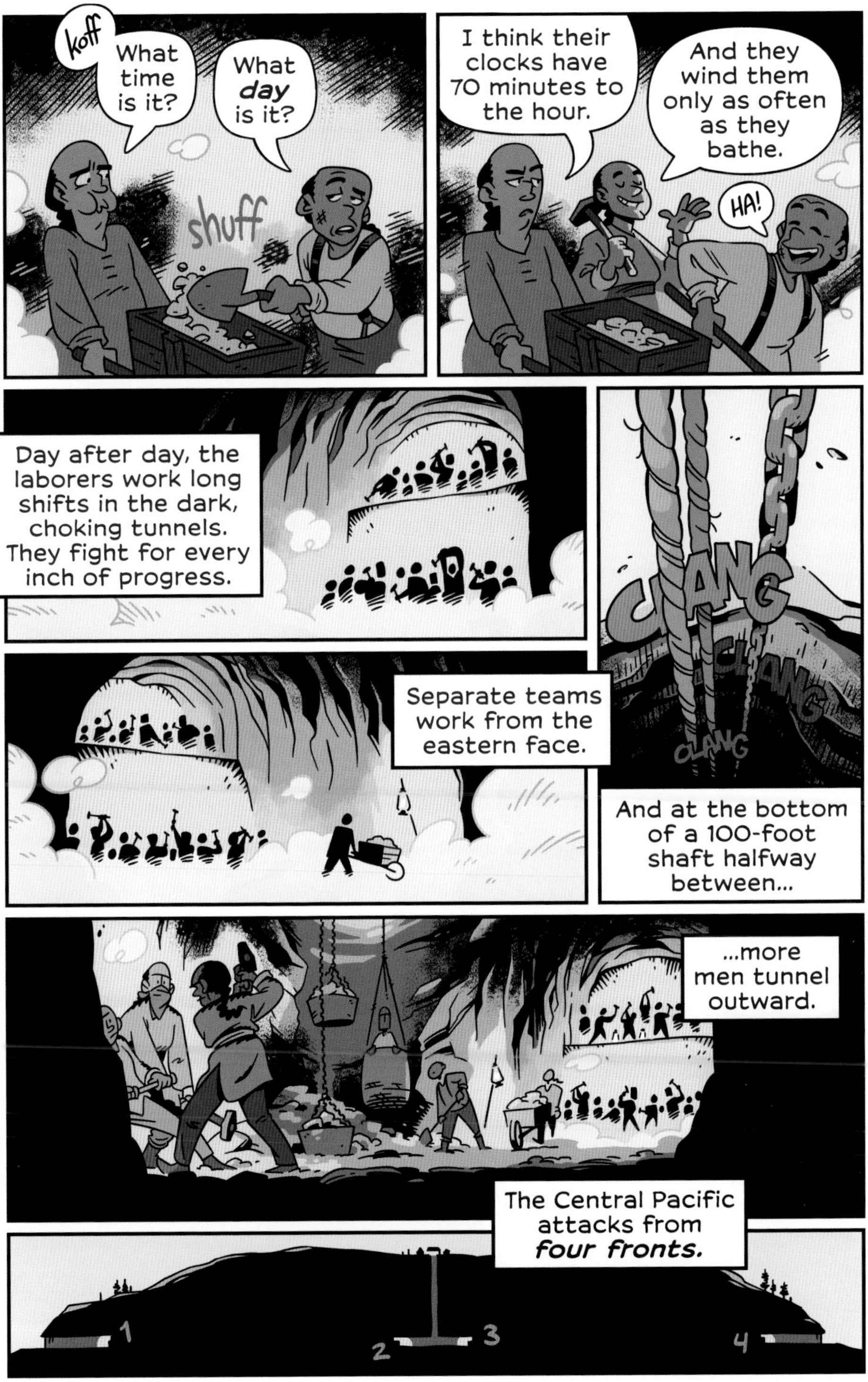
koff
What time is it?
What *day* is it?
shuff
I think their clocks have 70 minutes to the hour.
And they wind them only as often as they bathe.
HA!
Day after day, the laborers work long shifts in the dark, choking tunnels. They fight for every inch of progress.
CLANG
CLANG
CLANG
Separate teams work from the eastern face.
And at the bottom of a 100-foot shaft halfway between...
...more men tunnel outward.
The Central Pacific attacks from ***four fronts.***
1
2
3
4

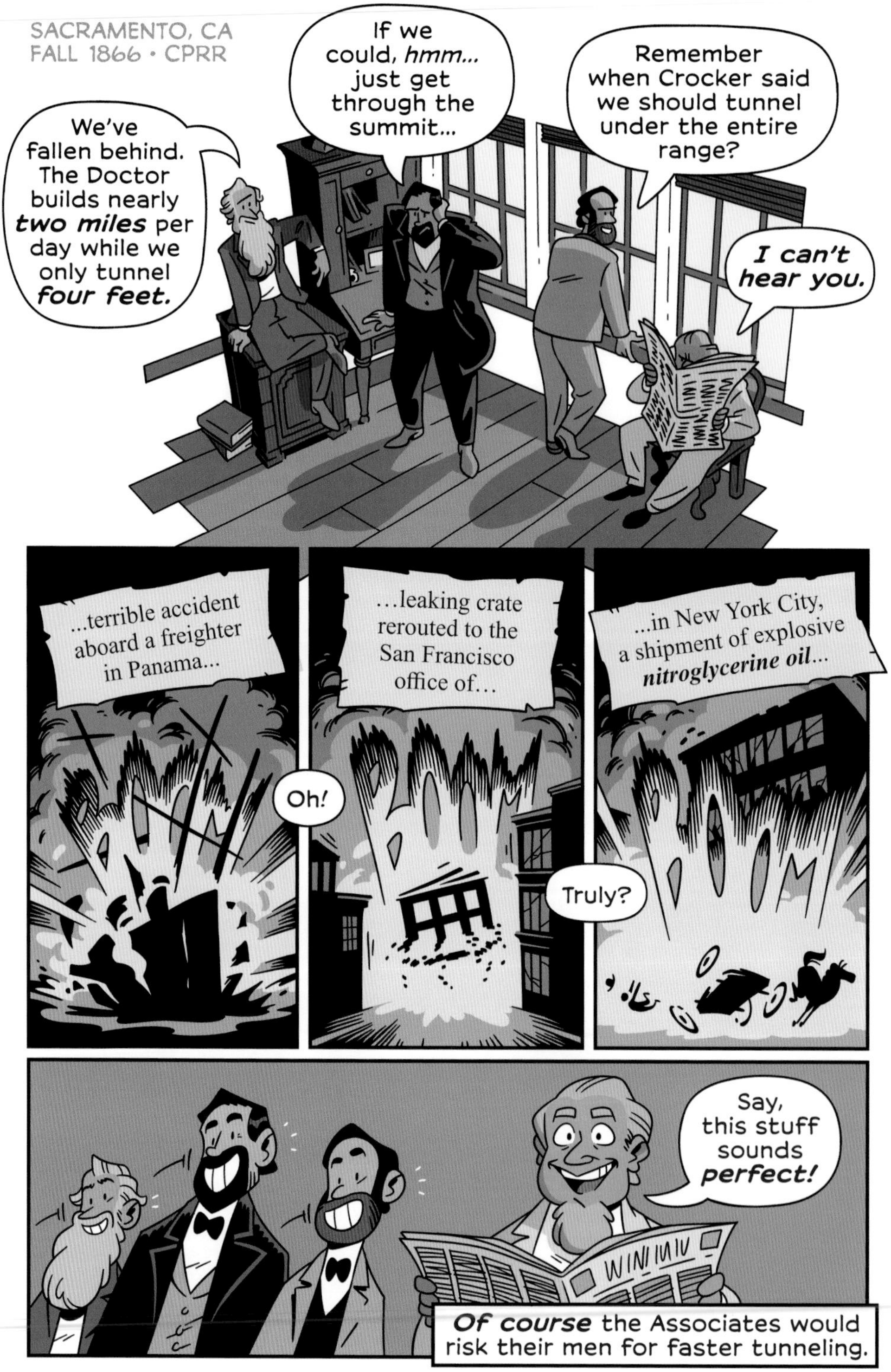
SACRAMENTO, CA
FALL 1866 • CPRR
We've fallen behind. The Doctor builds nearly **two miles** per day while we only tunnel **four feet.**
If we could, *hmm...* just get through the summit...
Remember when Crocker said we should tunnel under the entire range?
*I can't hear you.*
...terrible accident aboard a freighter in Panama...
Oh!
…leaking crate rerouted to the San Francisco office of…
Truly?
...in New York City, a shipment of explosive ***nitroglycerine oil***...
Say, this stuff sounds ***perfect!***
***Of course*** the Associates would risk their men for faster tunneling.

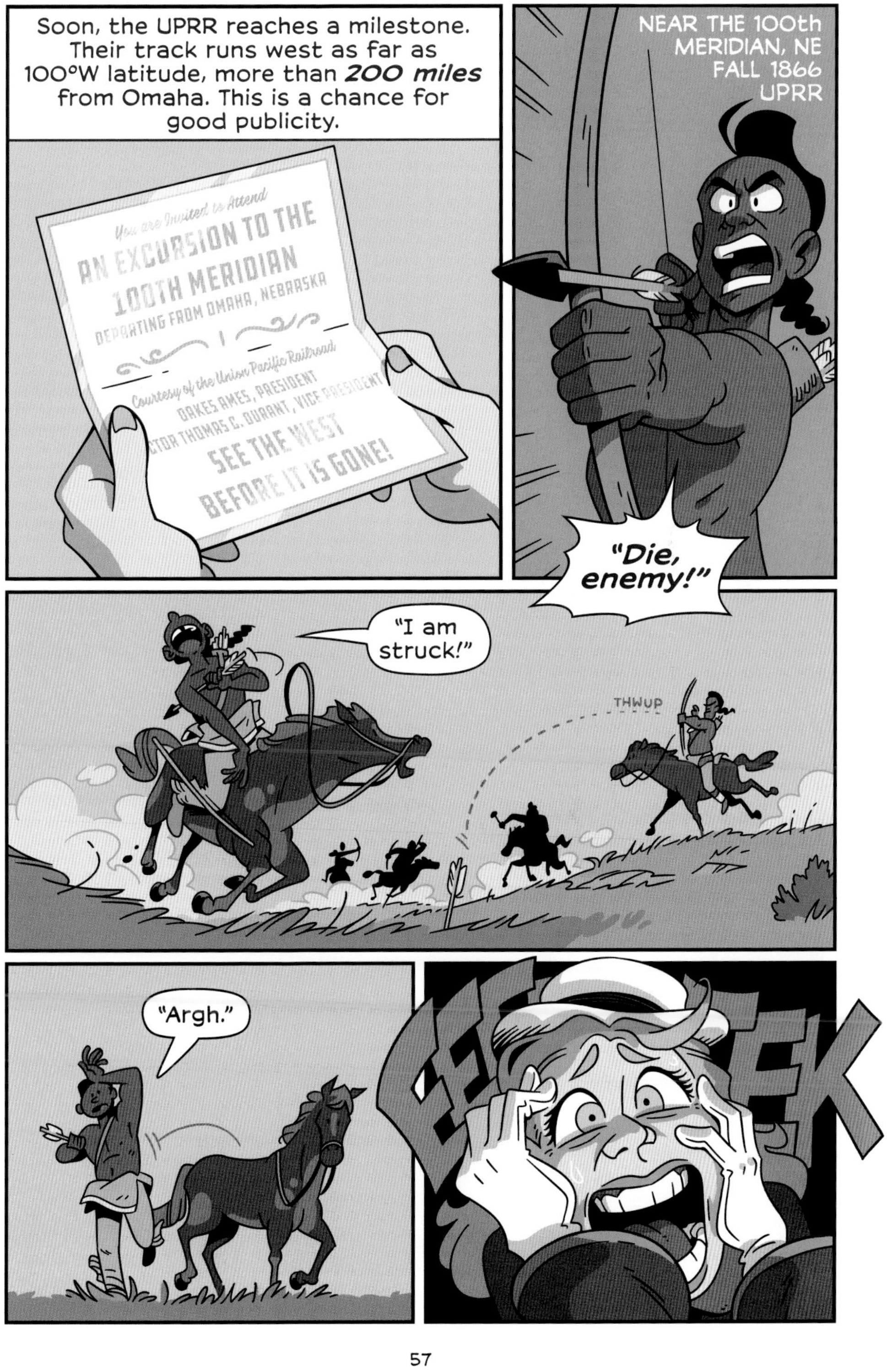

Soon, the UPRR reaches a milestone. Their track runs west as far as 100°W latitude, more than ***200 miles*** from Omaha. This is a chance for good publicity.
You are Invited to Attend
AN EXCURSION TO THE
100TH MERIDIAN
DEPARTING FROM OMAHA, NEBRASKA
Courtesy of the Union Pacific Railroad
OAKES AMES, PRESIDENT
THOMAS C. DURANT, VICE PRESIDENT
SEE THE WEST
BEFORE IT IS GONE!
NEAR THE 100th MERIDIAN, NE
FALL 1866
UPRR
"Die, enemy!"
"I am struck!"
THWUP
"Argh."

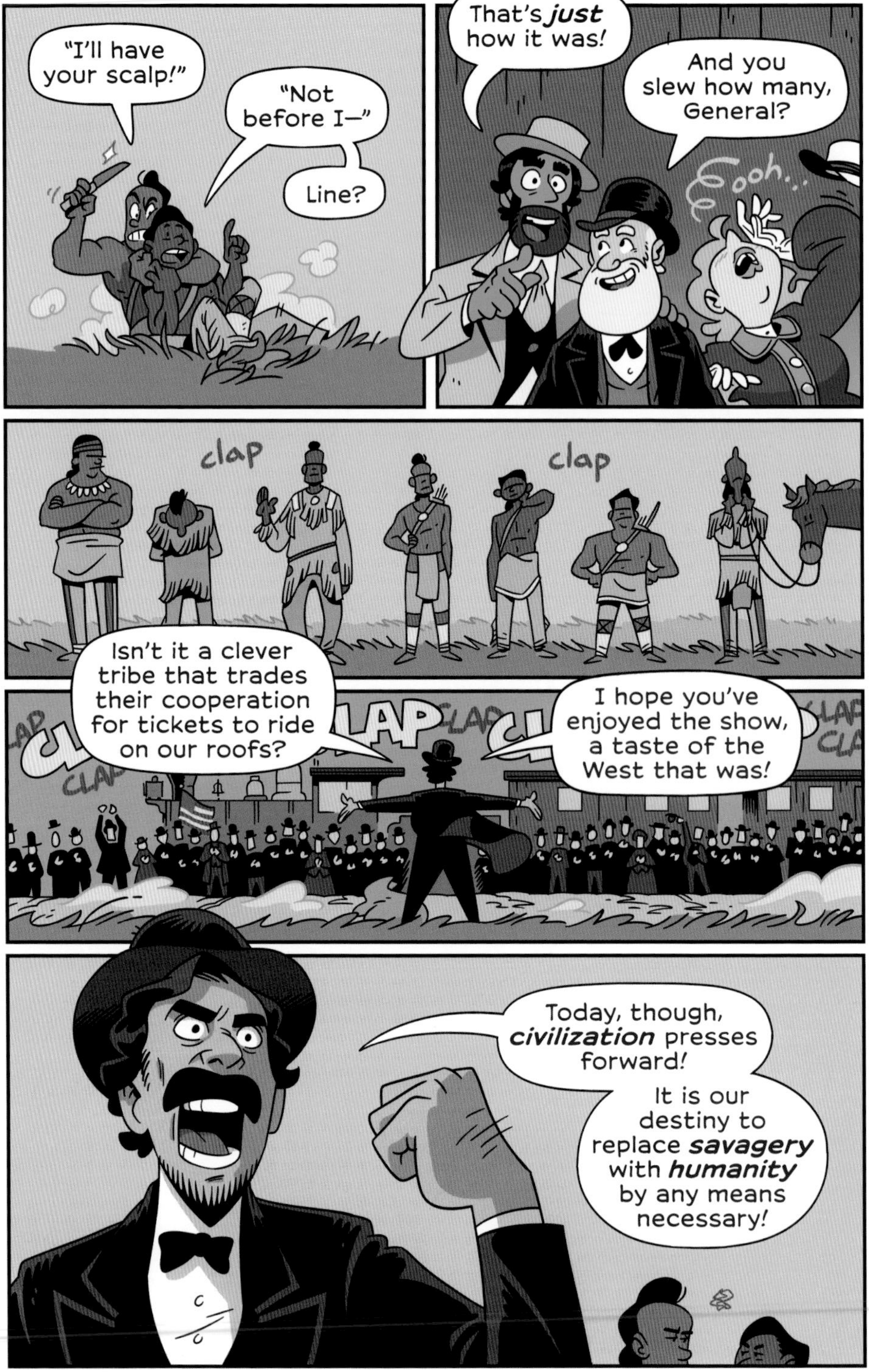
"I'll have your scalp!"
"Not before I—"
Line?
That's *just* how it was!
And you slew how many, General?
Oooh...
clap
clap
Isn't it a clever tribe that trades their cooperation for tickets to ride on our roofs?
CLAP
I hope you've enjoyed the show, a taste of the West that was!
Today, though, ***civilization*** presses forward!
It is our destiny to replace ***savagery*** with ***humanity*** by any means necessary!

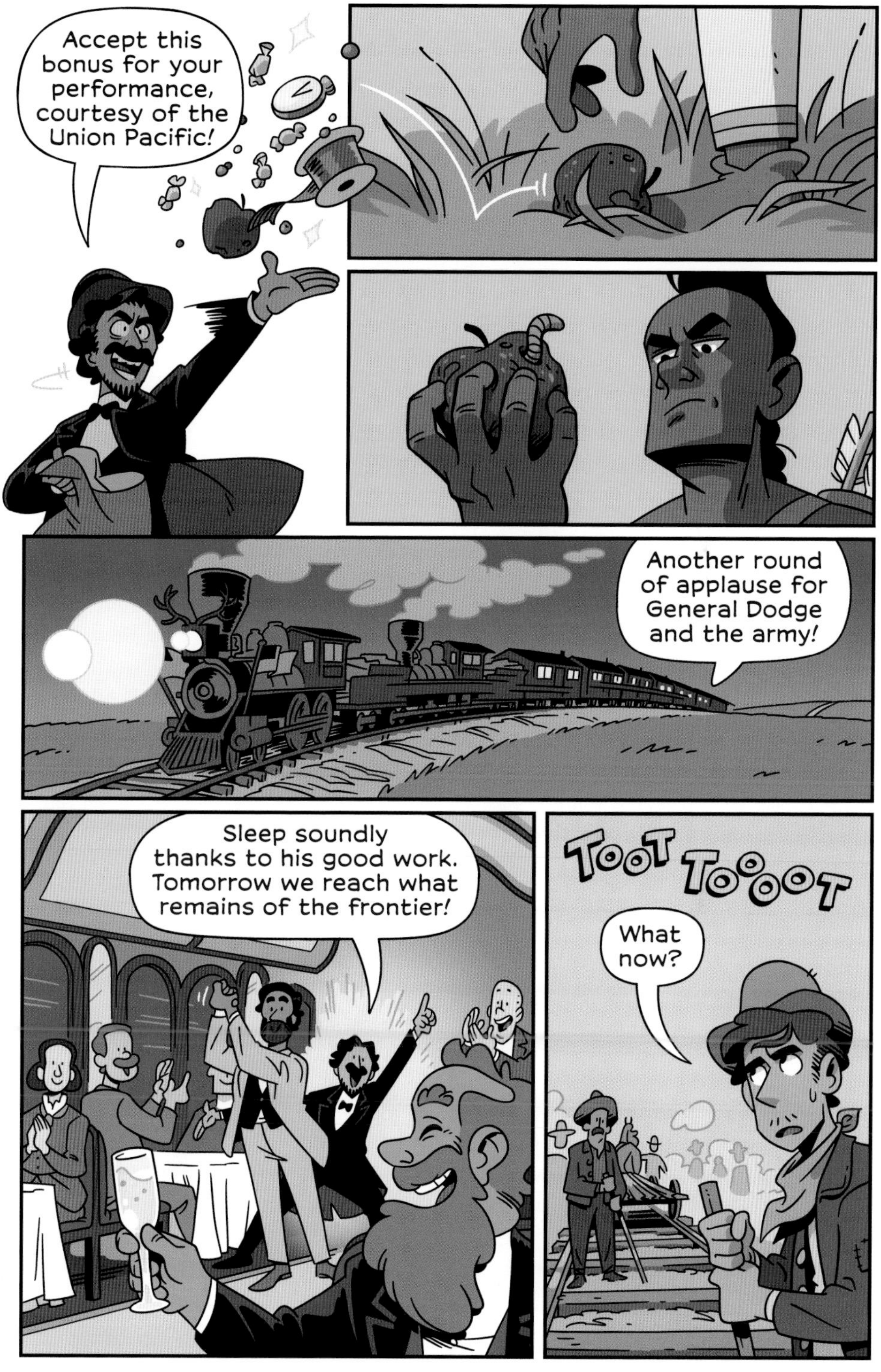
Accept this bonus for your performance, courtesy of the Union Pacific!
Another round of applause for General Dodge and the army!
Sleep soundly thanks to his good work. Tomorrow we reach what remains of the frontier!
TOOT TOOOOT
What now?

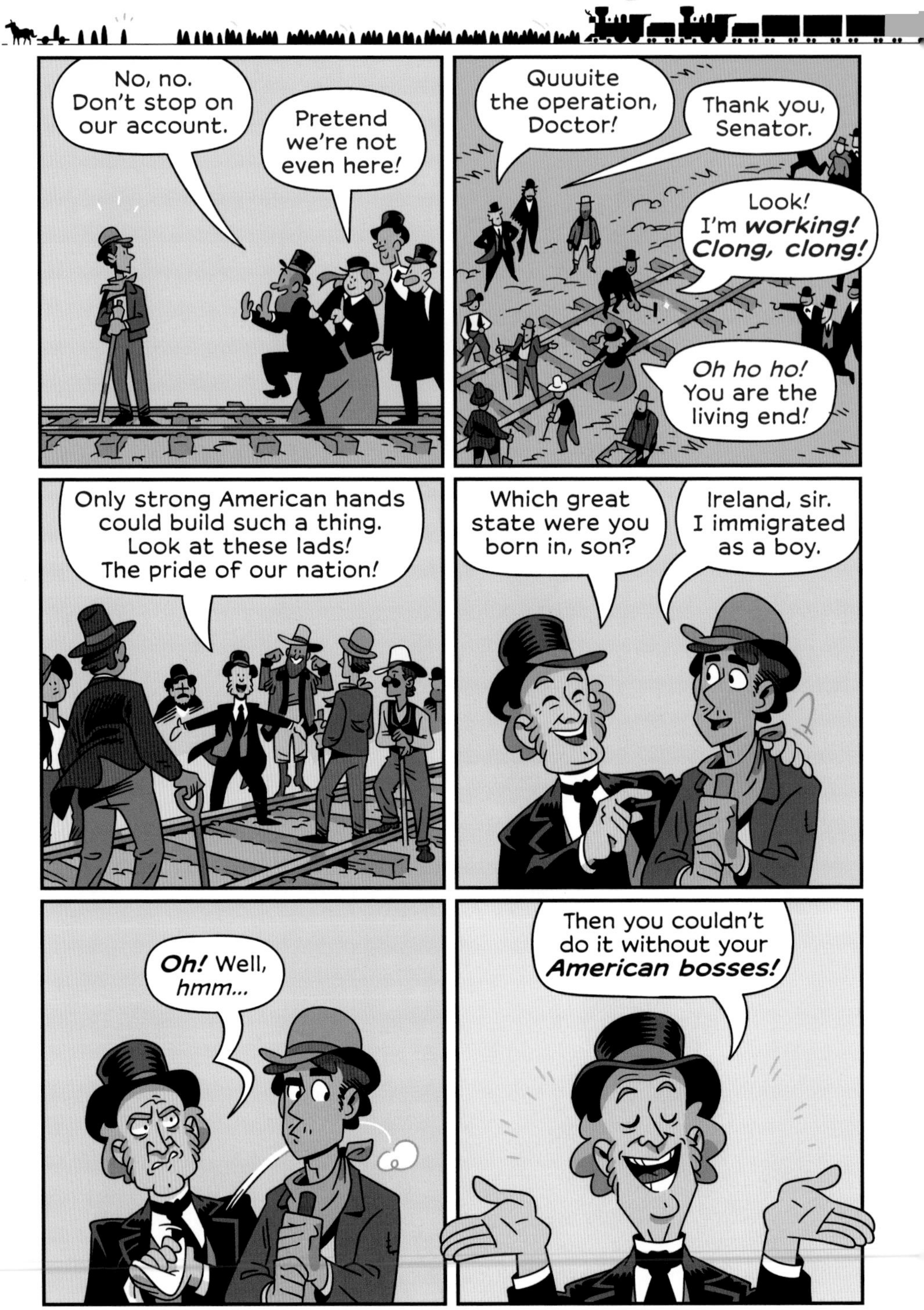
No, no. Don't stop on our account.
Pretend we're not even here!
Quuuite the operation, Doctor!
Thank you, Senator.
Look! I'm **working! Clong, clong!**
*Oh ho ho!* You are the living end!
Only strong American hands could build such a thing. Look at these lads! The pride of our nation!
Which great state were you born in, son?
Ireland, sir. I immigrated as a boy.
***Oh!*** Well, *hmm...*
Then you couldn't do it without your ***American bosses!***

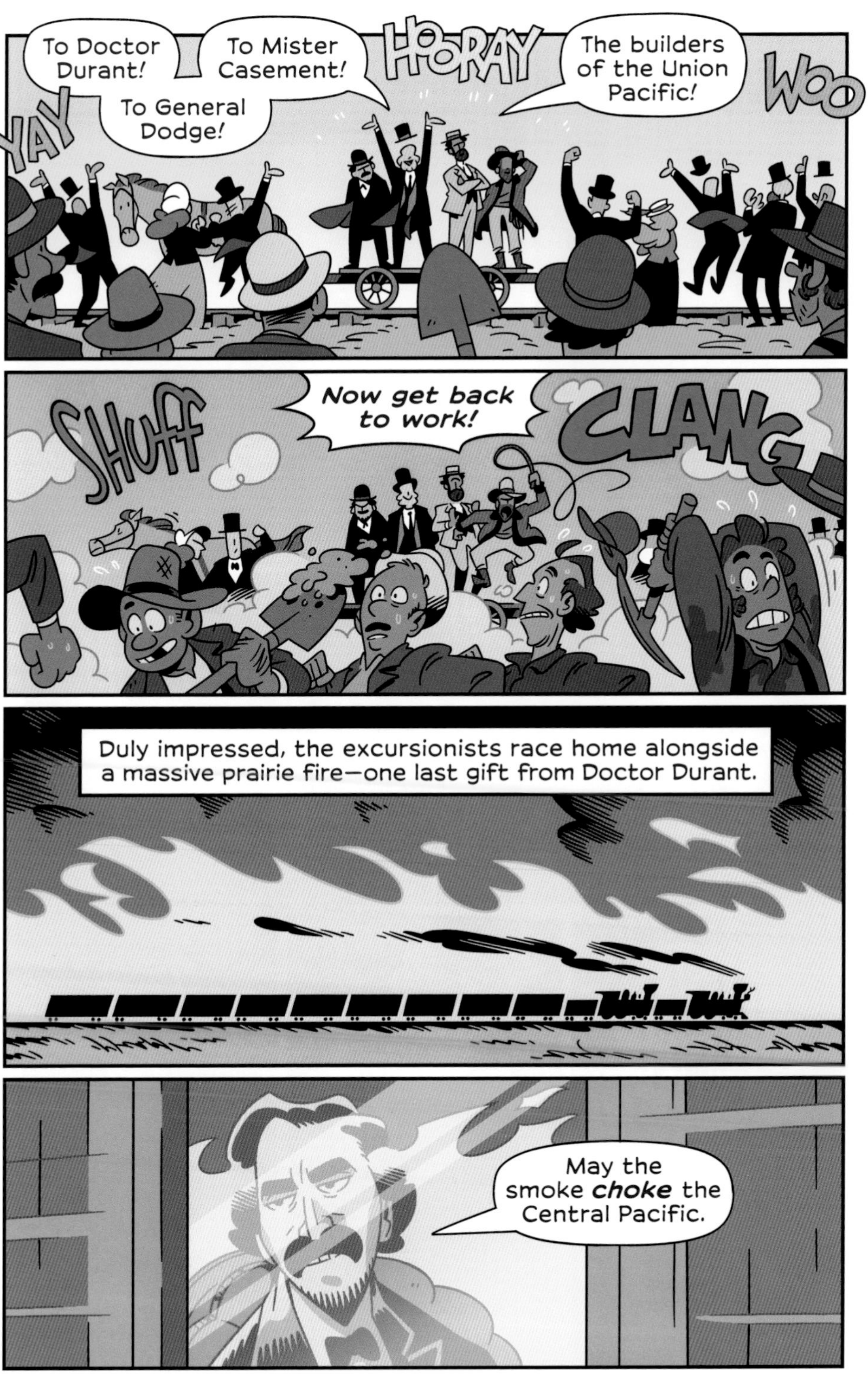
To Doctor Durant!
To General Dodge!
To Mister Casement!
HOORAY
The builders of the Union Pacific!
WOO
YAY
SHUFF
Now get back to work!
CLANG
Duly impressed, the excursionists race home alongside a massive prairie fire—one last gift from Doctor Durant.
May the smoke *choke* the Central Pacific.

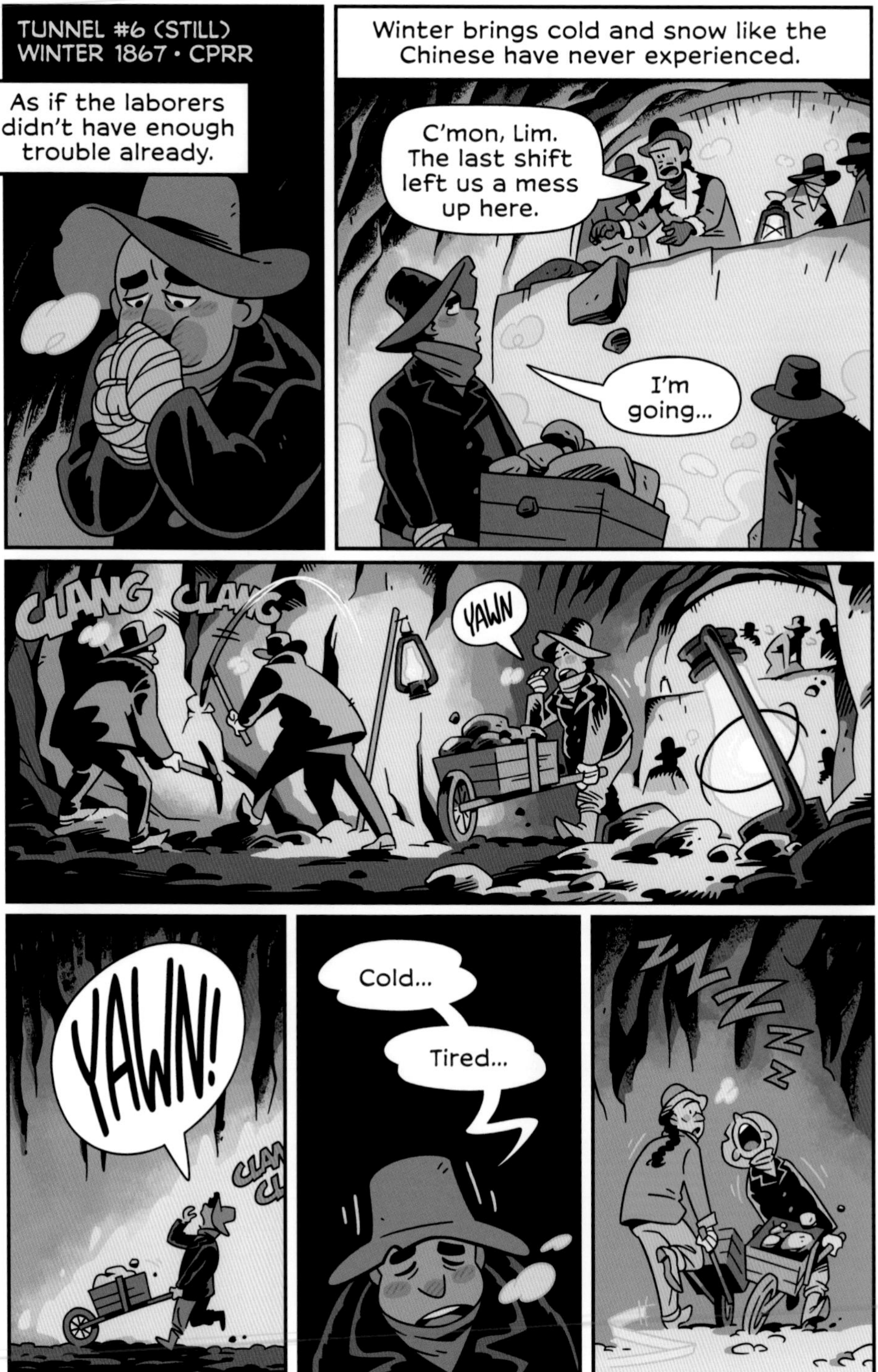
TUNNEL #6 (STILL)
WINTER 1867 • CPRR
As if the laborers didn't have enough trouble already.
Winter brings cold and snow like the Chinese have never experienced.
C'mon, Lim. The last shift left us a mess up here.
I'm going...
CLANG CLANG
YAWN
YAWN!
Cold...
Tired...
Z Z Z Z Z Z

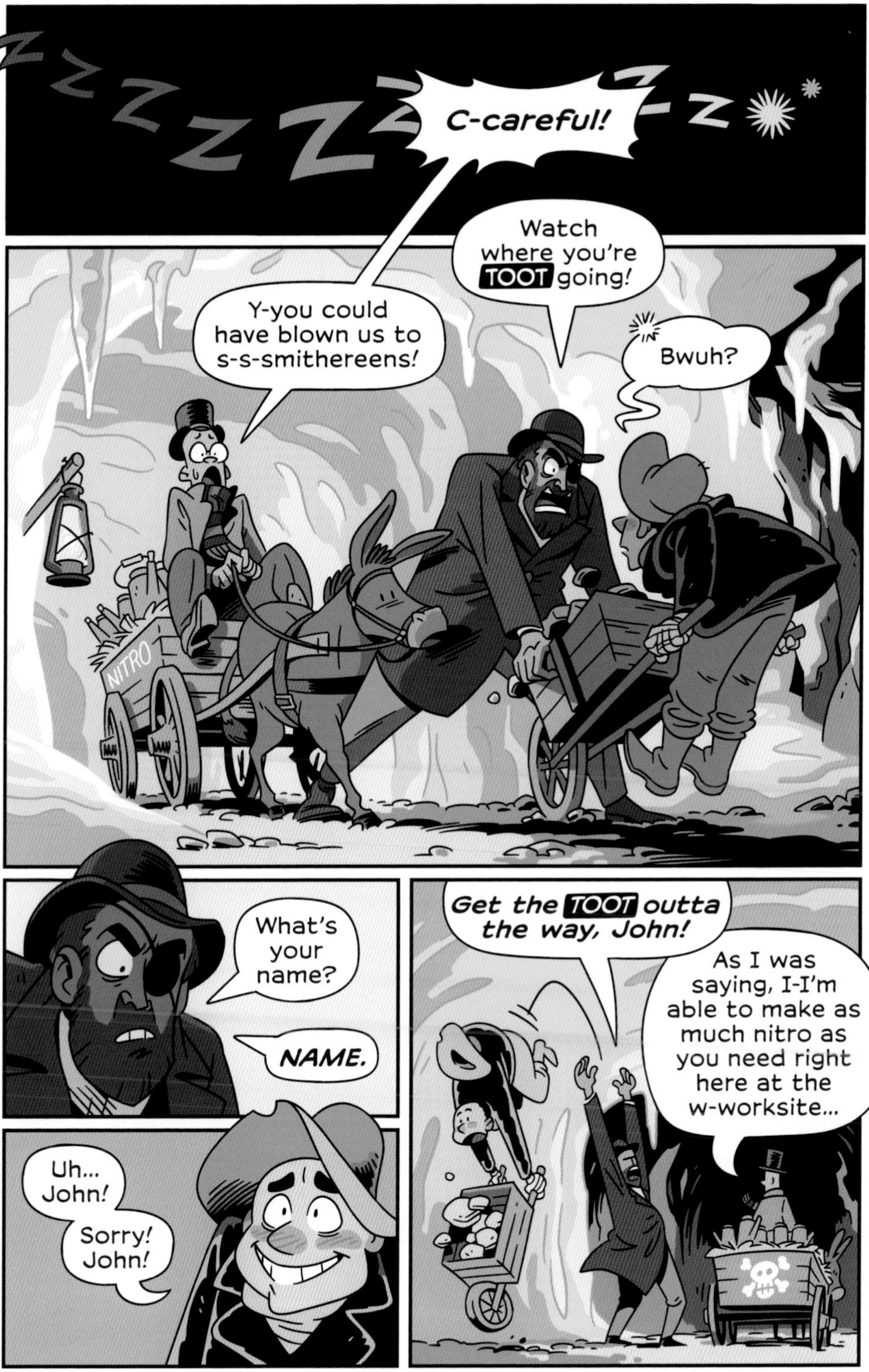
ZZZZZZZ
C-careful!
Z-Z
Y-you could have blown us to s-s-smithereens!
Watch where you're TOOT going!
Bwuh?
NITRO
What's your name?
NAME.
Uh... John!
Sorry! John!
Get the TOOT outta the way, John!
As I was saying, I-I'm able to make as much nitro as you need right here at the w-worksite...

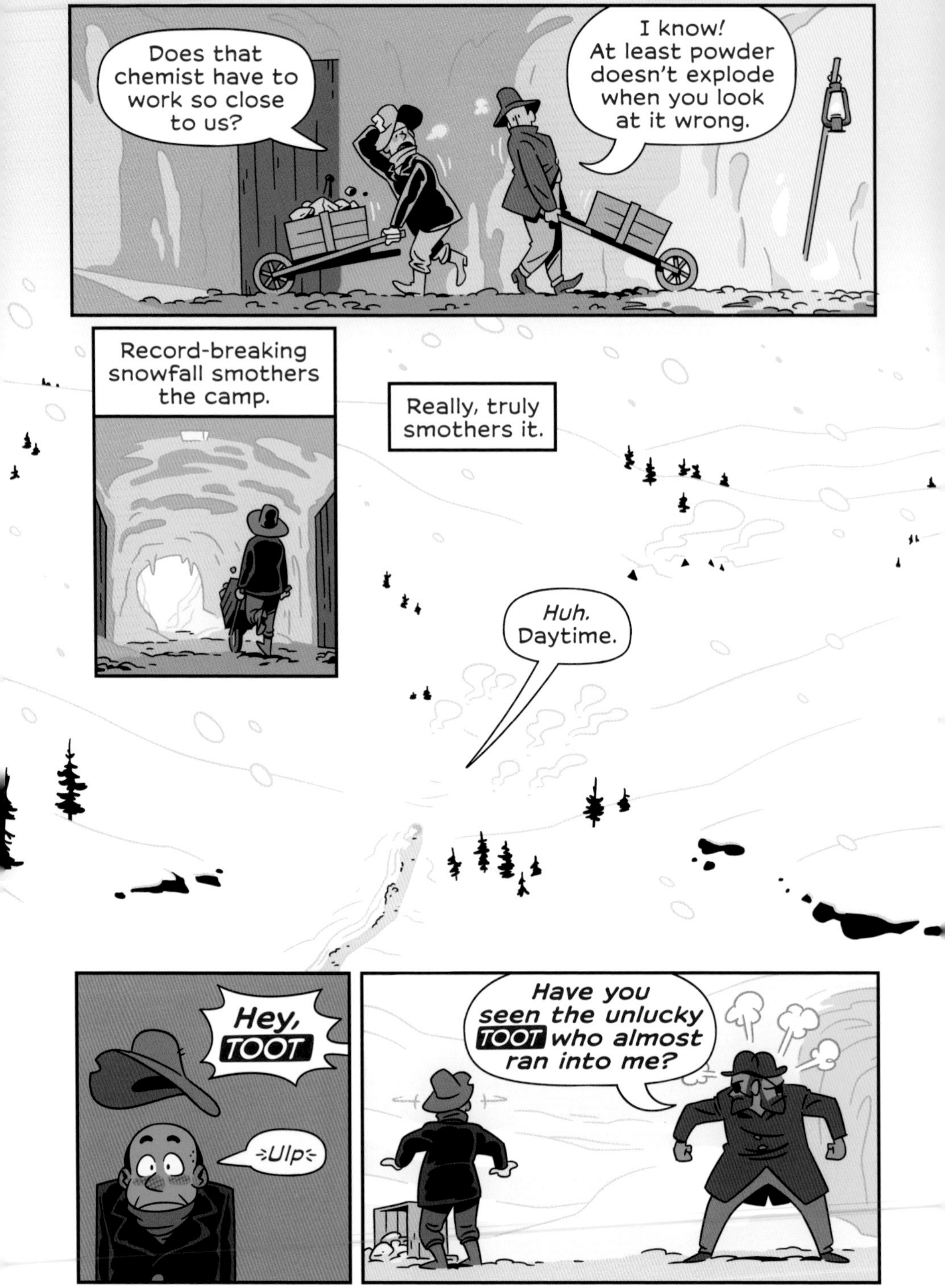
Does that chemist have to work so close to us?
I know! At least powder doesn't explode when you look at it wrong.
Record-breaking snowfall smothers the camp.
Really, truly smothers it.
Huh. Daytime.
Hey, TOOT
Ulp
Have you seen the unlucky TOOT who almost ran into me?

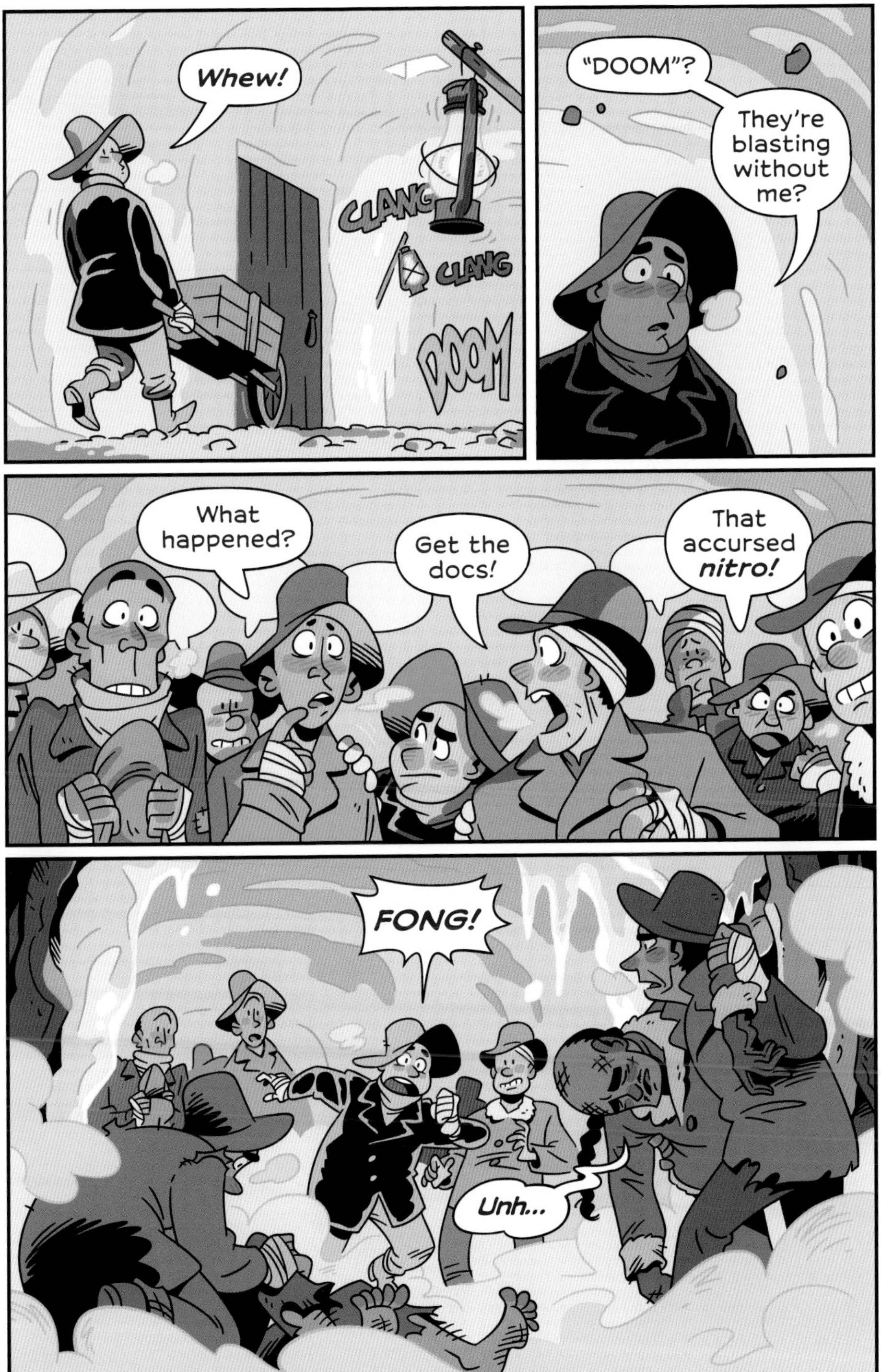
Whew!
CLANG
CLANG
DOOM
"DOOM"?
They're blasting without me?
What happened?
Get the docs!
That accursed *nitro!*
FONG!
Unh...

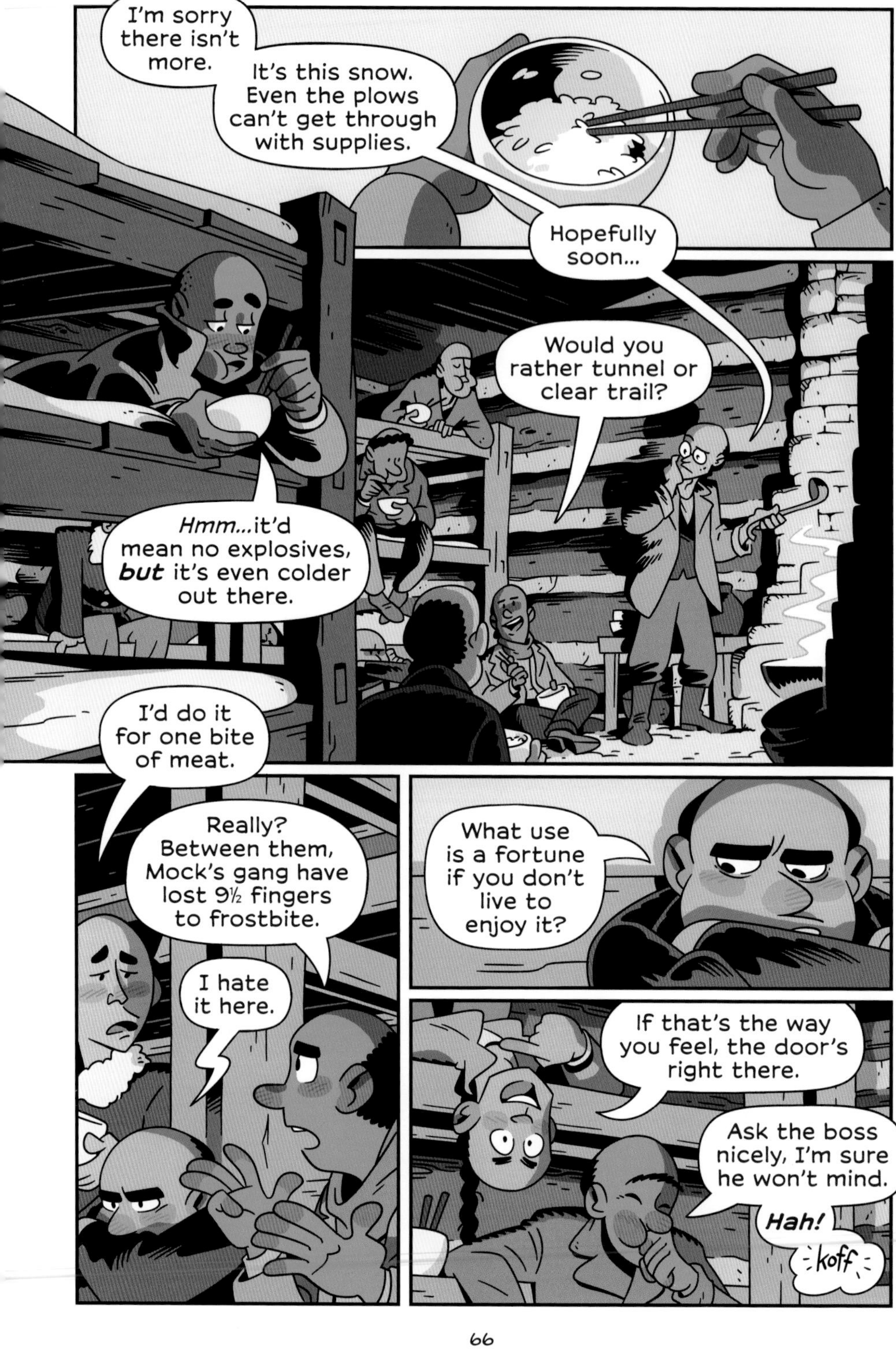

I'm sorry there isn't more.
It's this snow. Even the plows can't get through with supplies.
Hopefully soon...
Would you rather tunnel or clear trail?
*Hmm...*it'd mean no explosives, ***but*** it's even colder out there.
I'd do it for one bite of meat.
Really? Between them, Mock's gang have lost 9½ fingers to frostbite.
I hate it here.
What use is a fortune if you don't live to enjoy it?
If that's the way you feel, the door's right there.
Ask the boss nicely, I'm sure he won't mind.
***Hah!***
koff

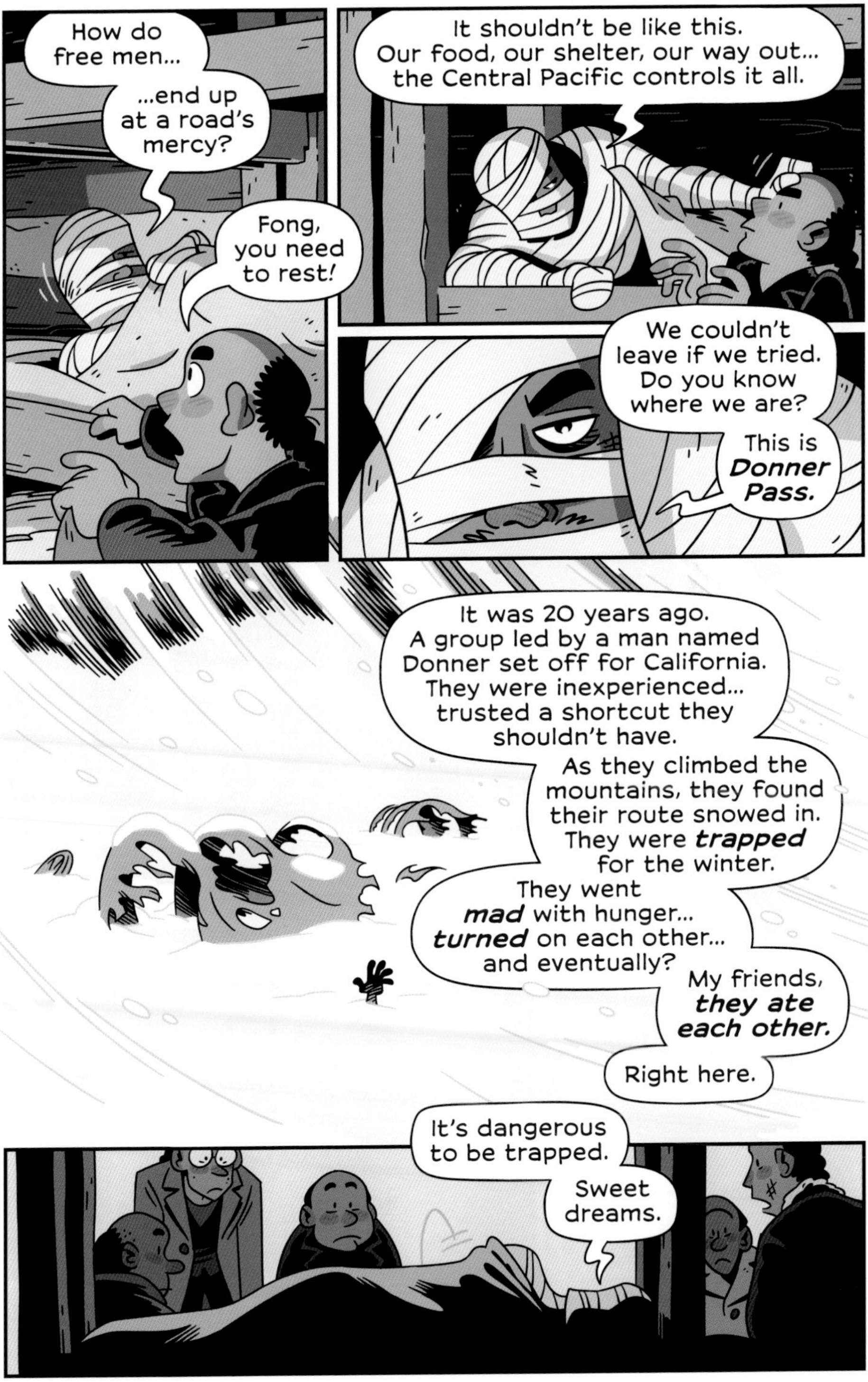
How do free men...
...end up at a road's mercy?
Fong, you need to rest!
It shouldn't be like this. Our food, our shelter, our way out... the Central Pacific controls it all.
We couldn't leave if we tried. Do you know where we are?
This is ***Donner Pass.***
It was 20 years ago. A group led by a man named Donner set off for California. They were inexperienced... trusted a shortcut they shouldn't have.
As they climbed the mountains, they found their route snowed in. They were ***trapped*** for the winter.
They went ***mad*** with hunger... ***turned*** on each other... and eventually?
My friends, ***they ate each other.***
Right here.
It's dangerous to be trapped.
Sweet dreams.

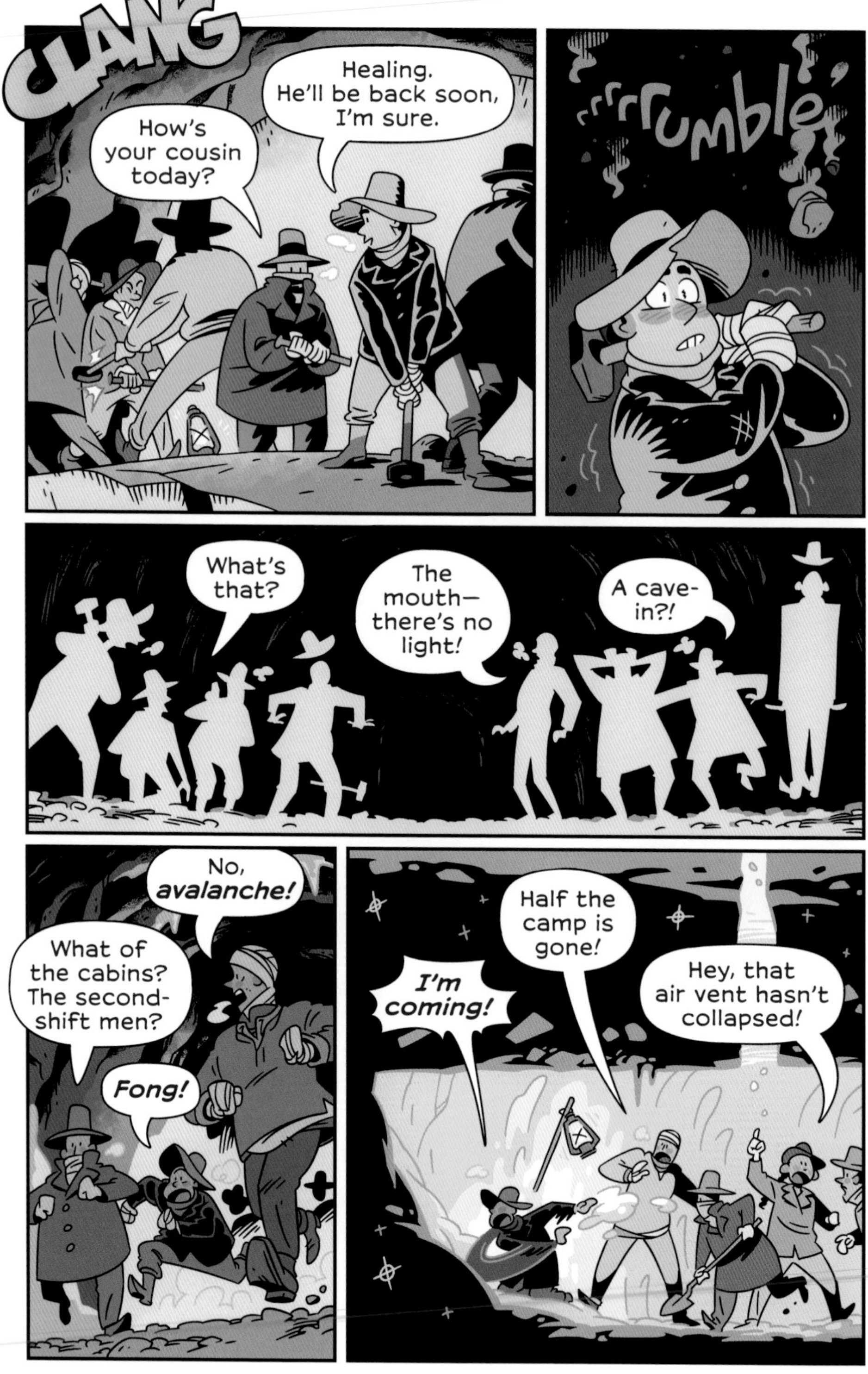
CLANG
How's your cousin today?
Healing. He'll be back soon, I'm sure.
rrrrrumble
What's that?
The mouth— there's no light!
A cave-in?!
No, *avalanche!*
What of the cabins? The second-shift men?
*Fong!*
*I'm coming!*
Half the camp is gone!
Hey, that air vent hasn't collapsed!

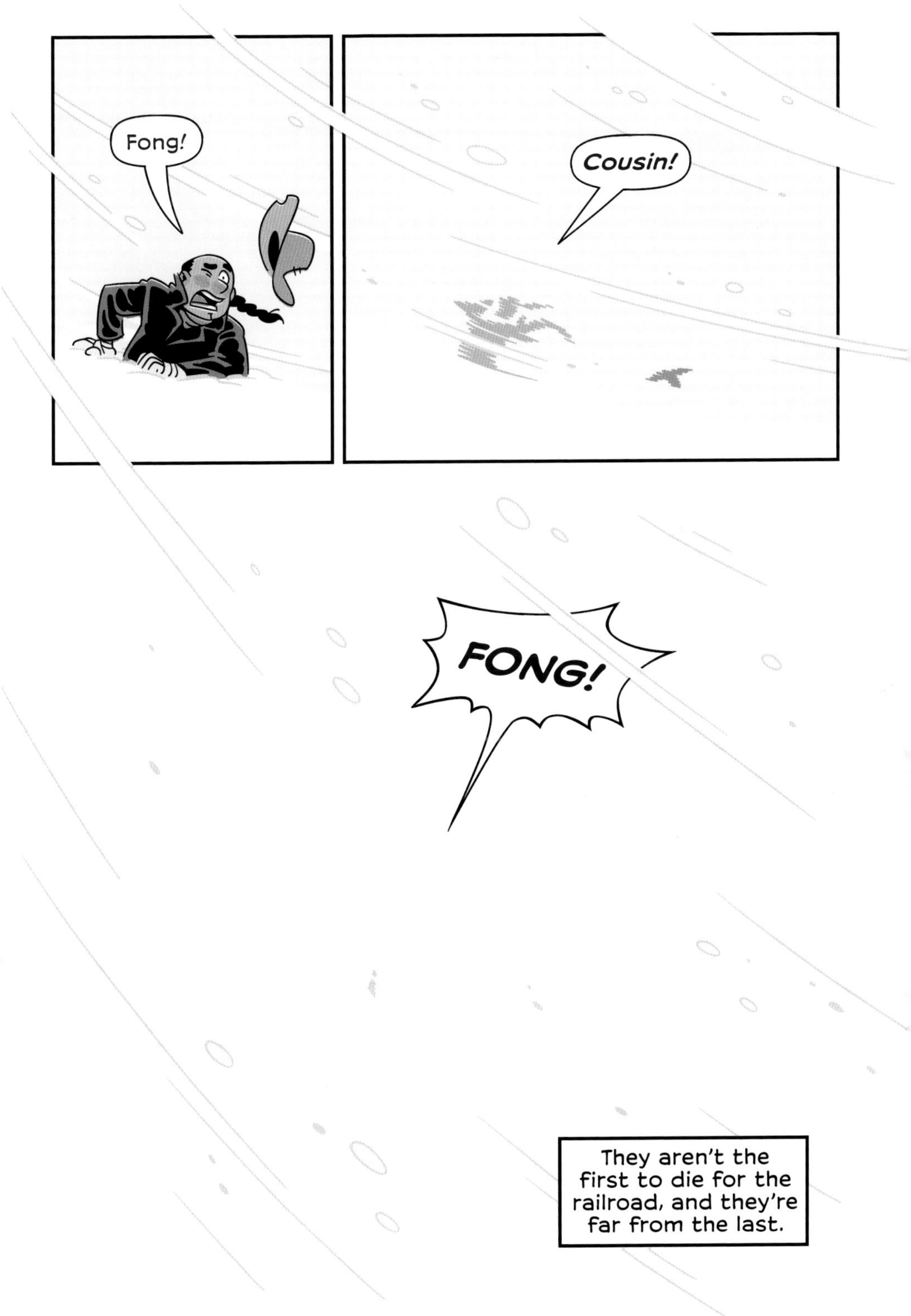
Fong!
Cousin!
FONG!
They aren't the first to die for the railroad, and they're far from the last.

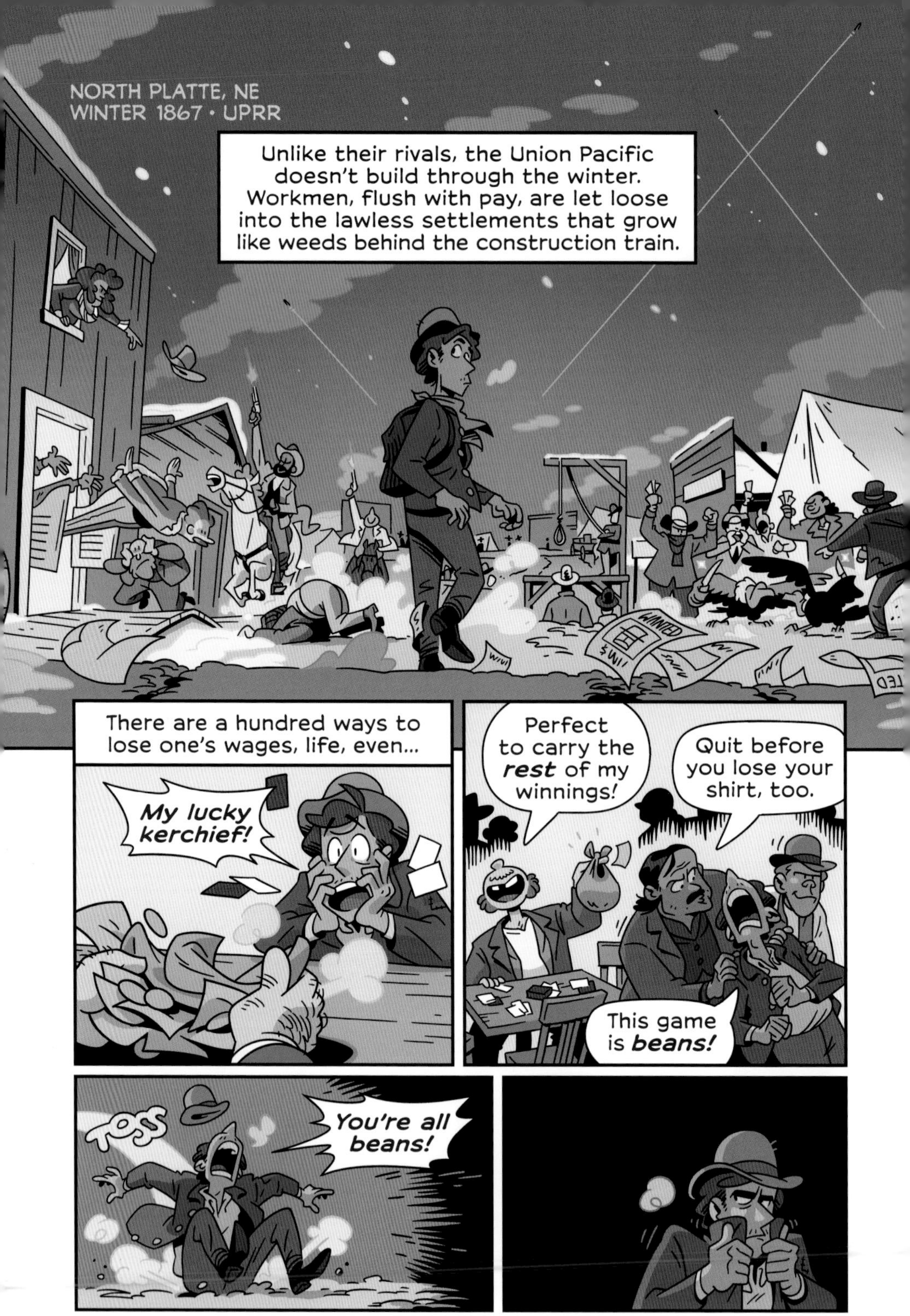
NORTH PLATTE, NE
WINTER 1867 • UPRR
Unlike their rivals, the Union Pacific doesn't build through the winter. Workmen, flush with pay, are let loose into the lawless settlements that grow like weeds behind the construction train.
WANTED
There are a hundred ways to lose one's wages, life, even...
My lucky kerchief!
Perfect to carry the rest of my winnings!
Quit before you lose your shirt, too.
This game is beans!
TOSS
You're all beans!

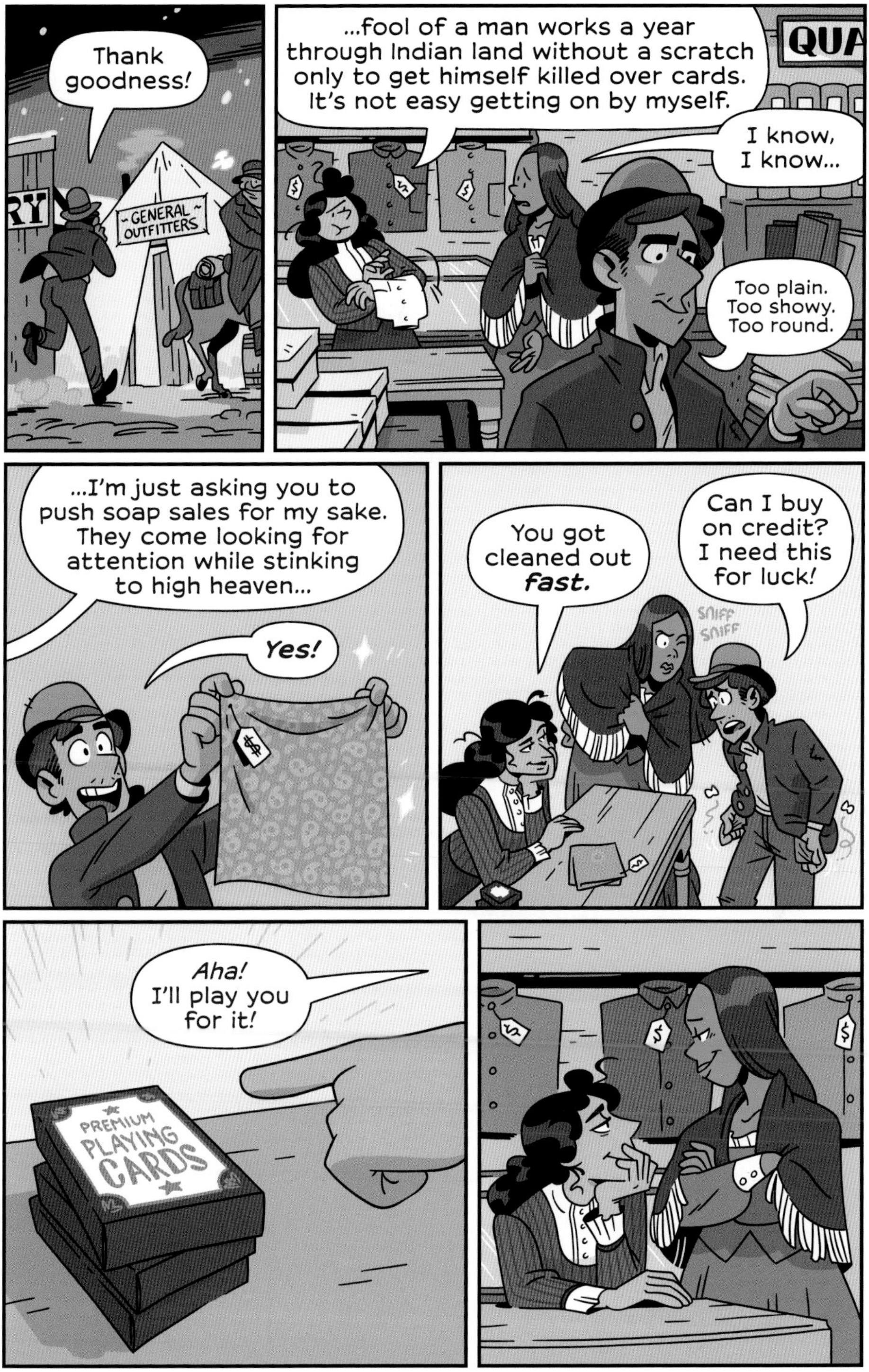
Thank goodness!
GENERAL OUTFITTERS
RY
QUA
...fool of a man works a year through Indian land without a scratch only to get himself killed over cards. It's not easy getting on by myself.
I know, I know...
Too plain. Too showy. Too round.
...I'm just asking you to push soap sales for my sake. They come looking for attention while stinking to high heaven...
Yes!
You got cleaned out fast.
Can I buy on credit? I need this for luck!
SNIFF SNIFF
Aha! I'll play you for it!
PREMIUM PLAYING CARDS

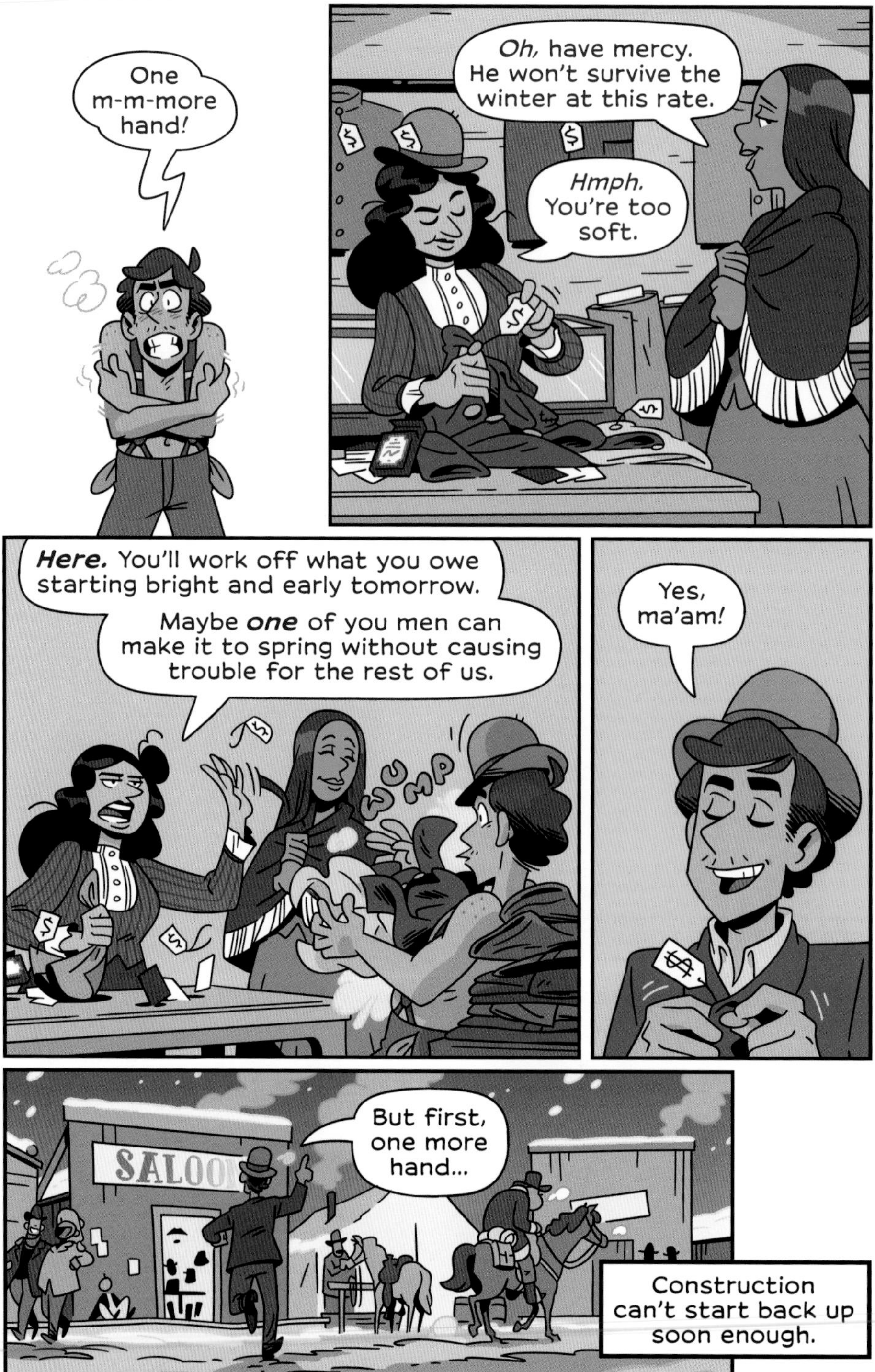
One
m-m-more
hand!
Oh, have mercy.
He won't survive the
winter at this rate.
Hmph.
You're too
soft.
Here. You'll work off what you owe
starting bright and early tomorrow.
Maybe one of you men can
make it to spring without causing
trouble for the rest of us.
WUMP
Yes,
ma'am!
SALOON
But first,
one more
hand...
Construction
can't start back up
soon enough.

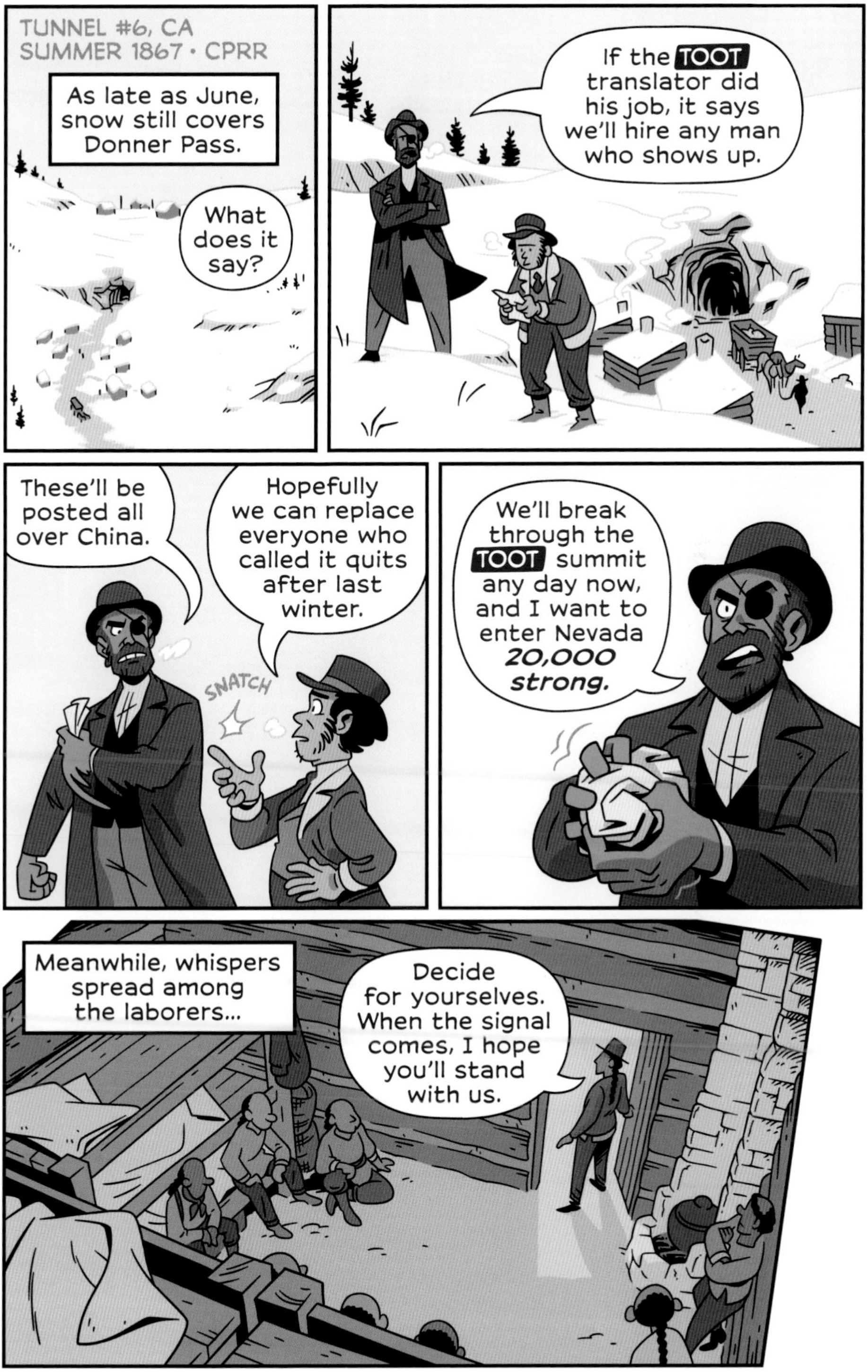
TUNNEL #6, CA
SUMMER 1867 • CPRR
As late as June, snow still covers Donner Pass.
What does it say?
If the TOOT translator did his job, it says we'll hire any man who shows up.
These'll be posted all over China.
Hopefully we can replace everyone who called it quits after last winter.
SNATCH
We'll break through the TOOT summit any day now, and I want to enter Nevada *20,000 strong.*
Meanwhile, whispers spread among the laborers...
Decide for yourselves. When the signal comes, I hope you'll stand with us.

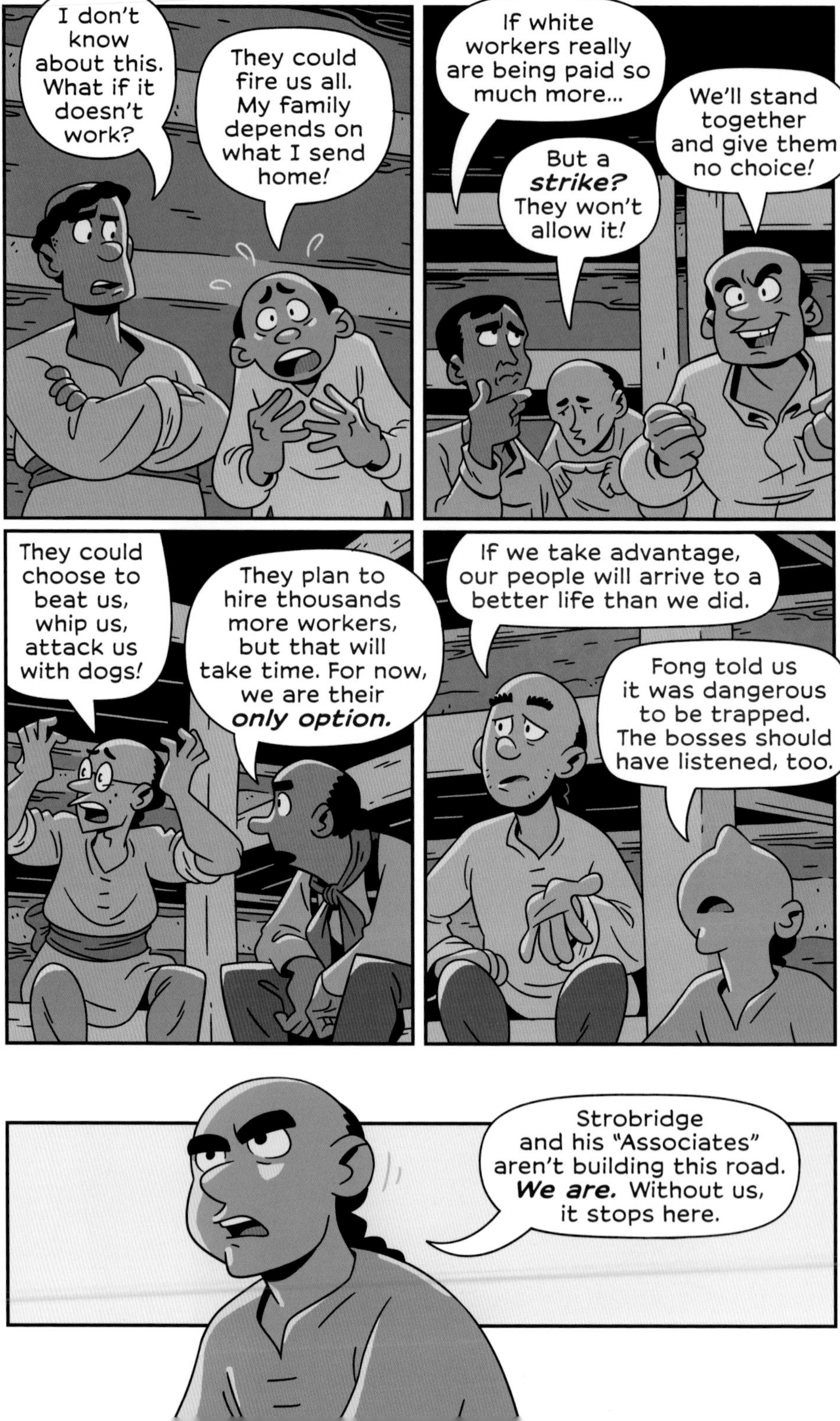
I don't know about this. What if it doesn't work?
They could fire us all. My family depends on what I send home!
If white workers really are being paid so much more...
But a *strike?* They won't allow it!
We'll stand together and give them no choice!
They could choose to beat us, whip us, attack us with dogs!
They plan to hire thousands more workers, but that will take time. For now, we are their *only option.*
If we take advantage, our people will arrive to a better life than we did.
Fong told us it was dangerous to be trapped. The bosses should have listened, too.
Strobridge and his "Associates" aren't building this road. *We are.* Without us, it stops here.

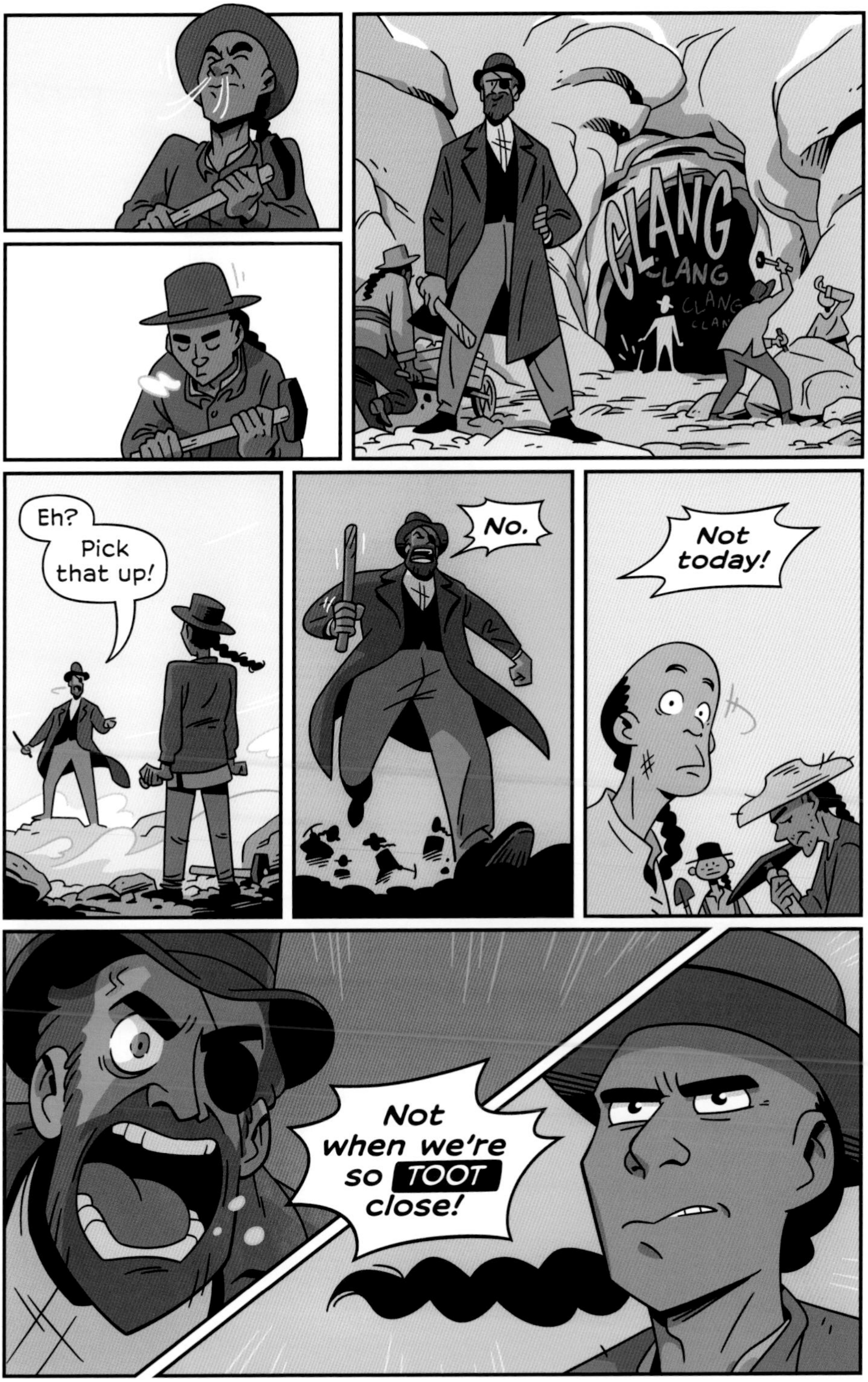
CLANG
CLANG
CLANG
CLAN
Eh? Pick that up!
No.
Not today!
Not when we're so TOOT close!

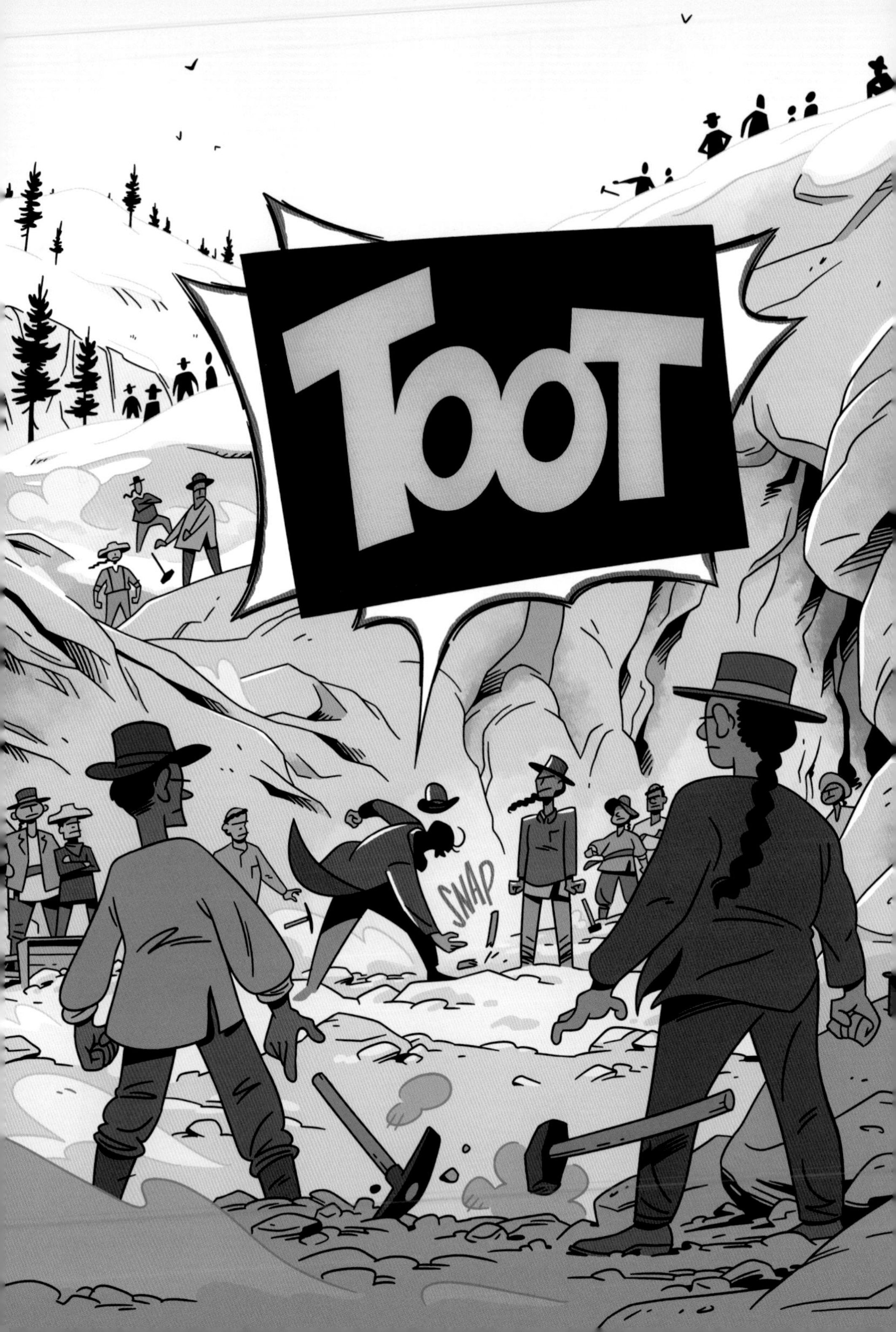
TOOT
SNAP

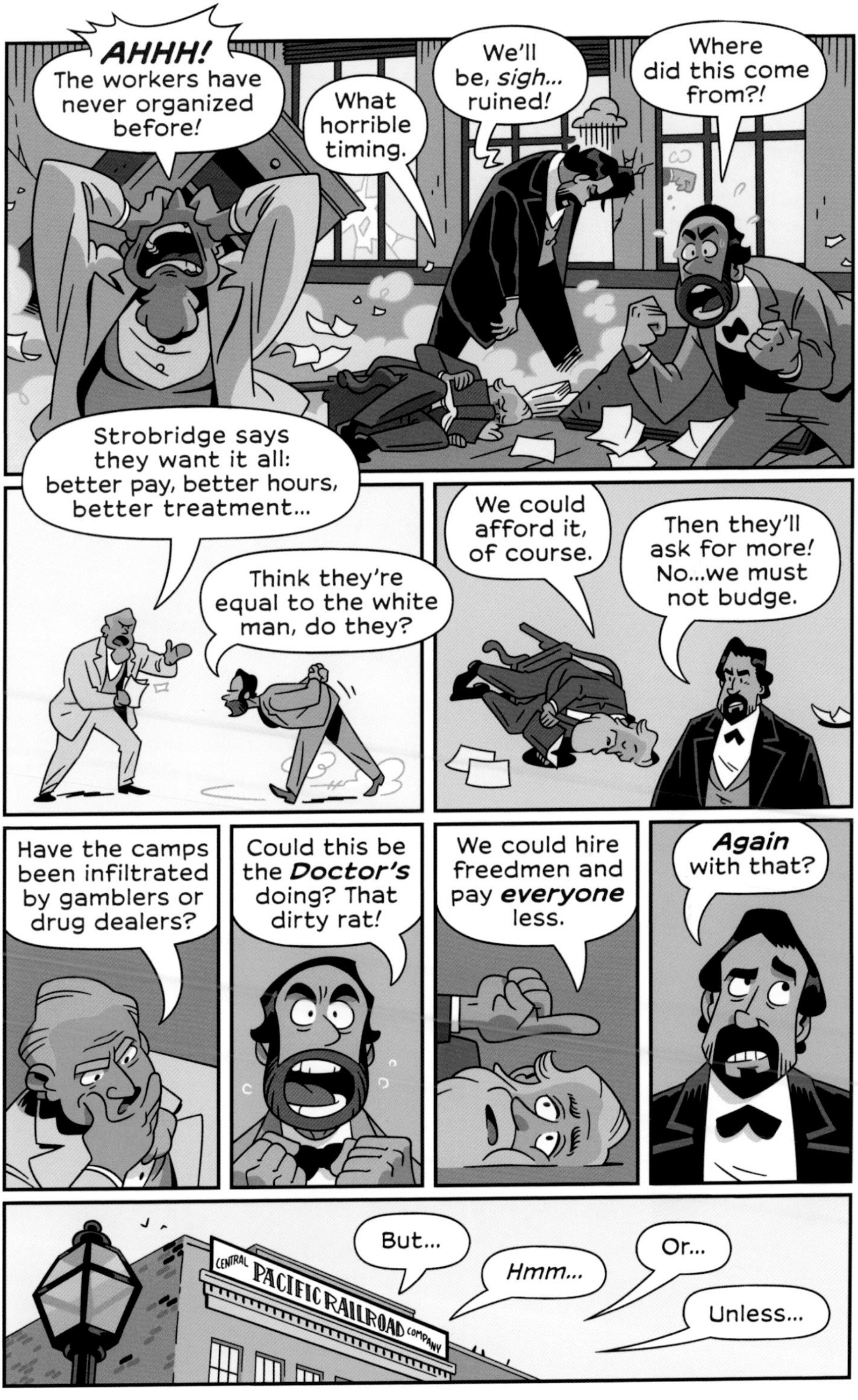

AHHH! The workers have never organized before!
What horrible timing.
We'll be, sigh... ruined!
Where did this come from?!
Strobridge says they want it all: better pay, better hours, better treatment...
Think they're equal to the white man, do they?
We could afford it, of course.
Then they'll ask for more! No...we must not budge.
Have the camps been infiltrated by gamblers or drug dealers?
Could this be the Doctor's doing? That dirty rat!
We could hire freedmen and pay everyone less.
Again with that?
CENTRAL PACIFIC RAILROAD COMPANY
But...
Hmm...
Or...
Unless...

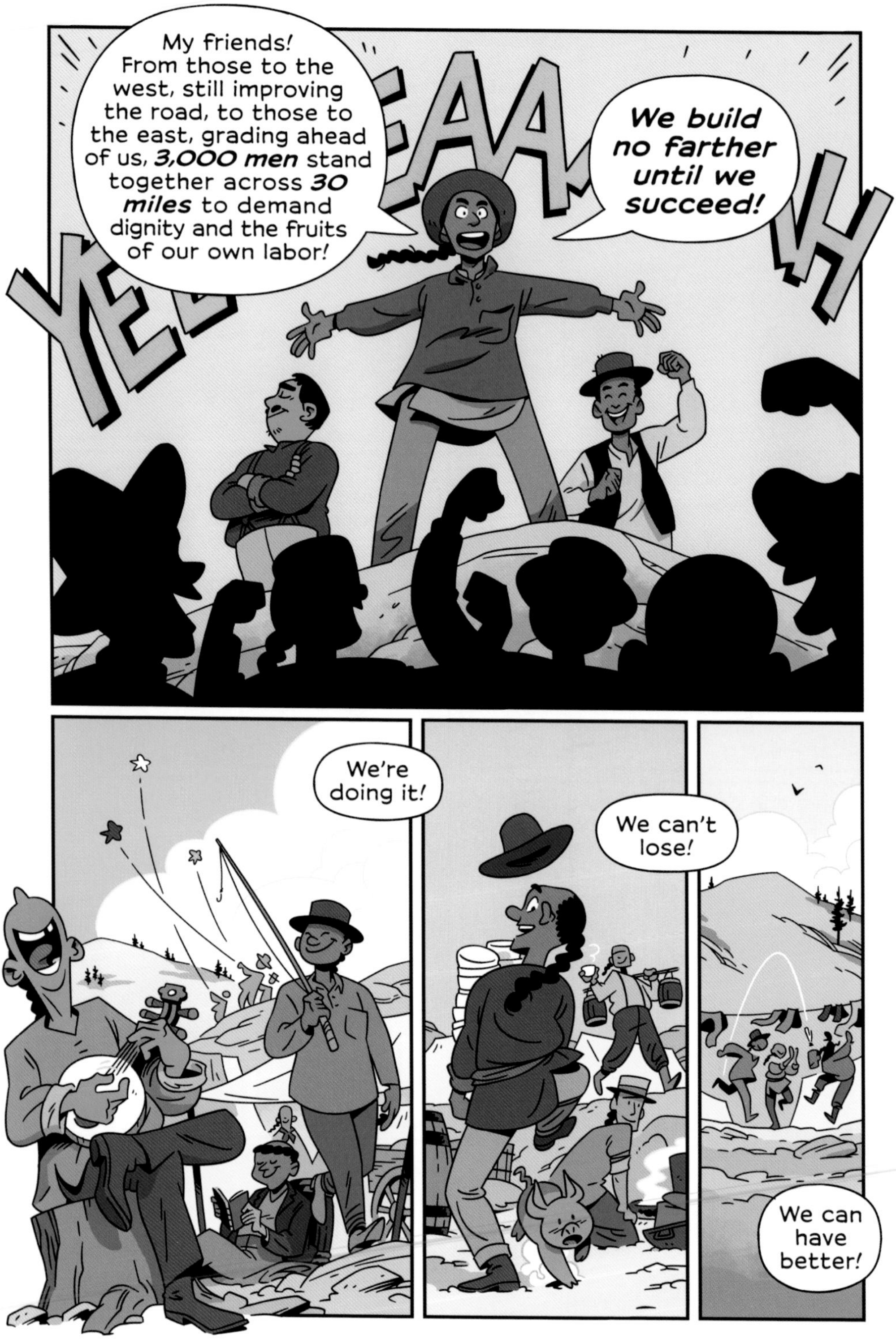
My friends! From those to the west, still improving the road, to those to the east, grading ahead of us, **3,000 men** stand together across **30 miles** to demand dignity and the fruits of our own labor!
YEEEAAAAHH
**We build no farther until we succeed!**
We're doing it!
We can't lose!
We can have better!

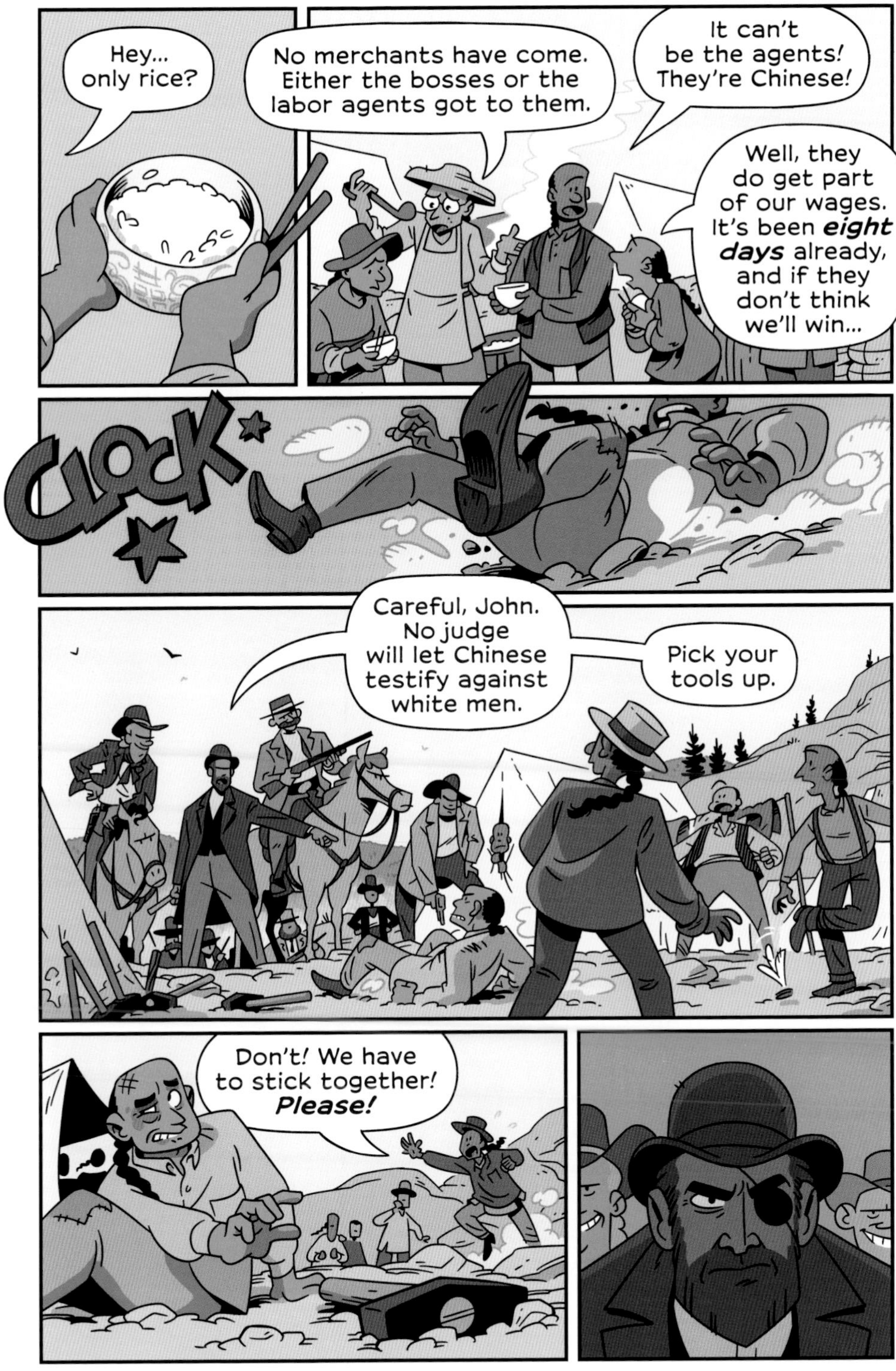
Hey... only rice?
No merchants have come. Either the bosses or the labor agents got to them.
It can't be the agents! They're Chinese!
Well, they do get part of our wages. It's been ***eight days*** already, and if they don't think we'll win...
CLOCK
Careful, John. No judge will let Chinese testify against white men.
Pick your tools up.
Don't! We have to stick together! ***Please!***

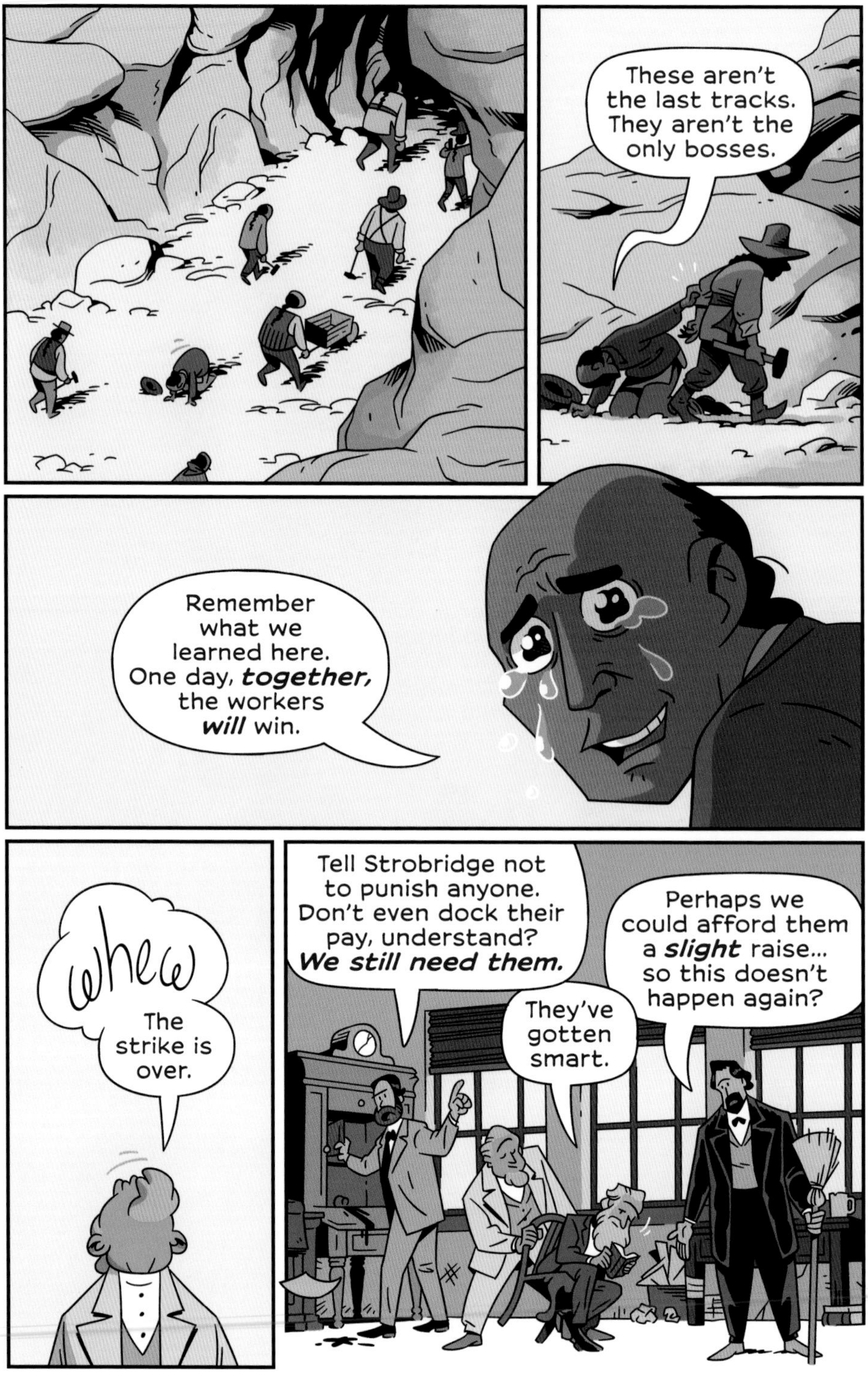
These aren't the last tracks. They aren't the only bosses.
Remember what we learned here. One day, ***together,*** the workers ***will*** win.
whew
The strike is over.
Tell Strobridge not to punish anyone. Don't even dock their pay, understand? ***We still need them.***
They've gotten smart.
Perhaps we could afford them a ***slight*** raise... so this doesn't happen again?

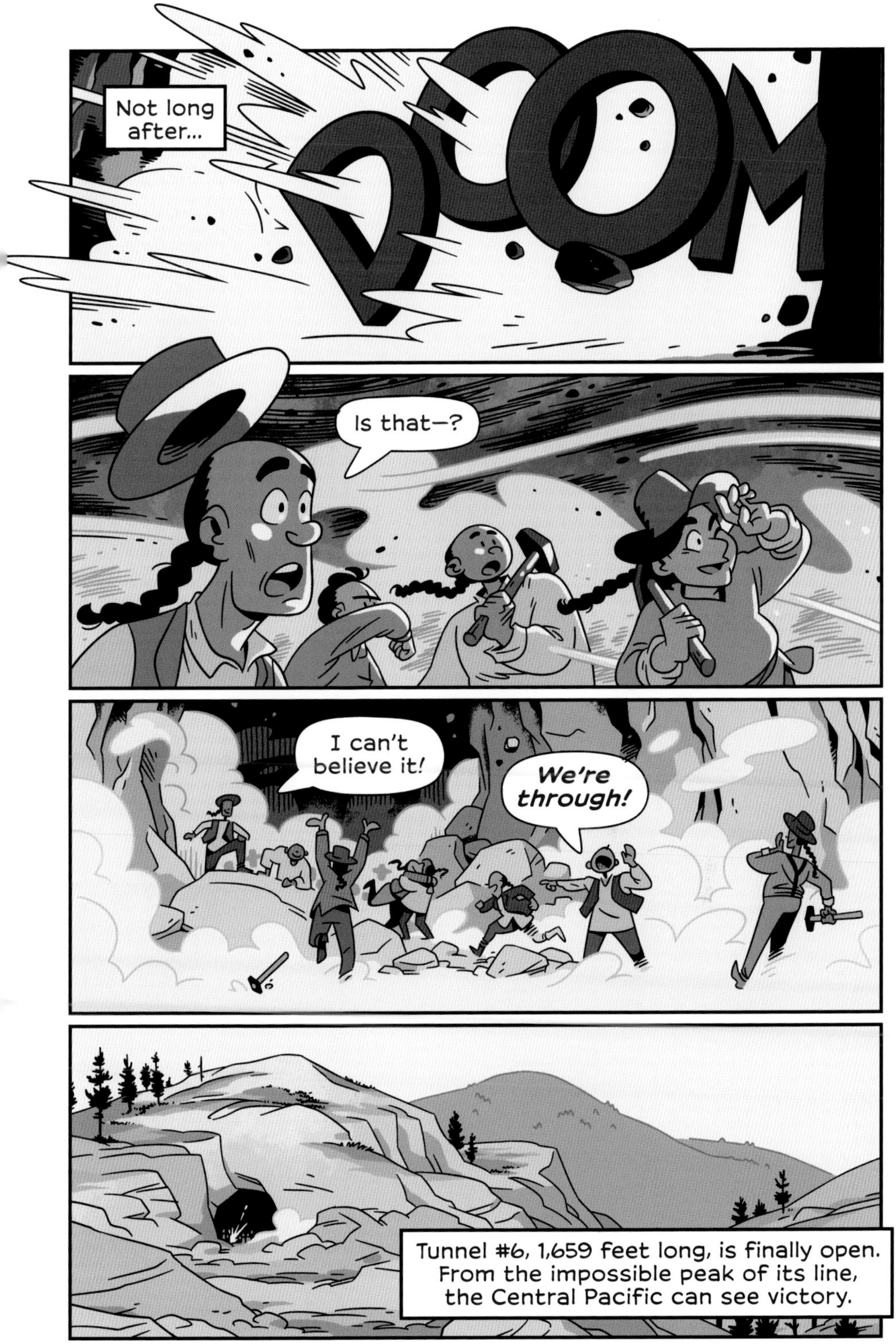
Not long after...
DOOM
Is that—?
I can't believe it!
We're through!
Tunnel #6, 1,659 feet long, is finally open.
From the impossible peak of its line,
the Central Pacific can see victory.

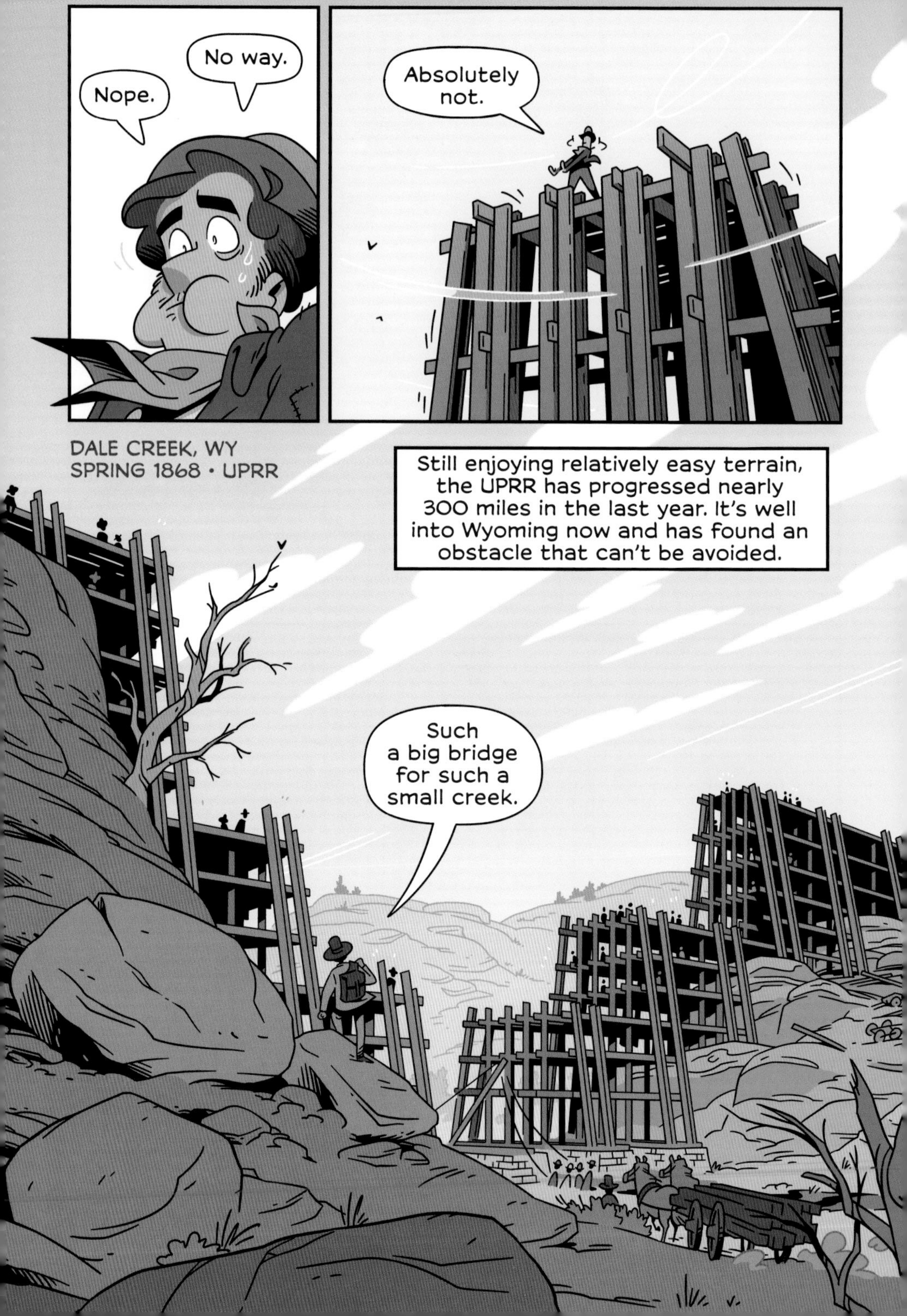
No way.
Nope.
Absolutely not.
DALE CREEK, WY
SPRING 1868 • UPRR
Still enjoying relatively easy terrain, the UPRR has progressed nearly 300 miles in the last year. It's well into Wyoming now and has found an obstacle that can't be avoided.
Such a big bridge for such a small creek.

Up she goes!

Good!

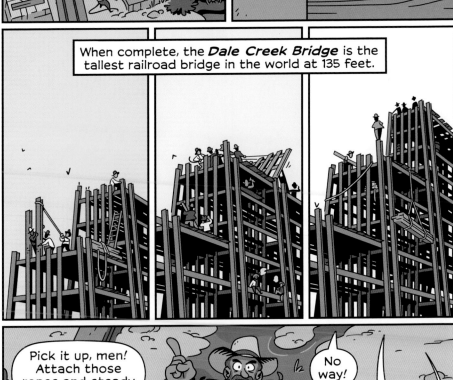

When complete, the **Dale Creek Bridge** is the tallest railroad bridge in the world at 135 feet.

Pick it up, men! Attach those ropes and steady this thing!

You want to get beaten by those Central Pacific Chinese?!

No way!

We'll show them!

Boo!

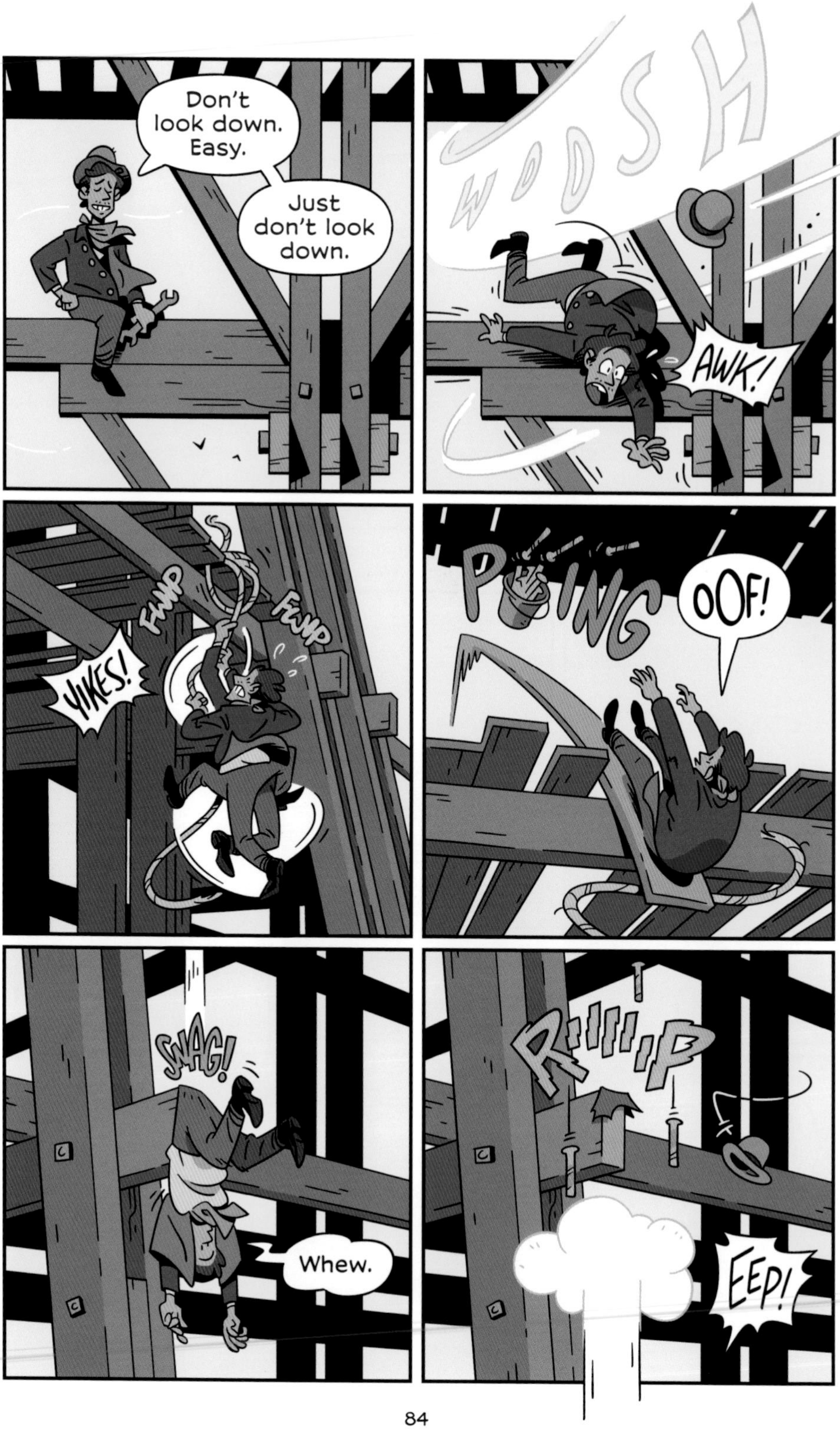
Don't look down. Easy.
Just don't look down.
WOOSH
AWK!
FWIP
FWIP
YIKES!
PTING
OOF!
SNAG!
Whew.
RIIIIP
EEP!

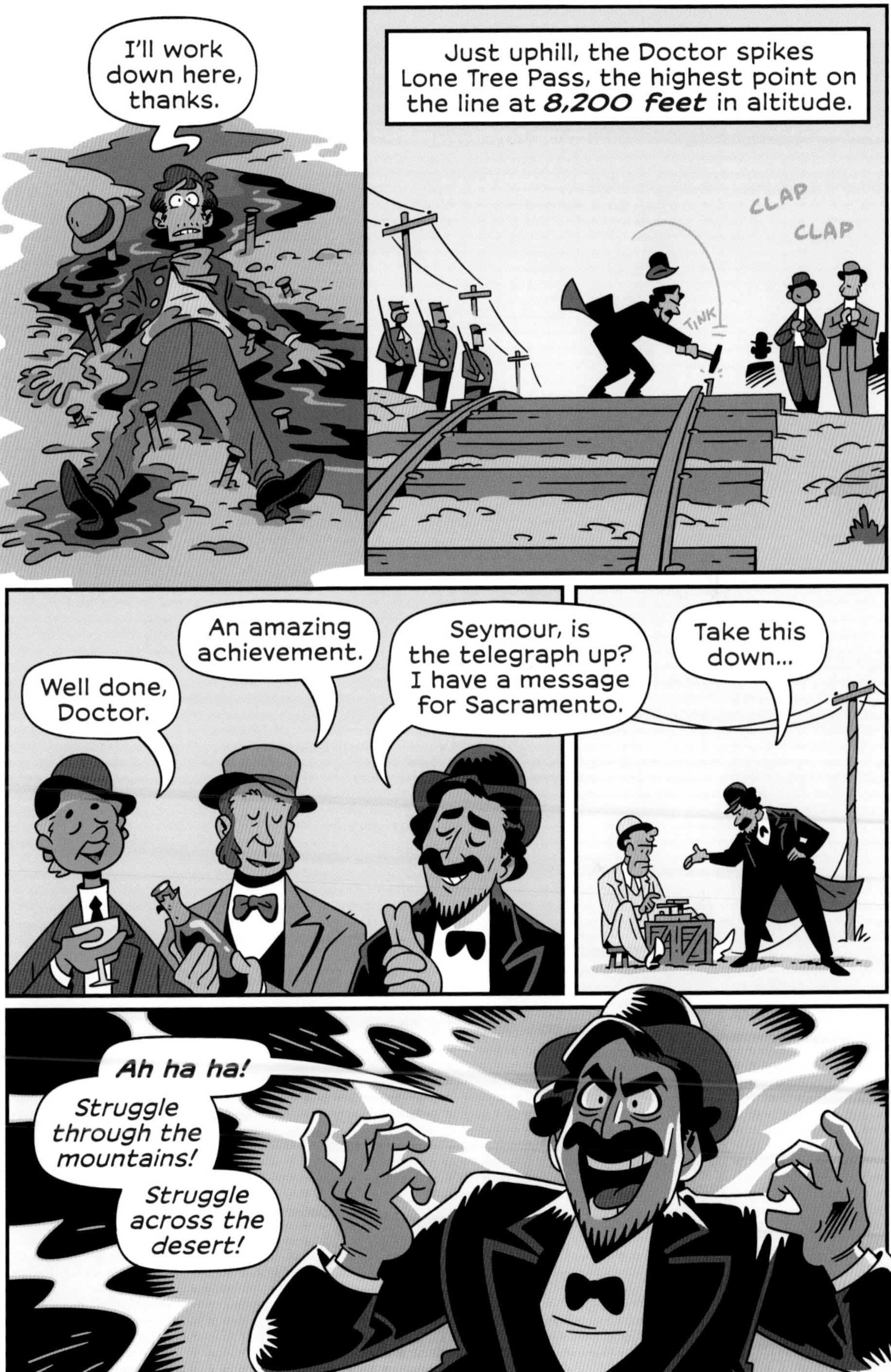
I'll work down here, thanks.
Just uphill, the Doctor spikes Lone Tree Pass, the highest point on the line at ***8,200 feet*** in altitude.
CLAP
CLAP
TINK
Well done, Doctor.
An amazing achievement.
Seymour, is the telegraph up? I have a message for Sacramento.
Take this down...
*Ah ha ha!*
*Struggle through the mountains!*
*Struggle across the desert!*

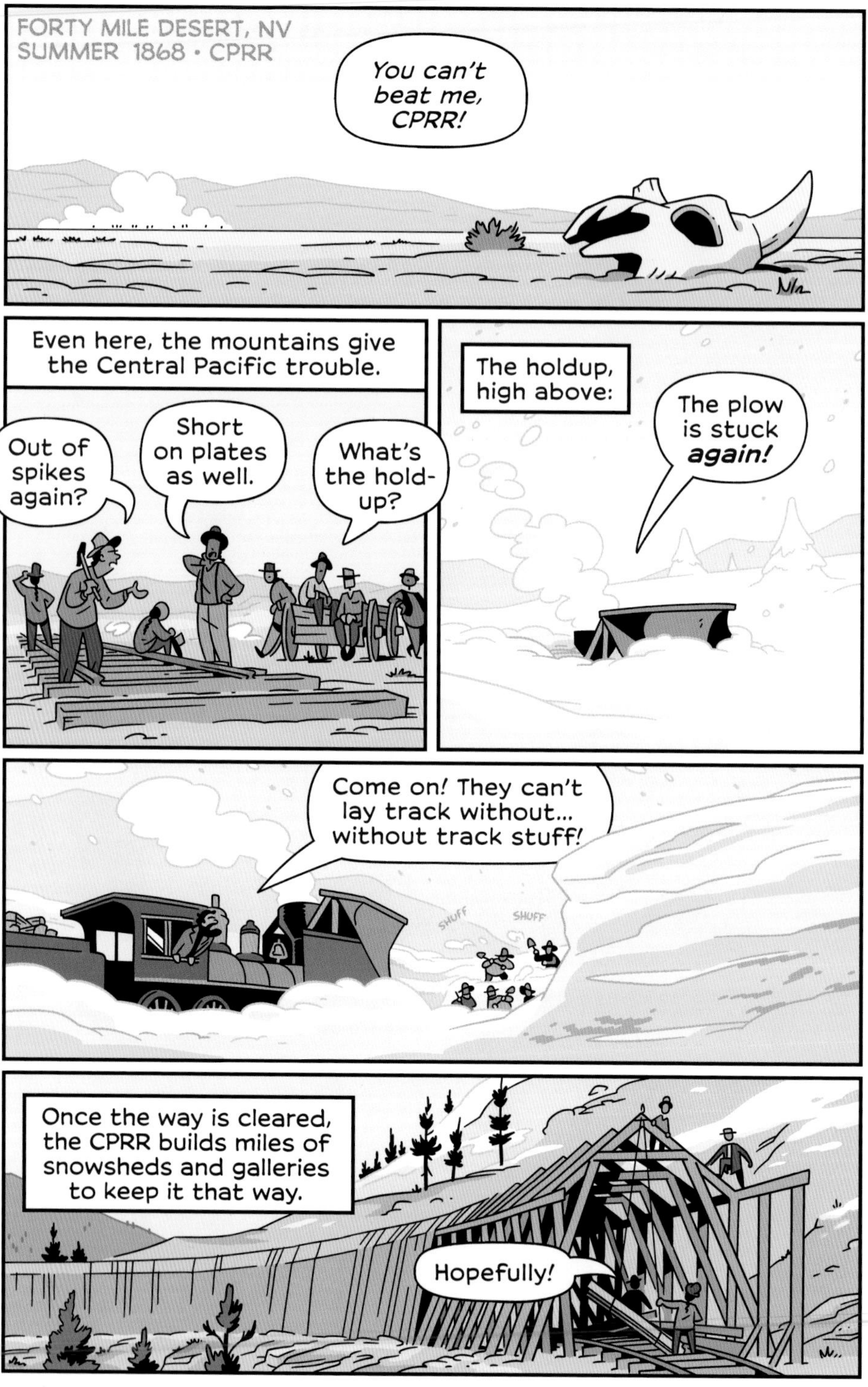
FORTY MILE DESERT, NV
SUMMER 1868 • CPRR
You can't beat me, CPRR!
Even here, the mountains give the Central Pacific trouble.
Out of spikes again?
Short on plates as well.
What's the hold-up?
The holdup, high above:
The plow is stuck again!
Come on! They can't lay track without... without track stuff!
SHUFF
SHUFF
Once the way is cleared, the CPRR builds miles of snowsheds and galleries to keep it that way.
Hopefully!

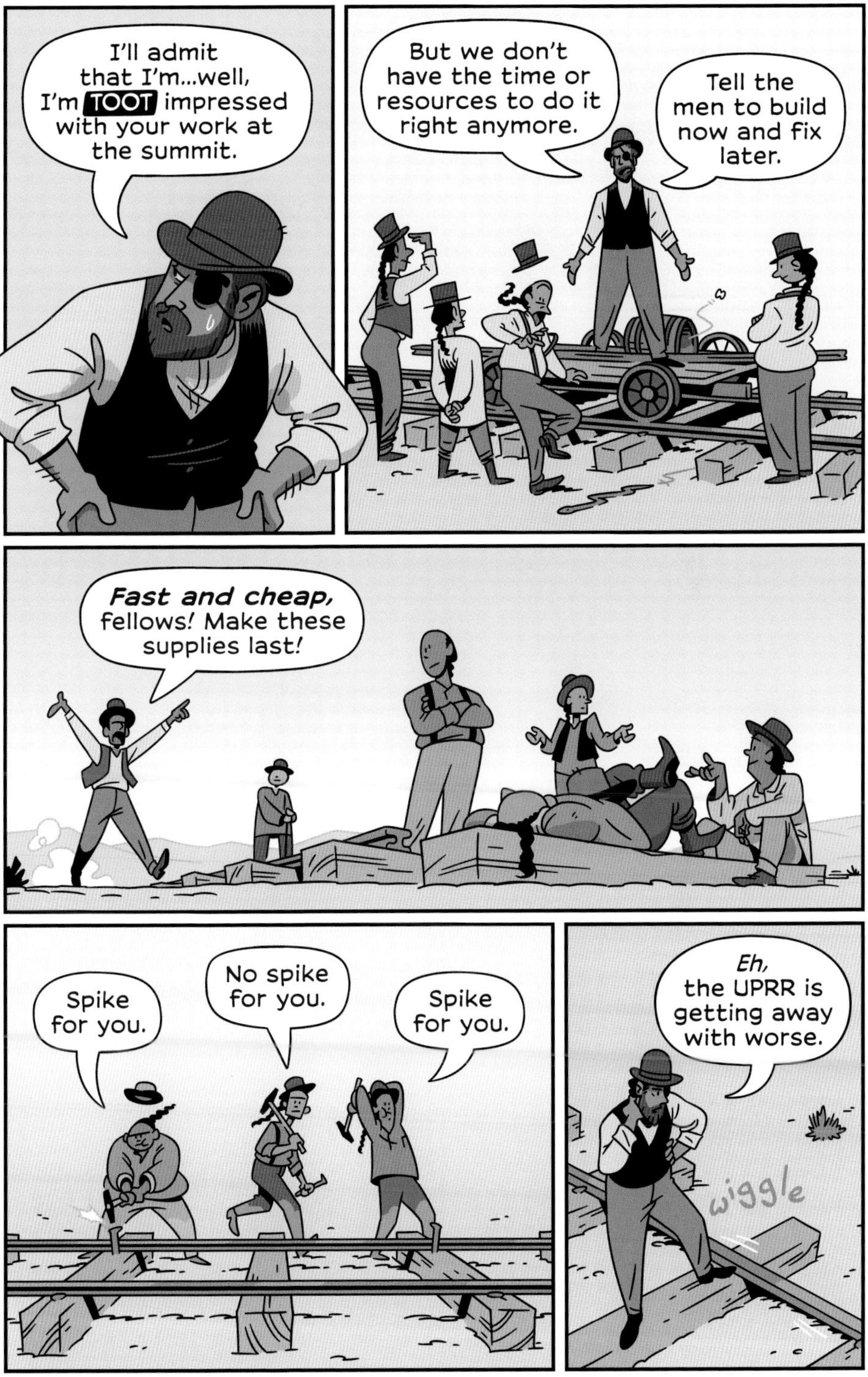
I'll admit that I'm...well, I'm TOOT impressed with your work at the summit.
But we don't have the time or resources to do it right anymore.
Tell the men to build now and fix later.
*Fast and cheap,* fellows! Make these supplies last!
Spike for you.
No spike for you.
Spike for you.
*Eh,* the UPRR is getting away with worse.
wiggle

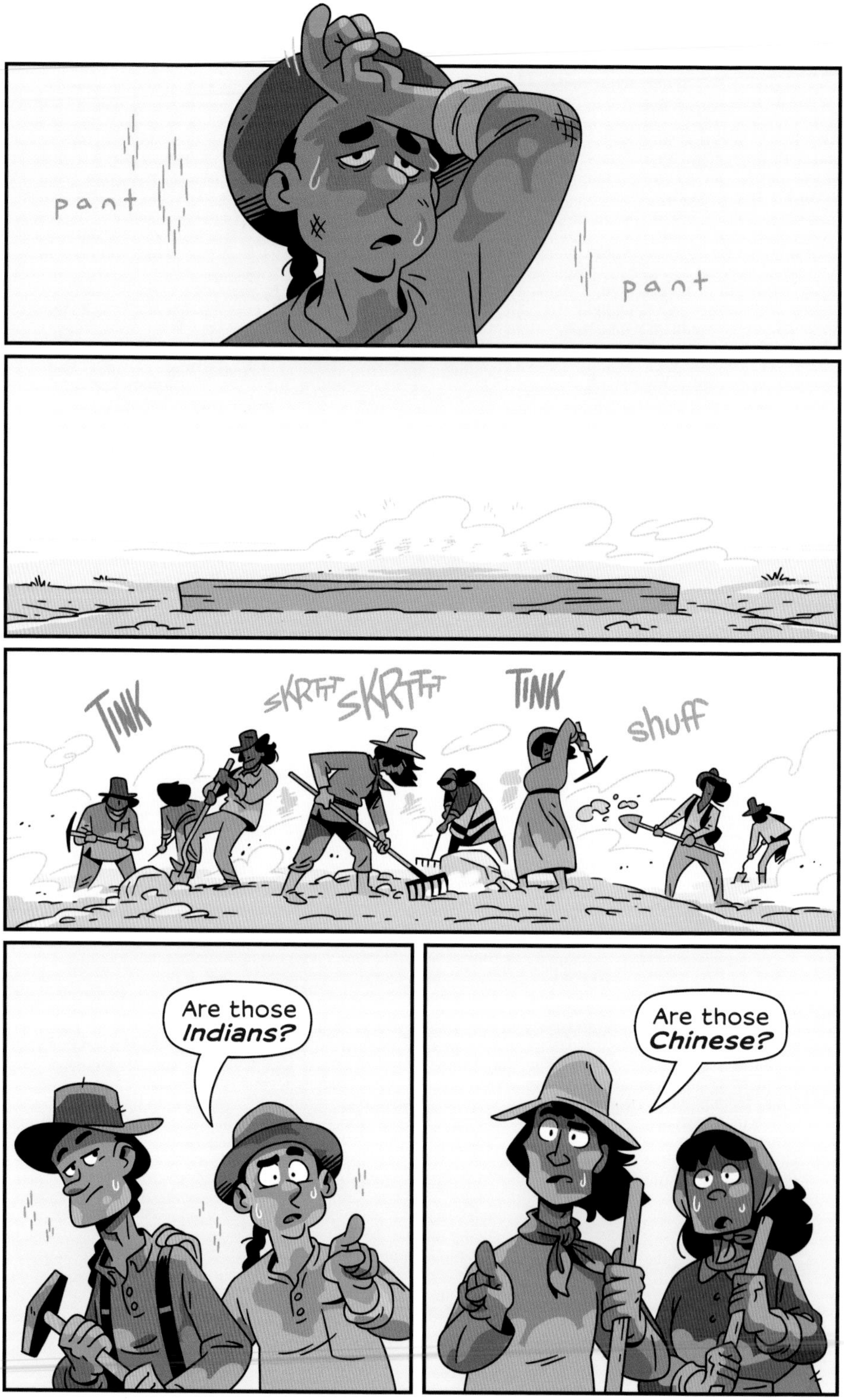
pant
pant
TINK
SKRTTT SKRTTT
TINK
shuff
Are those *Indians?*
Are those *Chinese?*

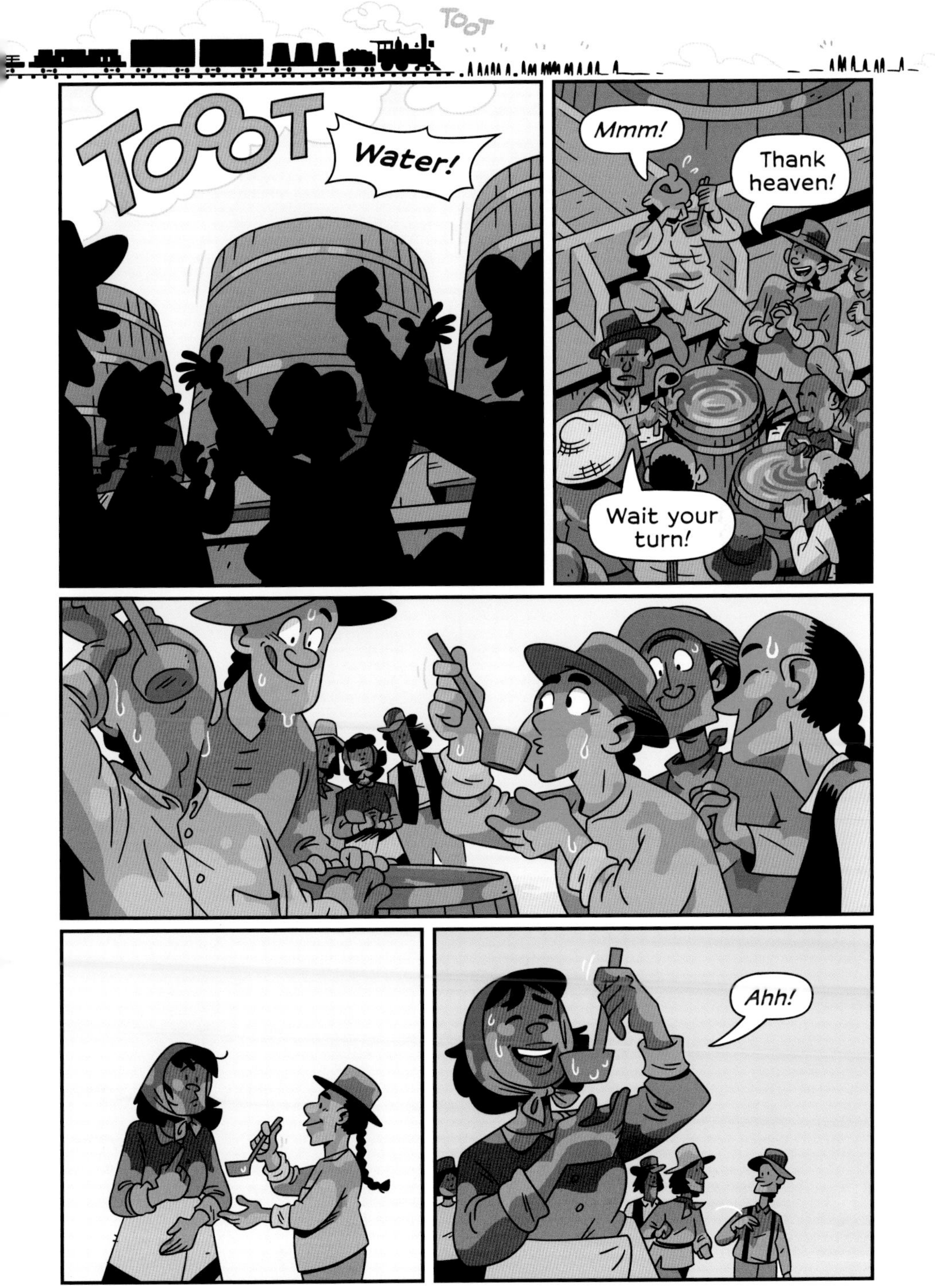
TOOT
TOOOT
Water!
Mmm!
Thank heaven!
Wait your turn!
Ahh!

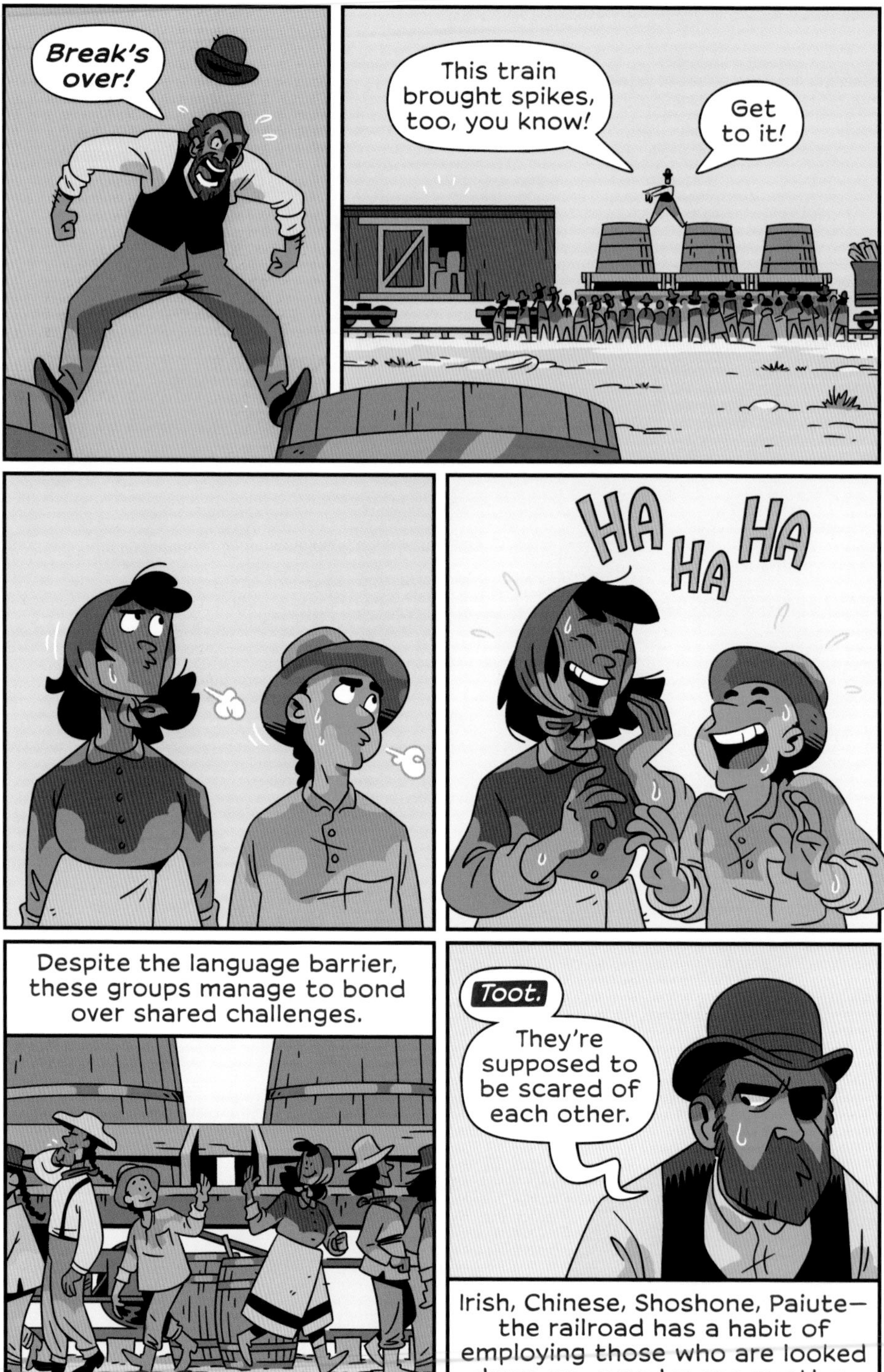
Break's over!
This train brought spikes, too, you know!
Get to it!
HA HA HA
Despite the language barrier, these groups manage to bond over shared challenges.
Toot.
They're supposed to be scared of each other.
Irish, Chinese, Shoshone, Paiute— the railroad has a habit of employing those who are looked down on, even by one another.

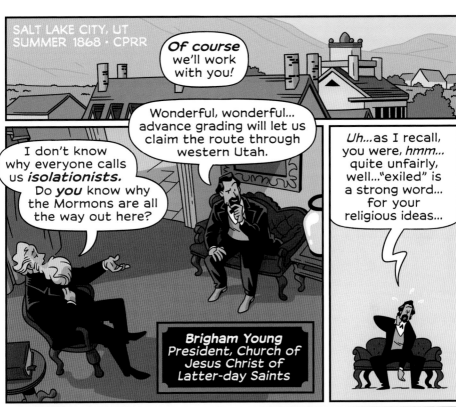

SALT LAKE CITY, UT
SUMMER 1868 · CPRR

*Of course* we'll work with you!

Wonderful, wonderful... advance grading will let us claim the route through western Utah.

I don't know why everyone calls us *isolationists.* Do *you* know why the Mormons are all the way out here?

*Uh...* as I recall, you were, *hmm...* quite unfairly, well..."exiled" is a strong word... for your religious ideas...

**Brigham Young**
*President, Church of Jesus Christ of Latter-day Saints*

And now America's titans of industry need our help! I could laugh! *Ha ha ha!*

*Uh...*
Ha ha ha!

*Ha ha!* And the Doctor has already contracted with us for the *eastern* canyons! What a blessing!

Mormon crews work for *both* railroads. The Church just wants rails to reach Salt Lake City.

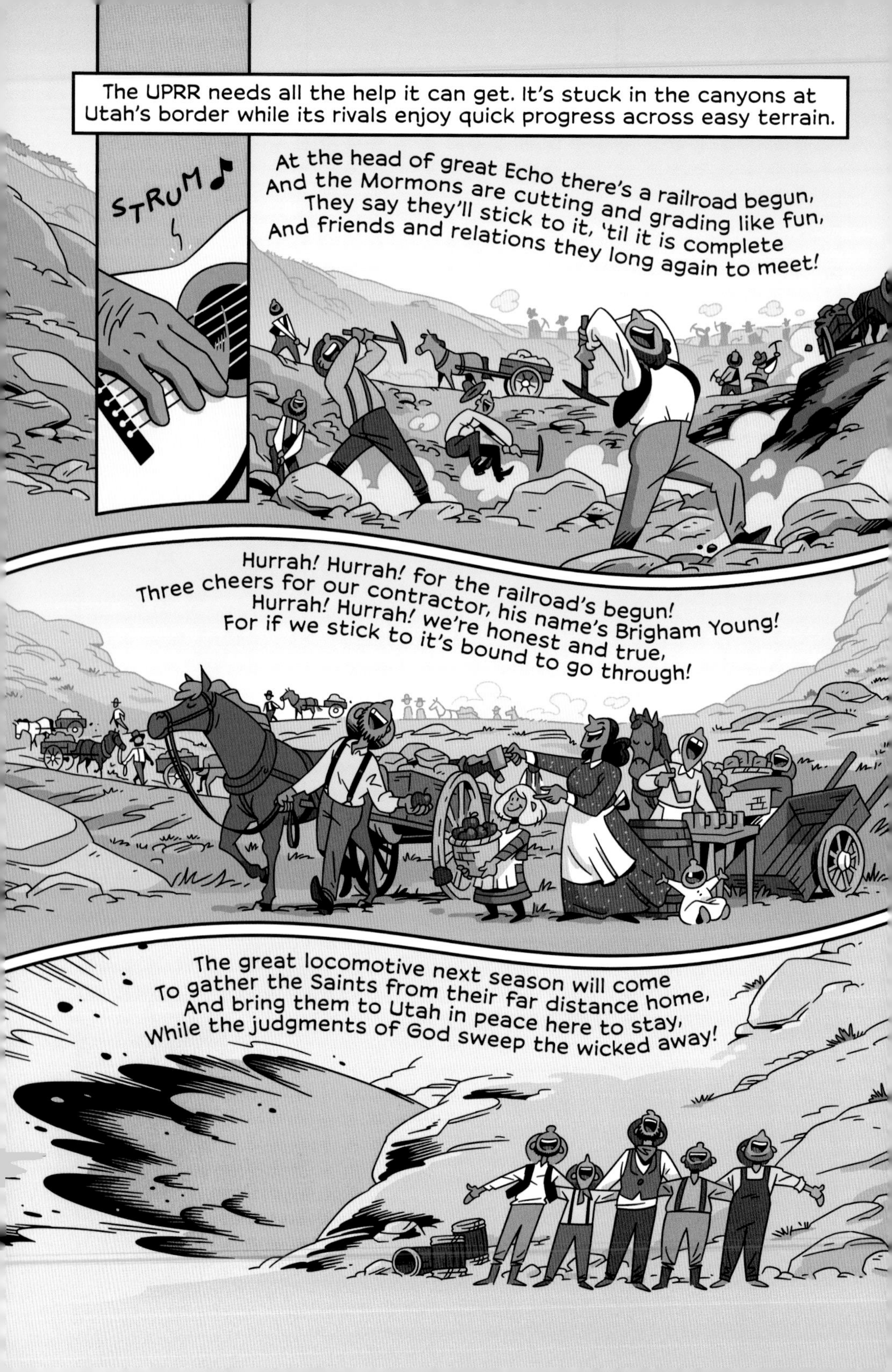
The UPRR needs all the help it can get. It's stuck in the canyons at Utah's border while its rivals enjoy quick progress across easy terrain.
STRUM
At the head of great Echo there's a railroad begun,
And the Mormons are cutting and grading like fun,
They say they'll stick to it, 'til it is complete
And friends and relations they long again to meet!
Hurrah! Hurrah! for the railroad's begun!
Three cheers for our contractor, his name's Brigham Young!
Hurrah! Hurrah! we're honest and true,
For if we stick to it's bound to go through!
The great locomotive next season will come
To gather the Saints from their far distance home,
And bring them to Utah in peace here to stay,
While the judgments of God sweep the wicked away!

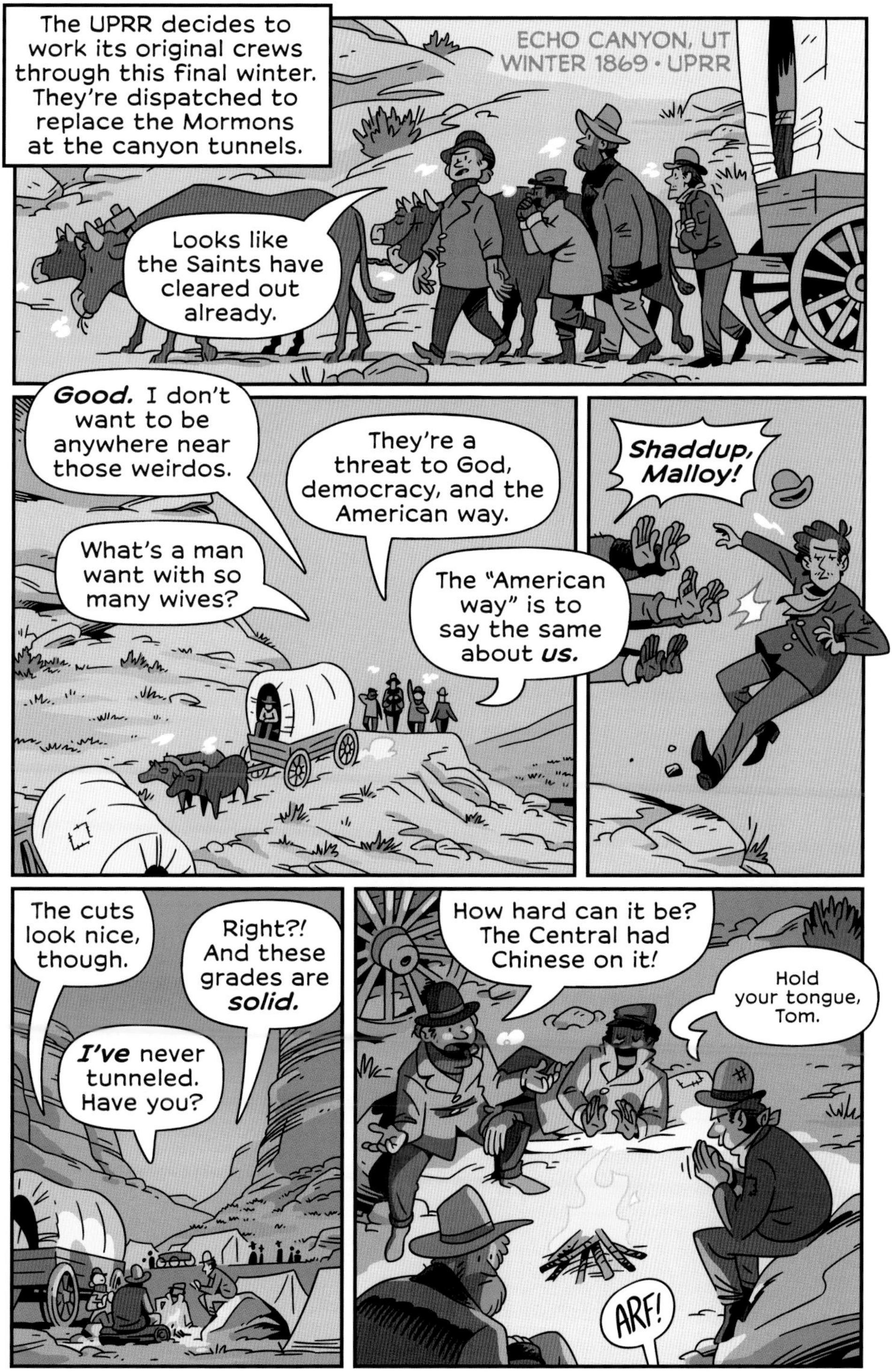
The UPRR decides to work its original crews through this final winter. They're dispatched to replace the Mormons at the canyon tunnels.
ECHO CANYON, UT WINTER 1869 • UPRR
Looks like the Saints have cleared out already.
*Good.* I don't want to be anywhere near those weirdos.
They're a threat to God, democracy, and the American way.
What's a man want with so many wives?
The "American way" is to say the same about *us.*
*Shaddup, Malloy!*
The cuts look nice, though.
Right?! And these grades are *solid.*
*I've* never tunneled. Have you?
How hard can it be? The Central had Chinese on it!
Hold your tongue, Tom.
ARF!

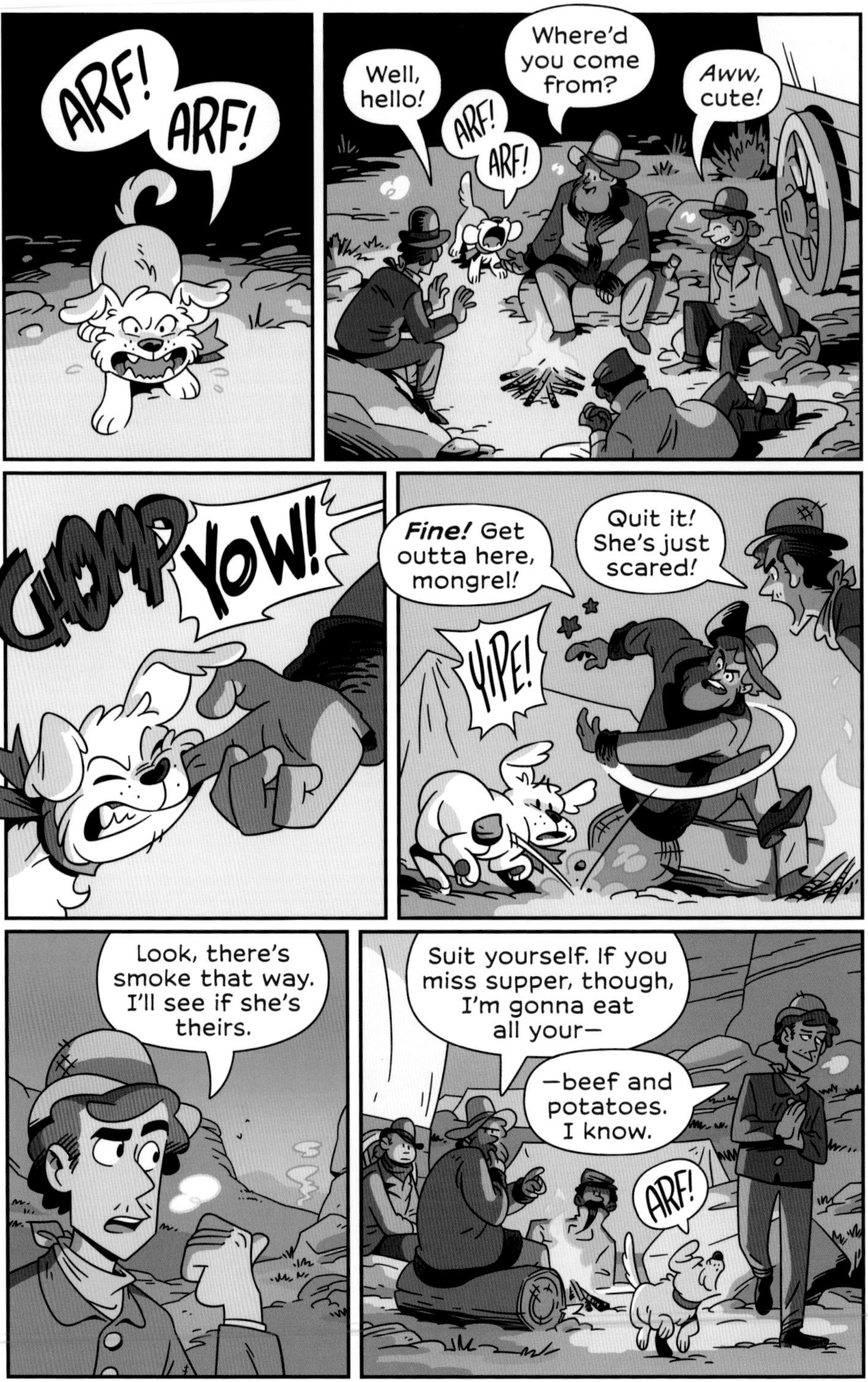
ARF!
ARF!
Well, hello!
ARF!
ARF!
Where'd you come from?
*Aww,* cute!
CHOMP
YOW!
***Fine!*** Get outta here, mongrel!
Quit it! She's just scared!
YIPE!
Look, there's smoke that way. I'll see if she's theirs.
Suit yourself. If you miss supper, though, I'm gonna eat all your—
—beef and potatoes. I know.
ARF!

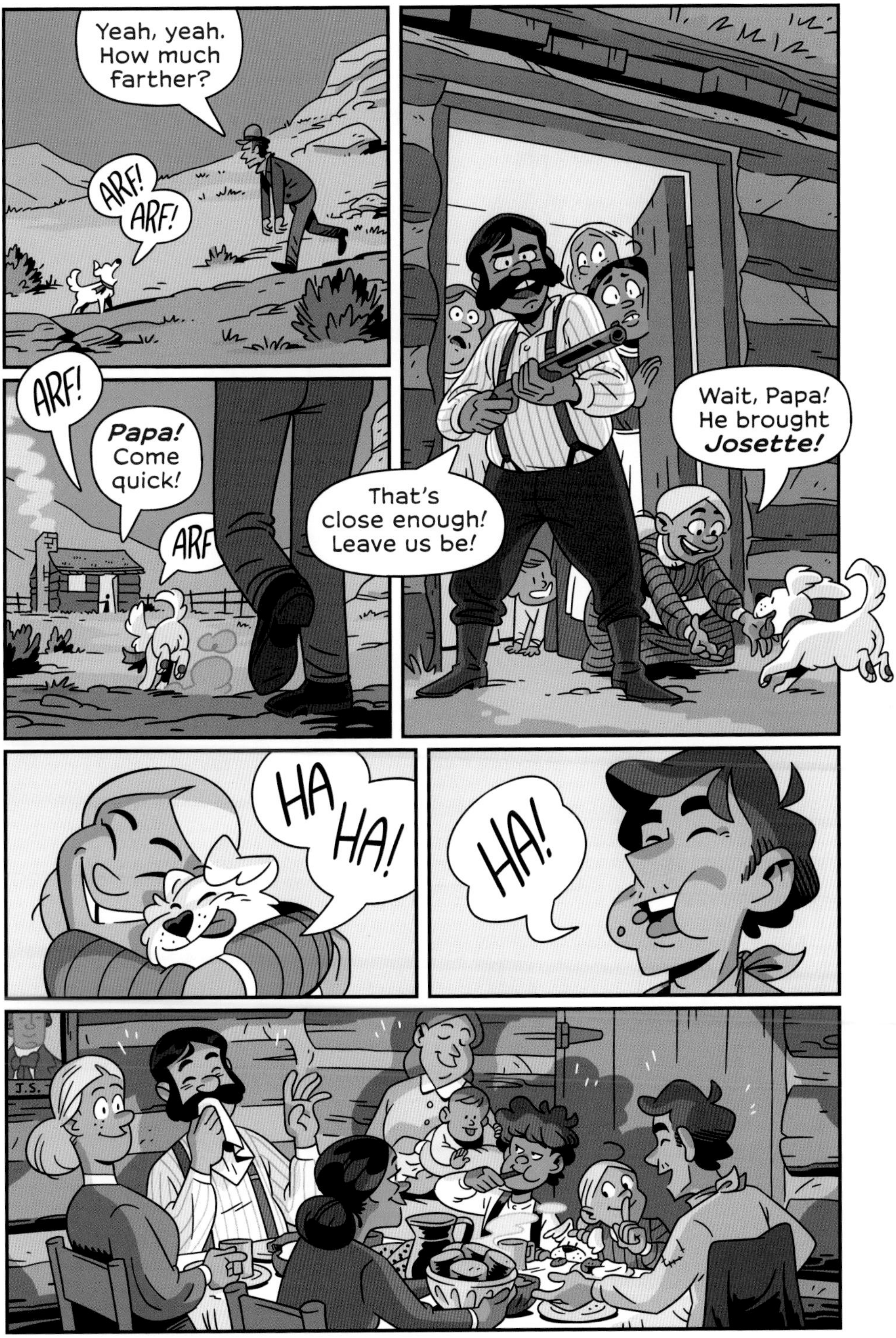
Yeah, yeah. How much farther?
ARF! ARF!
ARF!
Papa! Come quick!
ARF
That's close enough! Leave us be!
Wait, Papa! He brought Josette!
HA HA!
HA!

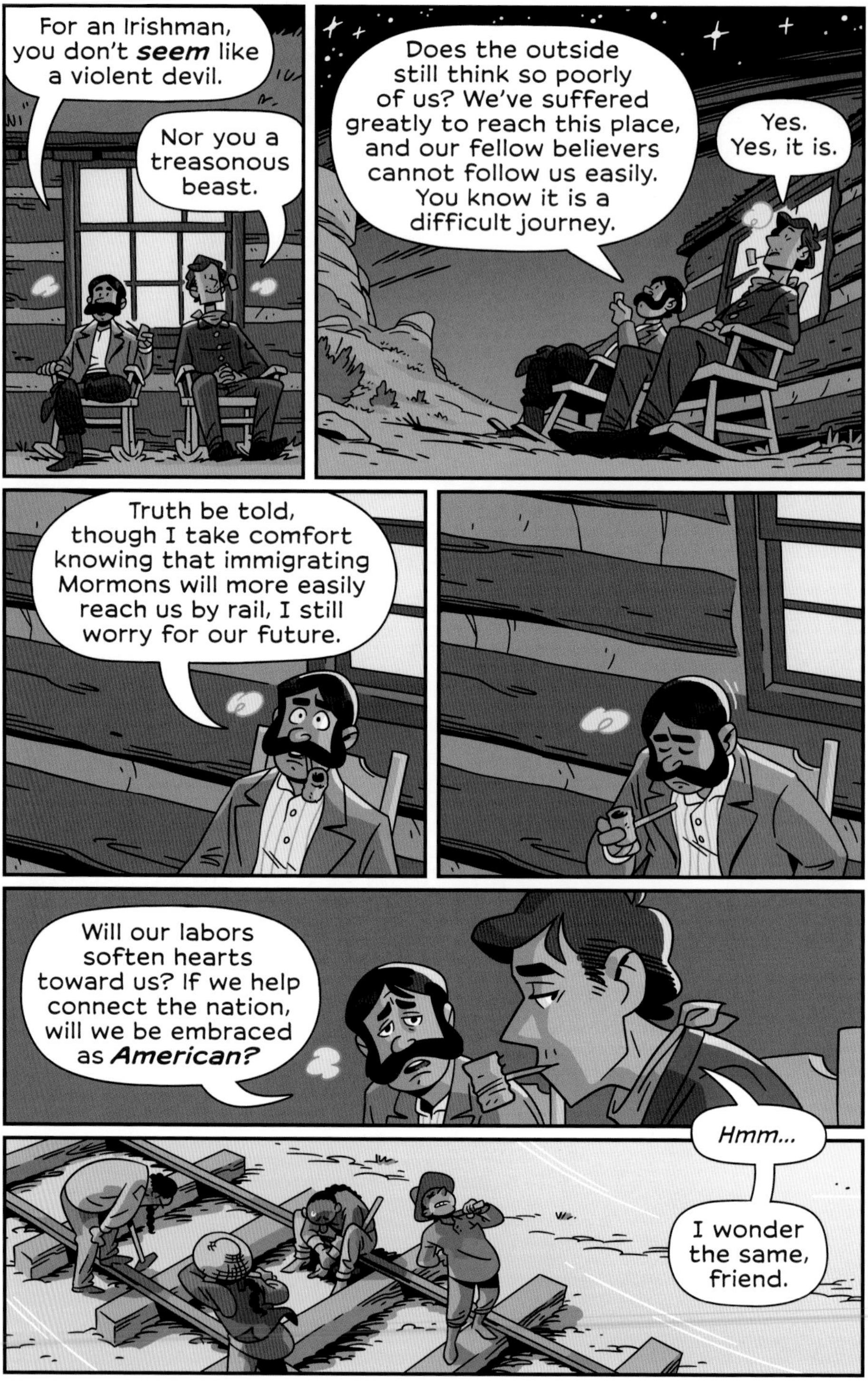

For an Irishman, you don't ***seem*** like a violent devil.
Nor you a treasonous beast.
Does the outside still think so poorly of us? We've suffered greatly to reach this place, and our fellow believers cannot follow us easily. You know it is a difficult journey.
Yes. Yes, it is.
Truth be told, though I take comfort knowing that immigrating Mormons will more easily reach us by rail, I still worry for our future.
Will our labors soften hearts toward us? If we help connect the nation, will we be embraced as ***American?***
*Hmm...*
I wonder the same, friend.

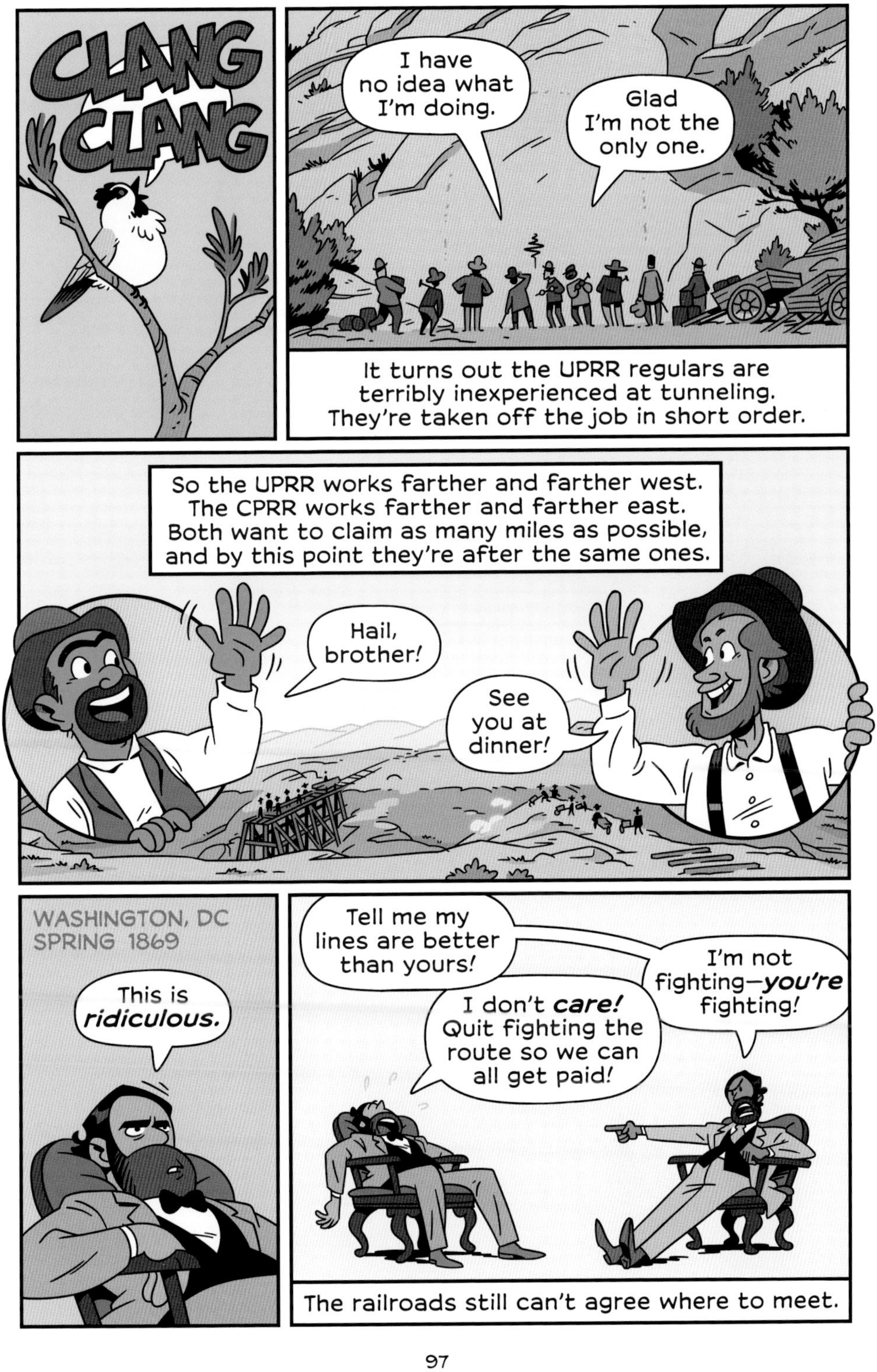
CLANG
CLANG
I have no idea what I'm doing.
Glad I'm not the only one.
It turns out the UPRR regulars are terribly inexperienced at tunneling. They're taken off the job in short order.
So the UPRR works farther and farther west. The CPRR works farther and farther east. Both want to claim as many miles as possible, and by this point they're after the same ones.
Hail, brother!
See you at dinner!
WASHINGTON, DC
SPRING 1869
This is *ridiculous.*
Tell me my lines are better than yours!
I'm not fighting—*you're* fighting!
I don't *care!* Quit fighting the route so we can all get paid!
The railroads still can't agree where to meet.

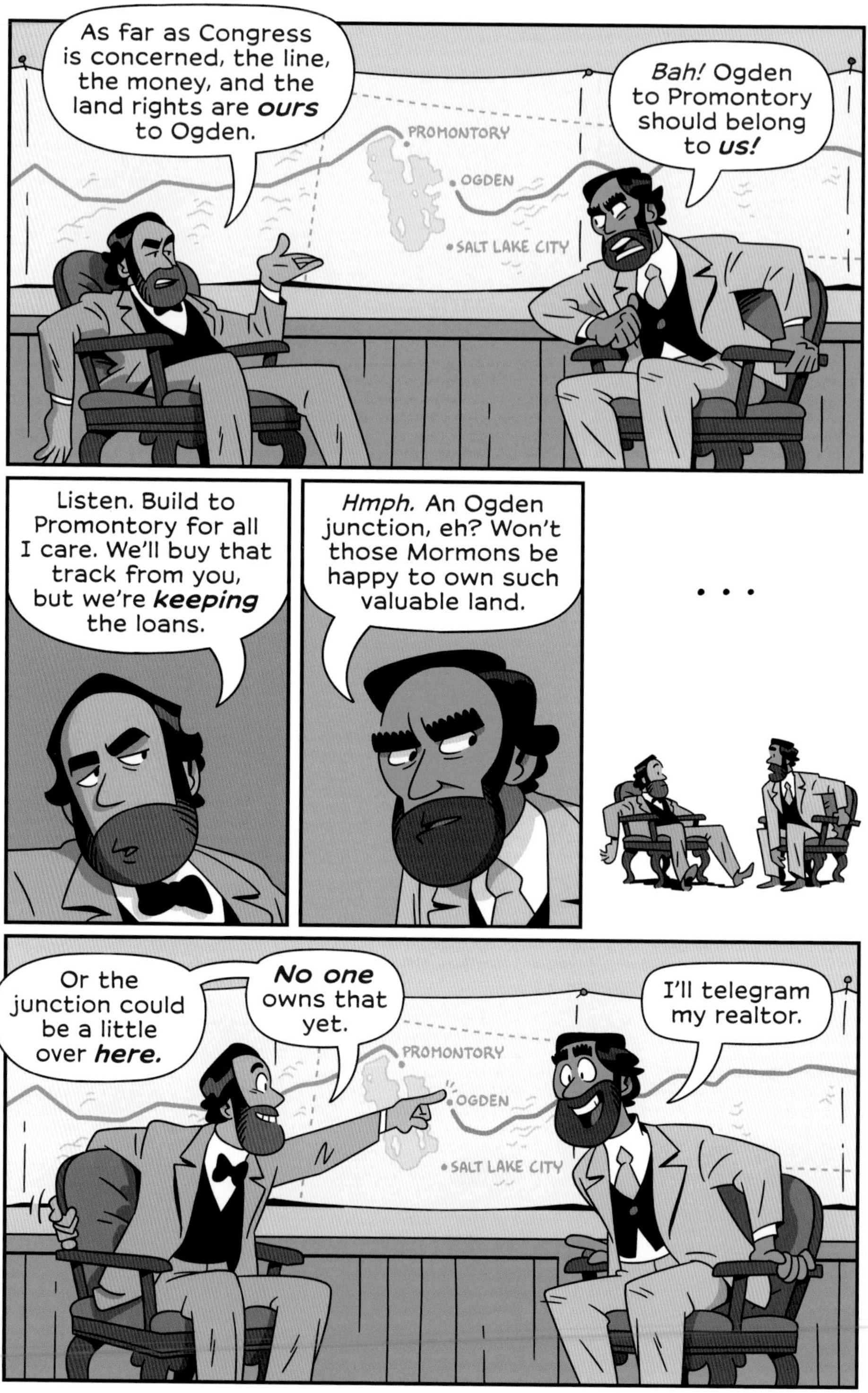
As far as Congress is concerned, the line, the money, and the land rights are ***ours*** to Ogden.
PROMONTORY
OGDEN
SALT LAKE CITY
*Bah!* Ogden to Promontory should belong to ***us!***
Listen. Build to Promontory for all I care. We'll buy that track from you, but we're ***keeping*** the loans.
*Hmph.* An Ogden junction, eh? Won't those Mormons be happy to own such valuable land.
. . .
Or the junction could be a little over ***here.***
***No one*** owns that yet.
I'll telegram my realtor.
PROMONTORY
OGDEN
SALT LAKE CITY

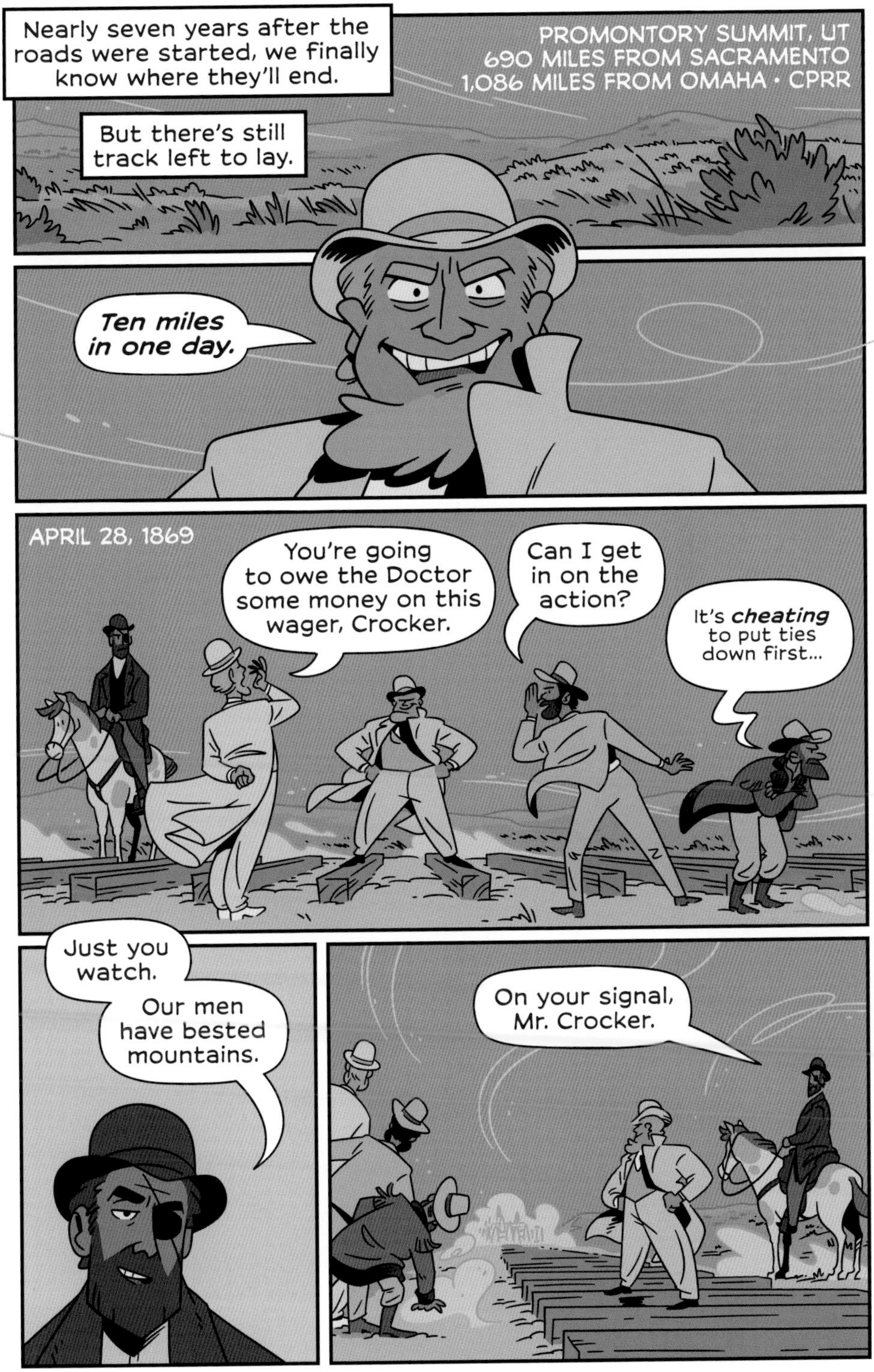
Nearly seven years after the roads were started, we finally know where they'll end.
PROMONTORY SUMMIT, UT
690 MILES FROM SACRAMENTO
1,086 MILES FROM OMAHA • CPRR
But there's still track left to lay.
Ten miles in one day.
APRIL 28, 1869
You're going to owe the Doctor some money on this wager, Crocker.
Can I get in on the action?
It's cheating to put ties down first...
Just you watch.
Our men have bested mountains.
On your signal, Mr. Crocker.

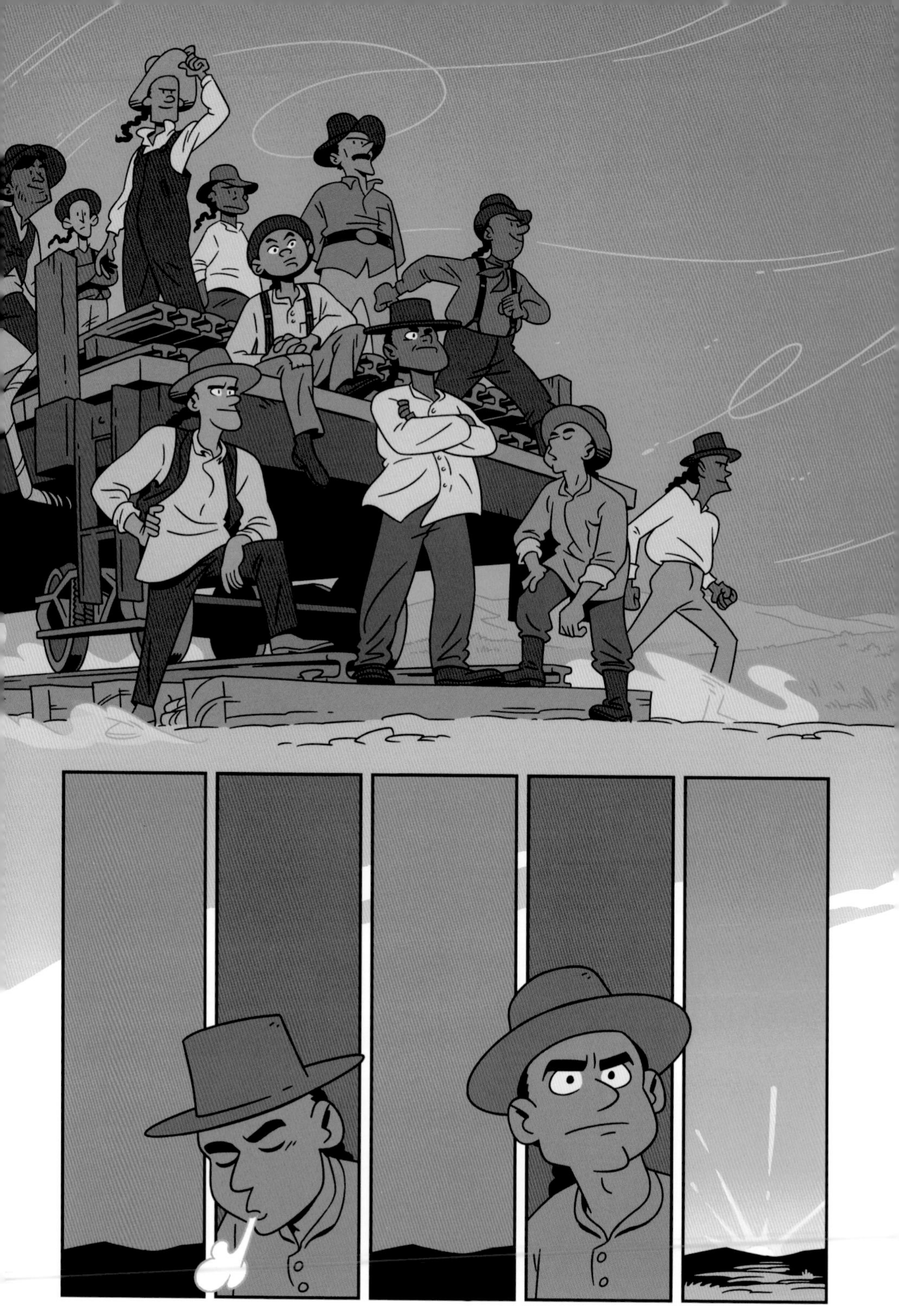

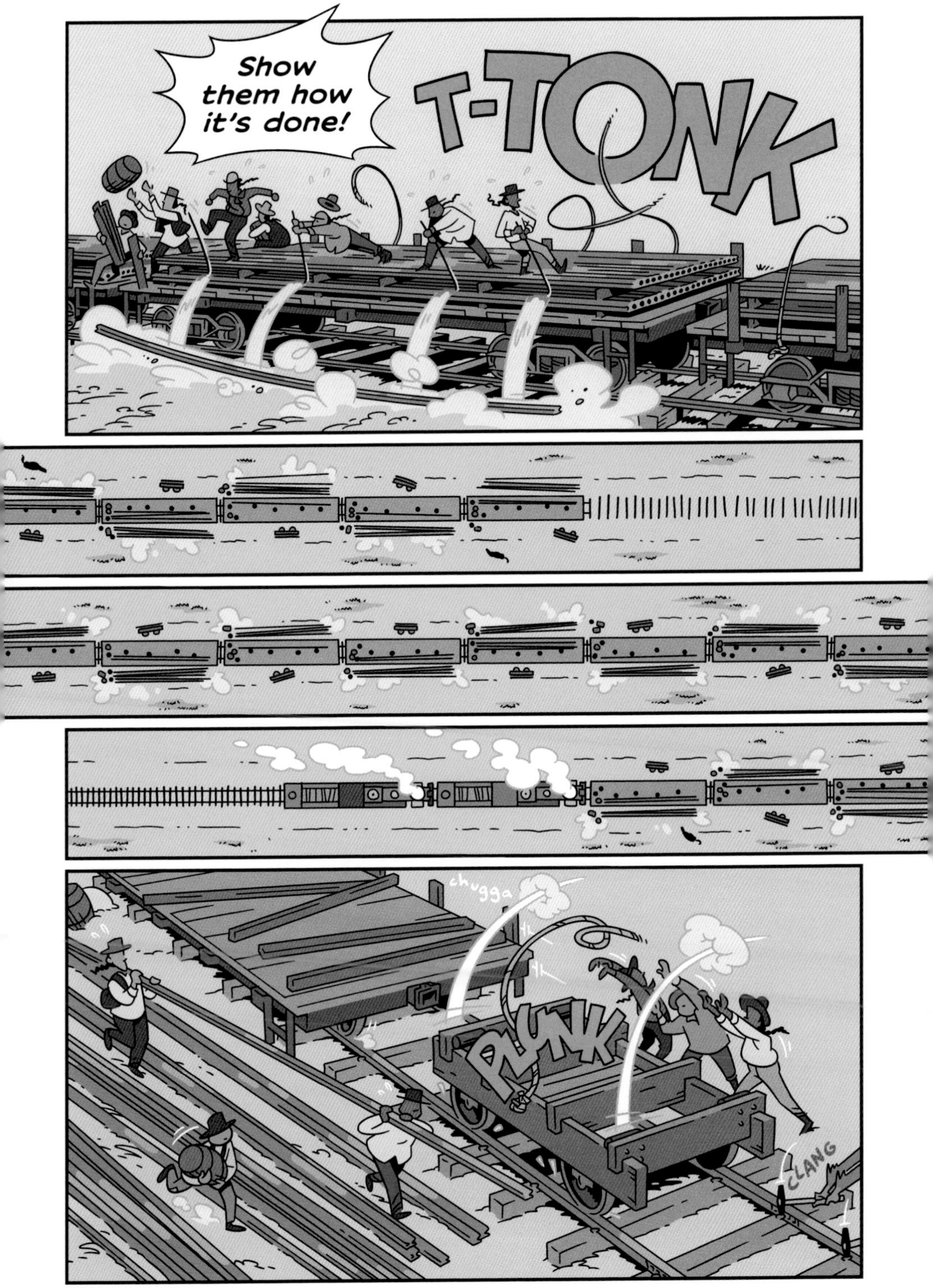
Show them how it's done!
T-TONK
chugga
PLUNK
CLANG

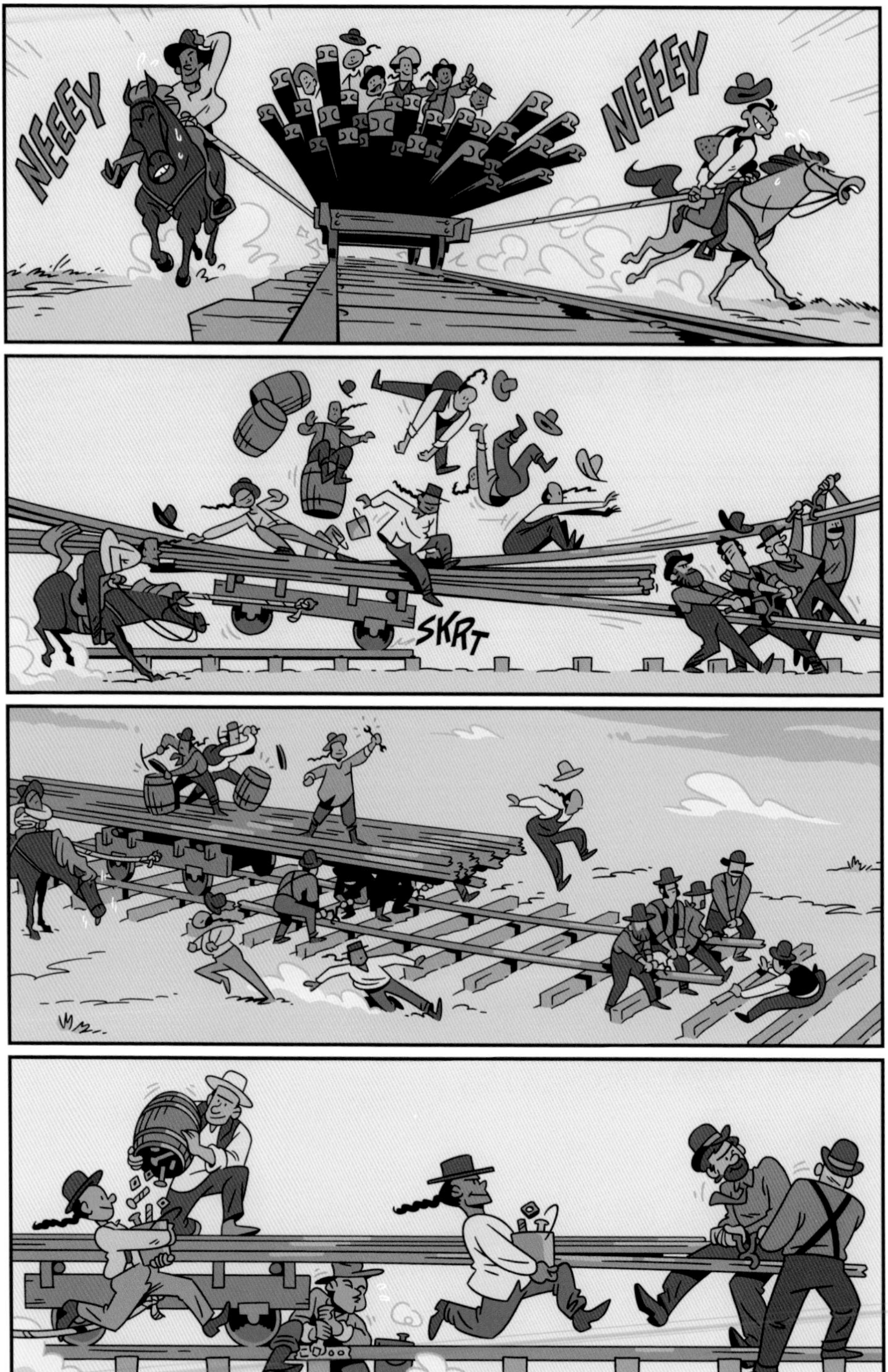
NEEEY
NEEEY
SKRT

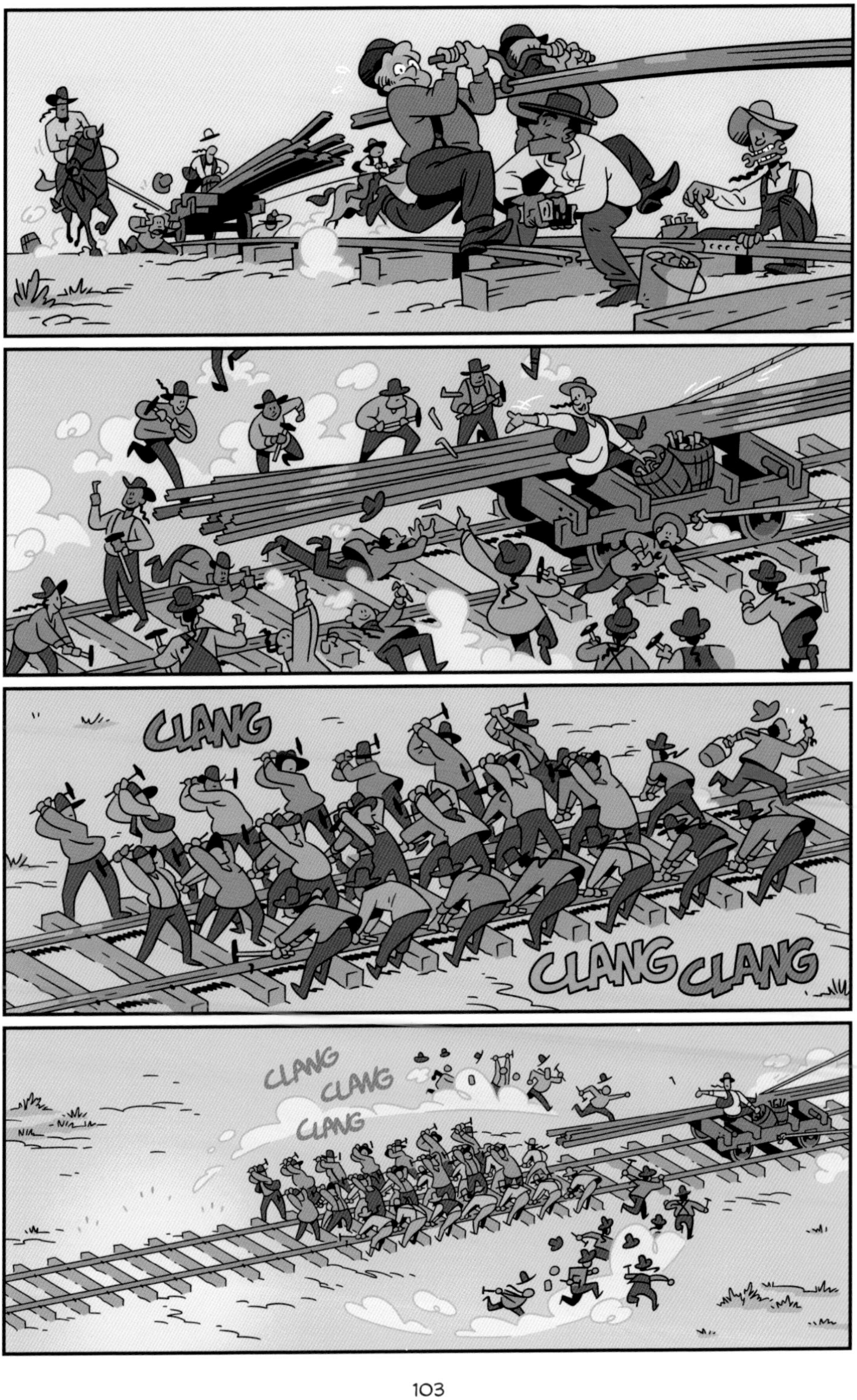
CLANG
CLANG
CLANG
CLANG
CLANG
CLANG

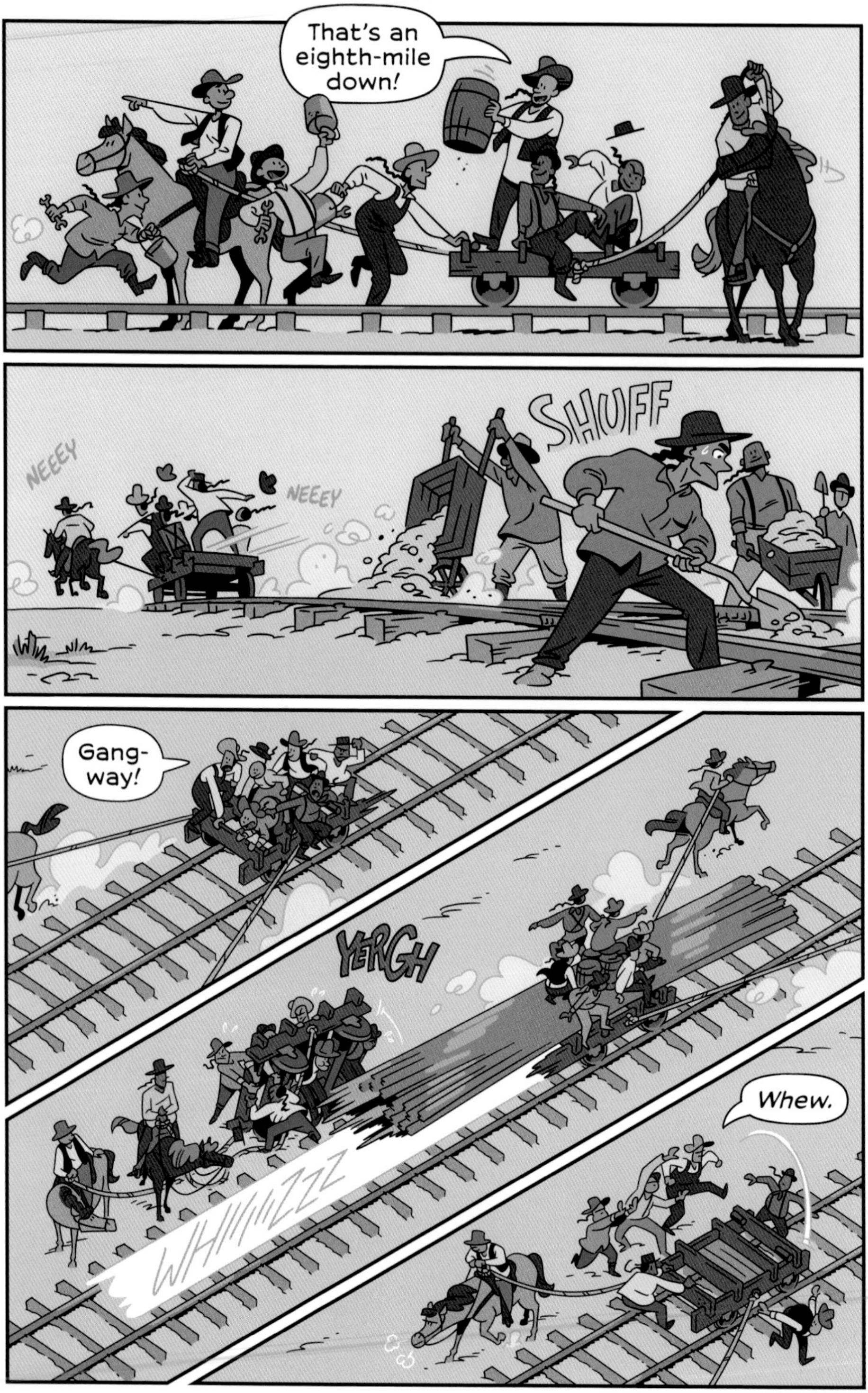
That's an eighth-mile down!
NEEEY
NEEEY
SHUFF
Gang-way!
YERGH
WHMMZZZ
Whew.

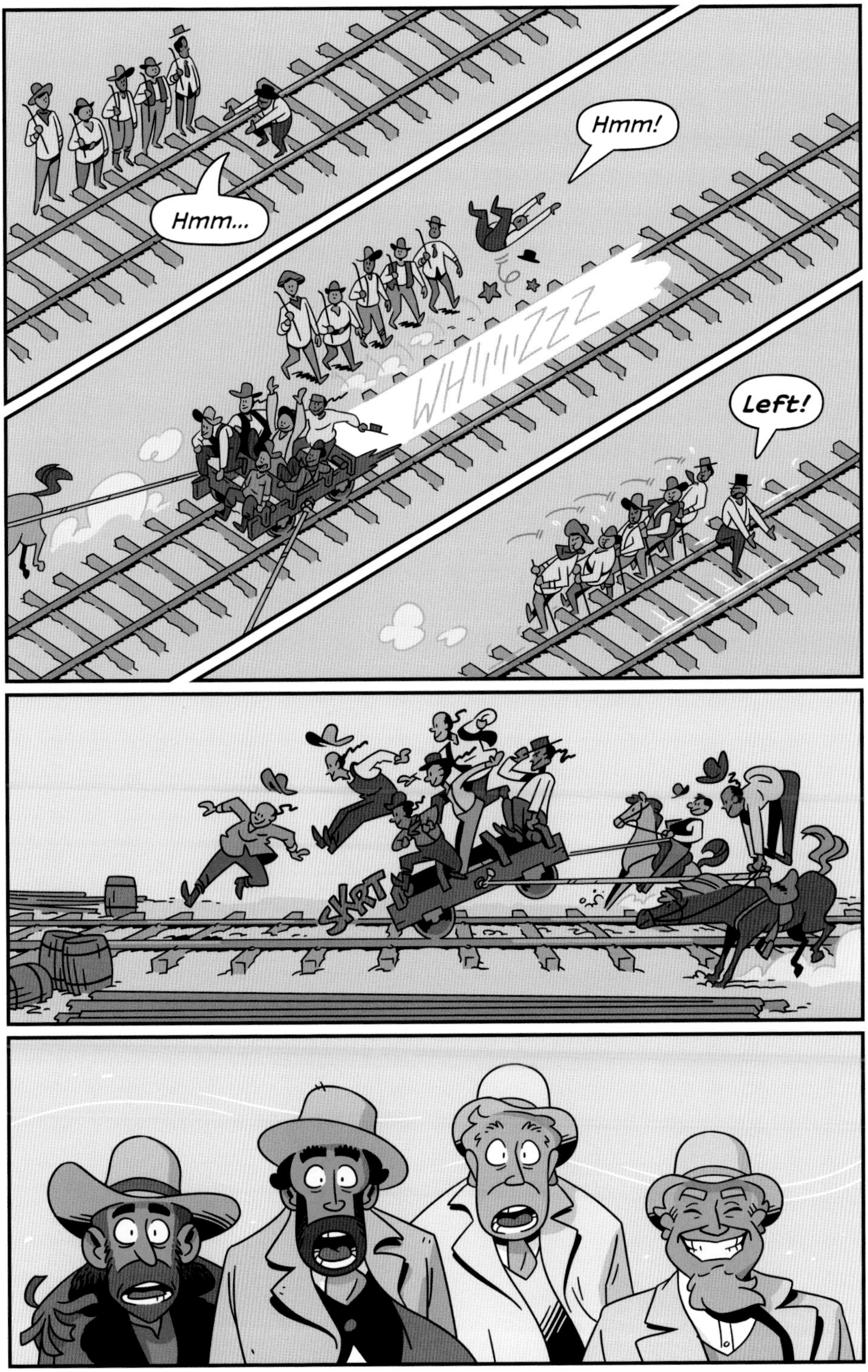
Hmm...
Hmm!
WHRRRZZZ
Left!
SKRT

Keep at it, men! We're on track for *one mile in one* TOOT *hour!*

WOO HOORAY YEAH

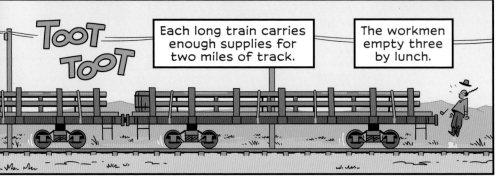

TOOT TOOT

Each long train carries enough supplies for two miles of track.

The workmen empty three by lunch.

And that's how the Central Pacific laid ten miles (and 56 feet) of track before dinner.

It's not far to the end now.

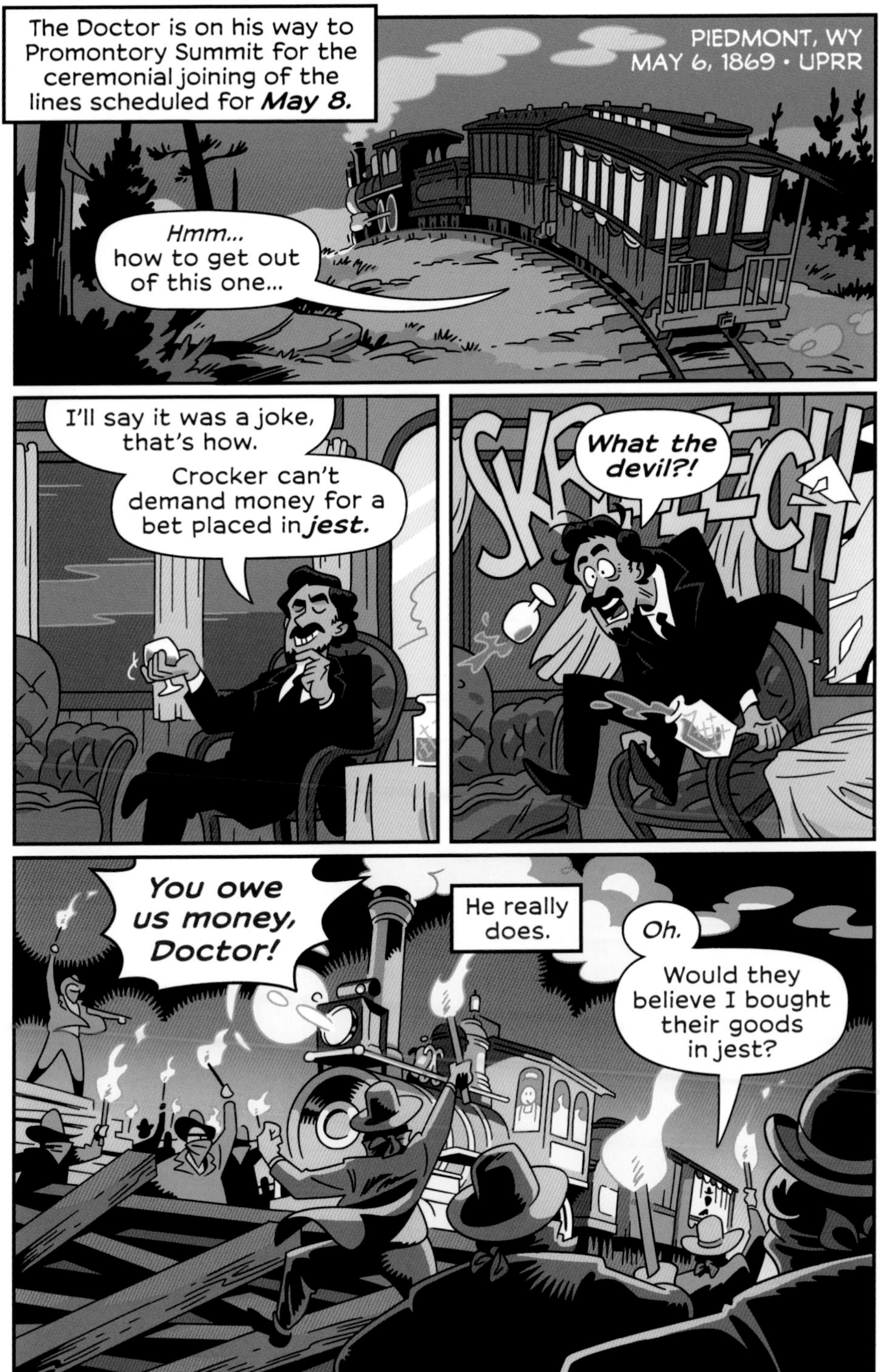
The Doctor is on his way to Promontory Summit for the ceremonial joining of the lines scheduled for ***May 8.***
PIEDMONT, WY
MAY 6, 1869 • UPRR
*Hmm...* how to get out of this one...
I'll say it was a joke, that's how.
Crocker can't demand money for a bet placed in ***jest.***
SKREEECH
***What the devil?!***
***You owe us money, Doctor!***
He really does.
*Oh.*
Would they believe I bought their goods in jest?

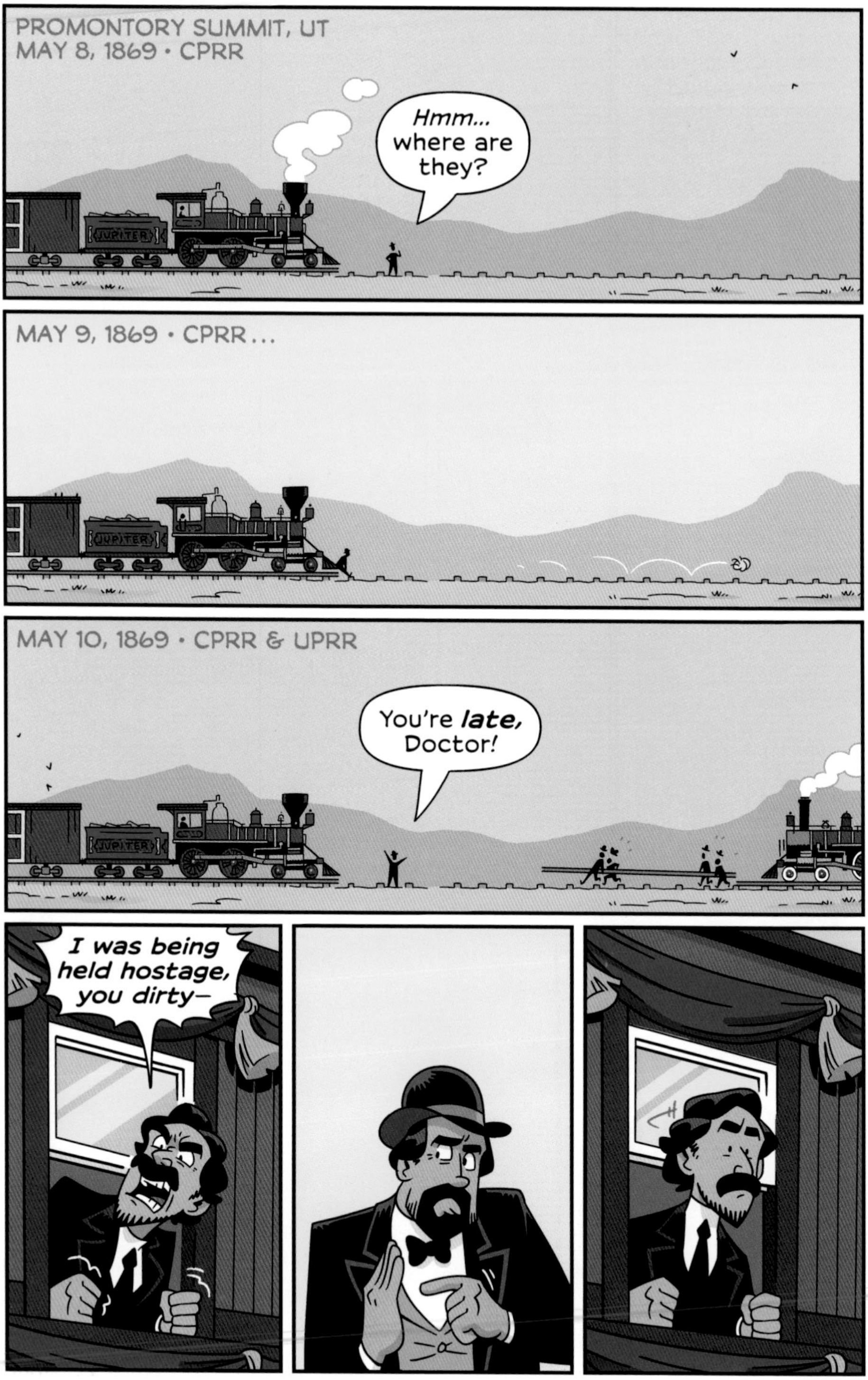
PROMONTORY SUMMIT, UT
MAY 8, 1869 • CPRR
Hmm... where are they?
JUPITER
MAY 9, 1869 • CPRR...
JUPITER
MAY 10, 1869 • CPRR & UPRR
You're *late,* Doctor!
JUPITER
*I was being held hostage, you dirty—*

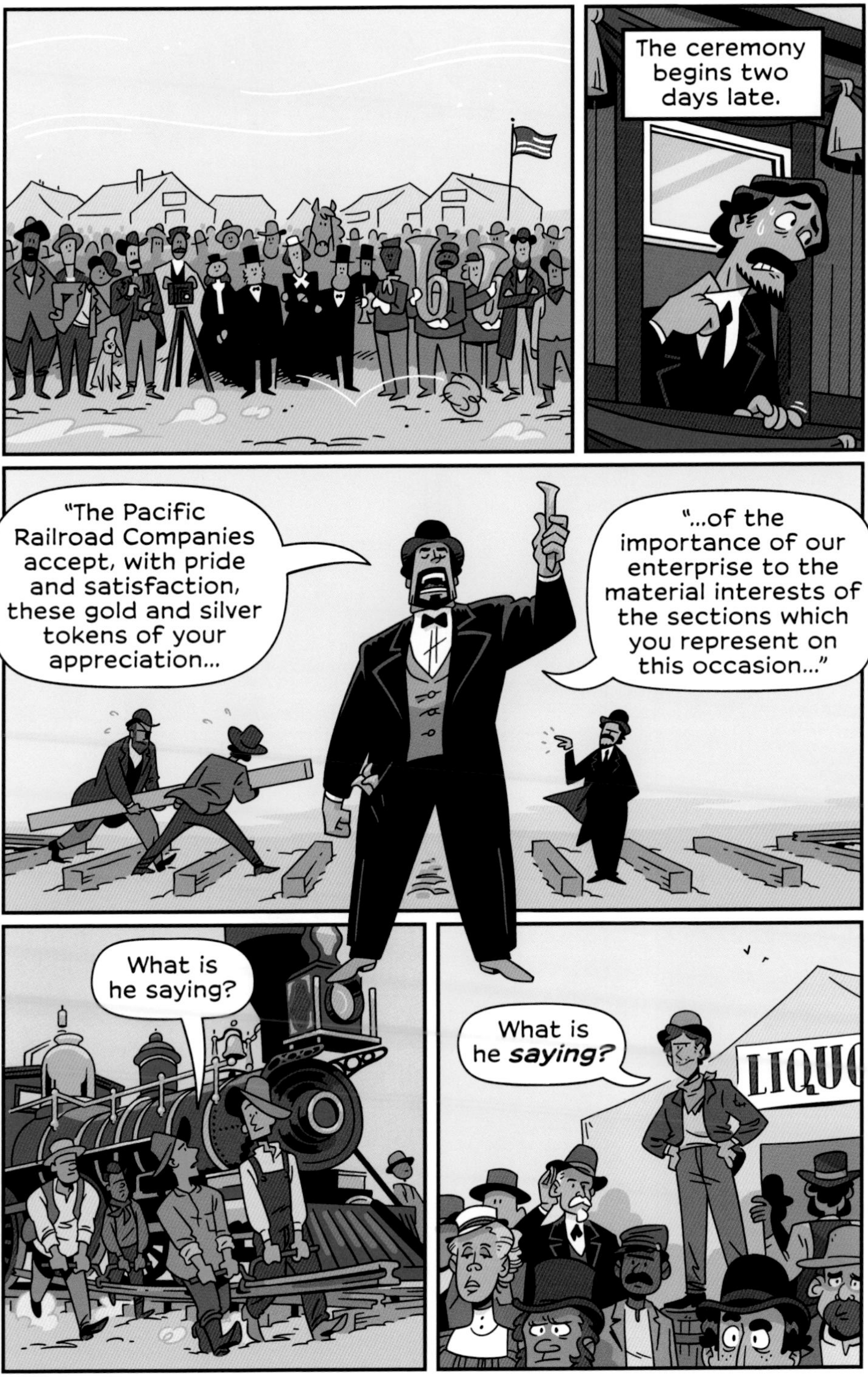
The ceremony begins two days late.
"The Pacific Railroad Companies accept, with pride and satisfaction, these gold and silver tokens of your appreciation...
"...of the importance of our enterprise to the material interests of the sections which you represent on this occasion..."
What is he saying?
What is he *saying?*
LIQU

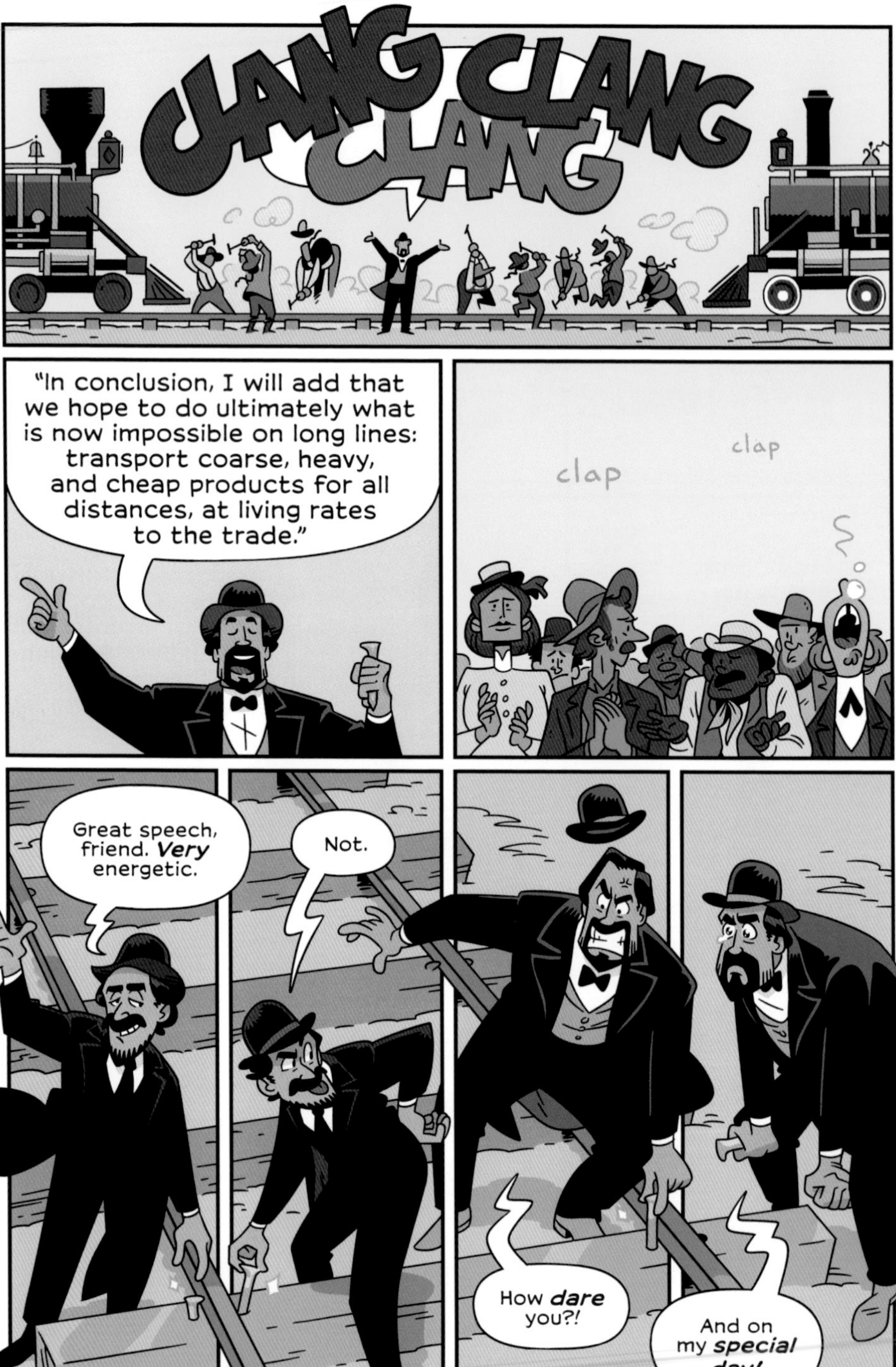
CLANG CLANG
CLANG
"In conclusion, I will add that we hope to do ultimately what is now impossible on long lines: transport coarse, heavy, and cheap products for all distances, at living rates to the trade."
clap
clap
Great speech, friend. *Very* energetic.
Not.
How *dare* you?!
And on my *special day!*

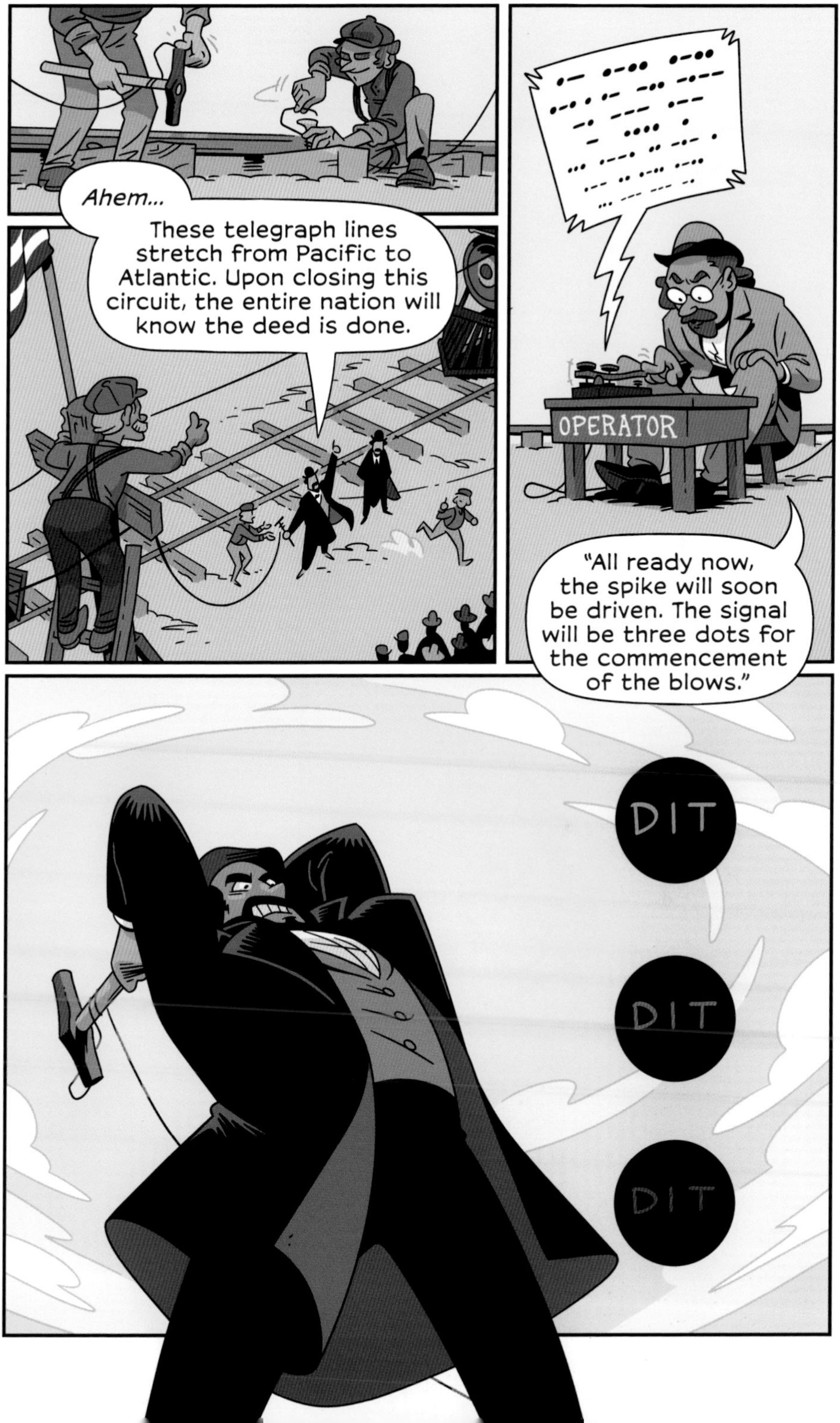
Ahem...
These telegraph lines stretch from Pacific to Atlantic. Upon closing this circuit, the entire nation will know the deed is done.
OPERATOR
"All ready now, the spike will soon be driven. The signal will be three dots for the commencement of the blows."
DIT
DIT
DIT

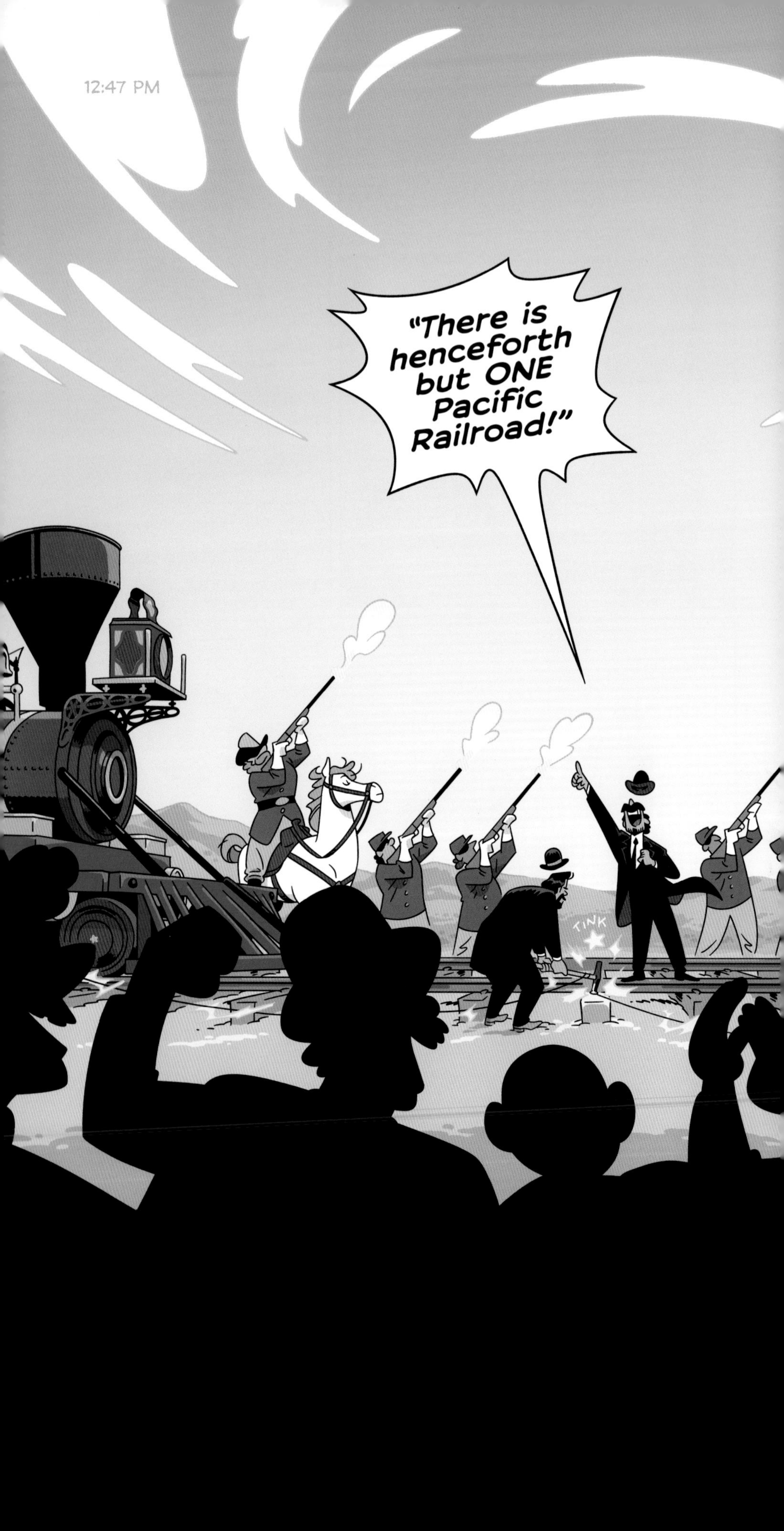
12:47 PM
"There is henceforth but ONE Pacific Railroad!"
TINK

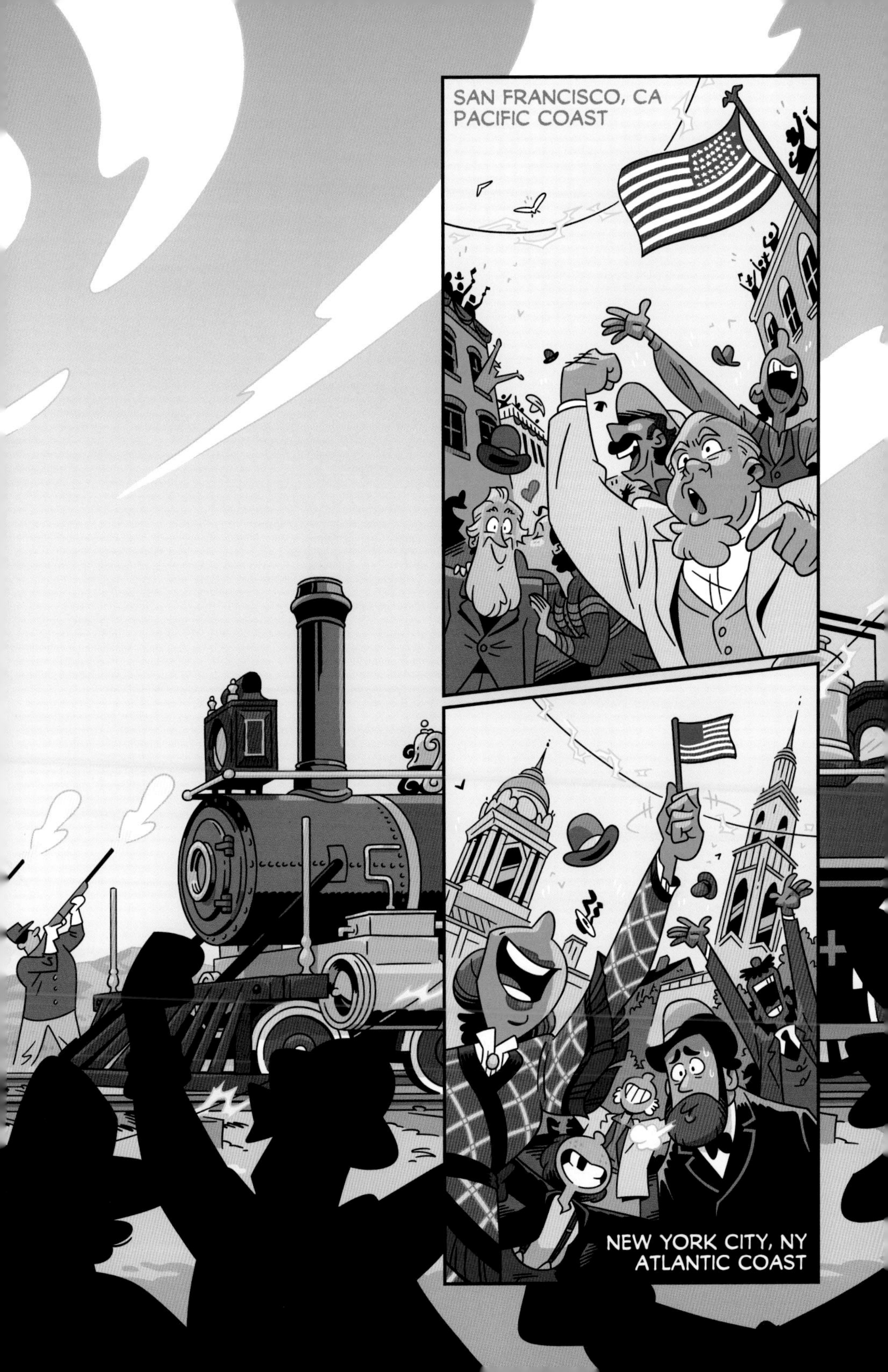
SAN FRANCISCO, CA
PACIFIC COAST
NEW YORK CITY, NY
ATLANTIC COAST

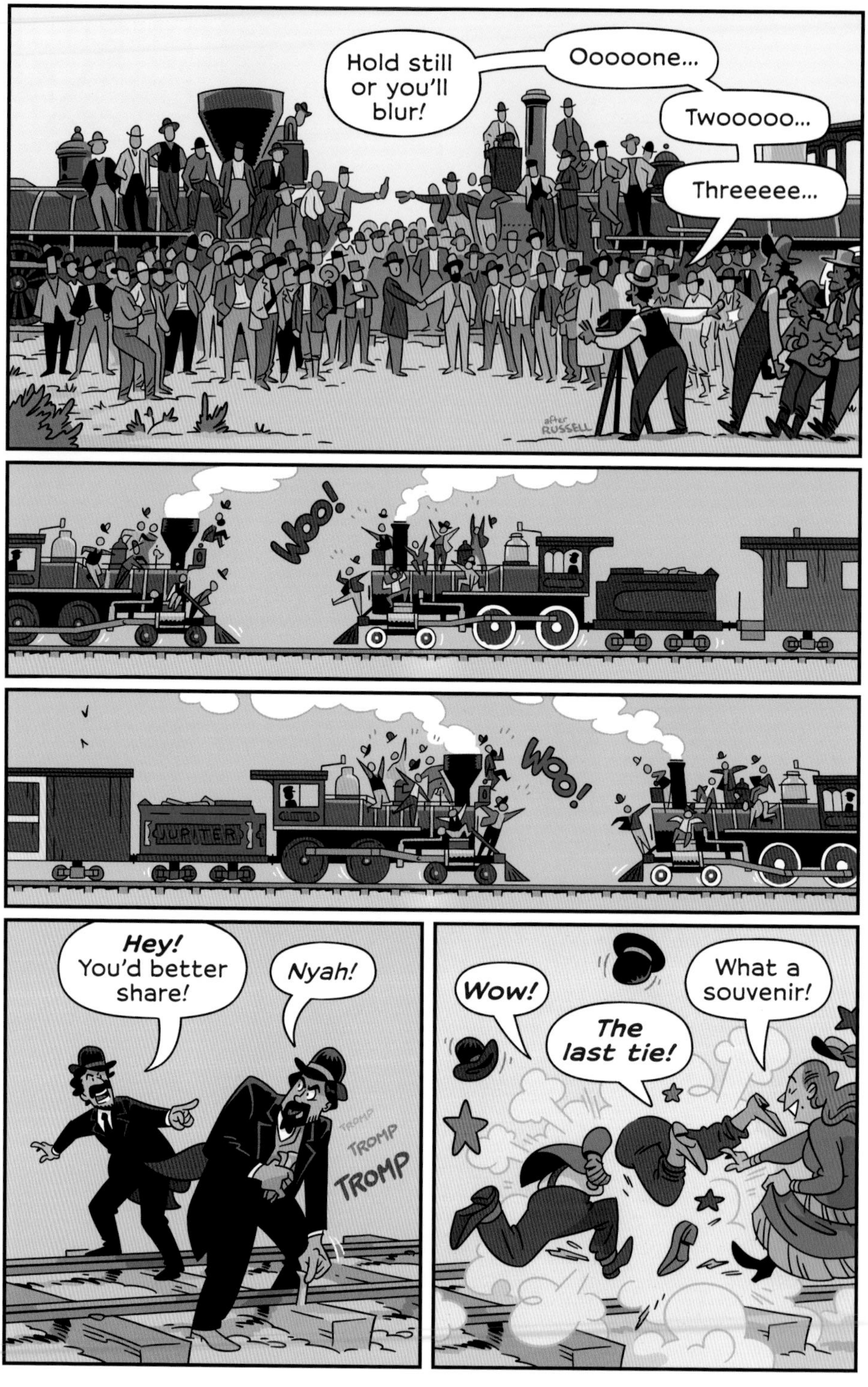
Hold still or you'll blur!
Ooooone...
Twooooo...
Threeeee...
after RUSSELL
WOO!
JUPITER
WOO!
Hey! You'd better share!
Nyah!
TROMP
TROMP
TROMP
Wow!
The last tie!
What a souvenir!

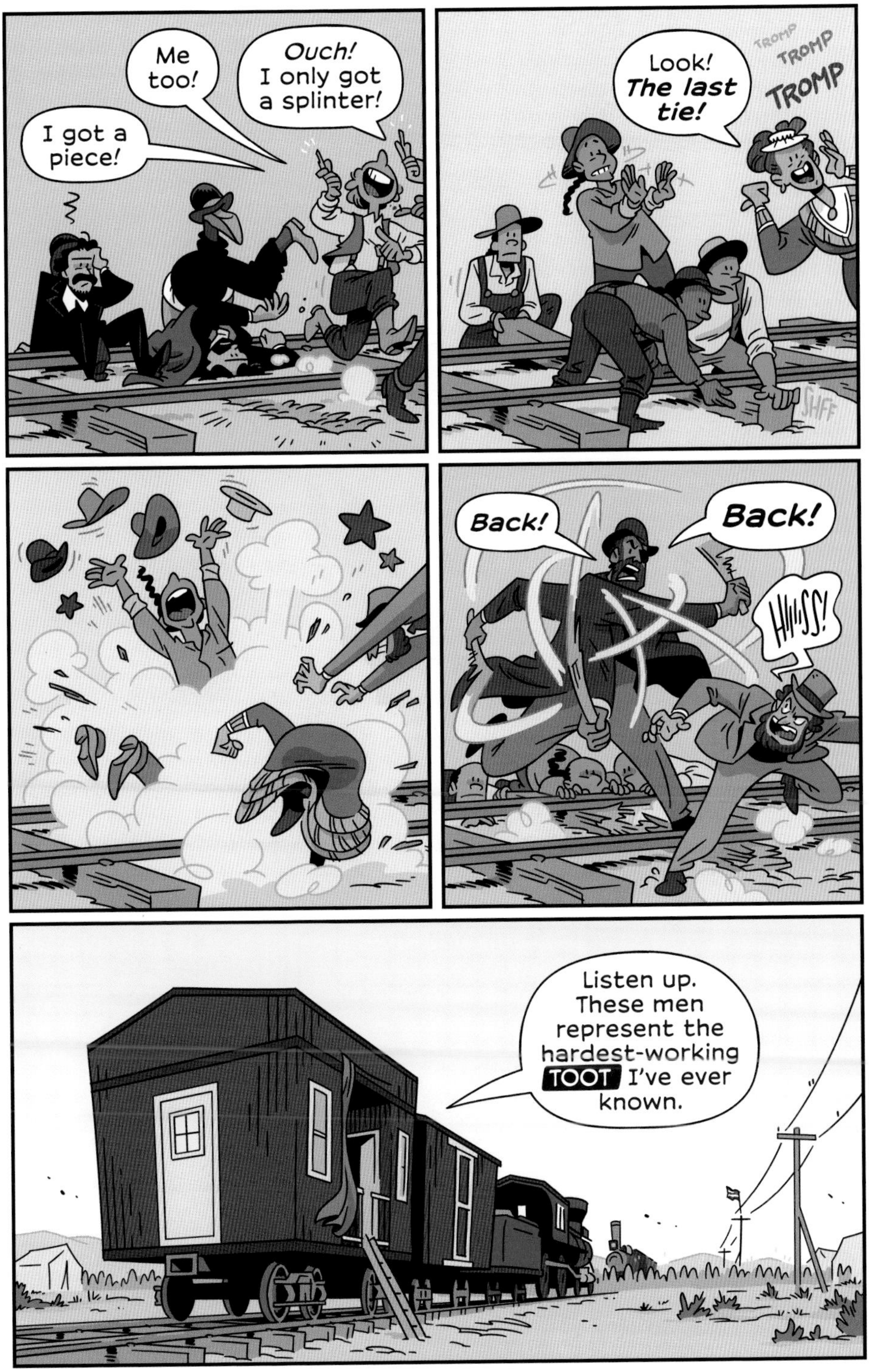
I got a piece!
Me too!
Ouch! I only got a splinter!
Look! The last tie!
TROMP
TROMP
TROMP
SHFF
Back!
Back!
HWSS!
Listen up. These men represent the hardest-working TOOT I've ever known.

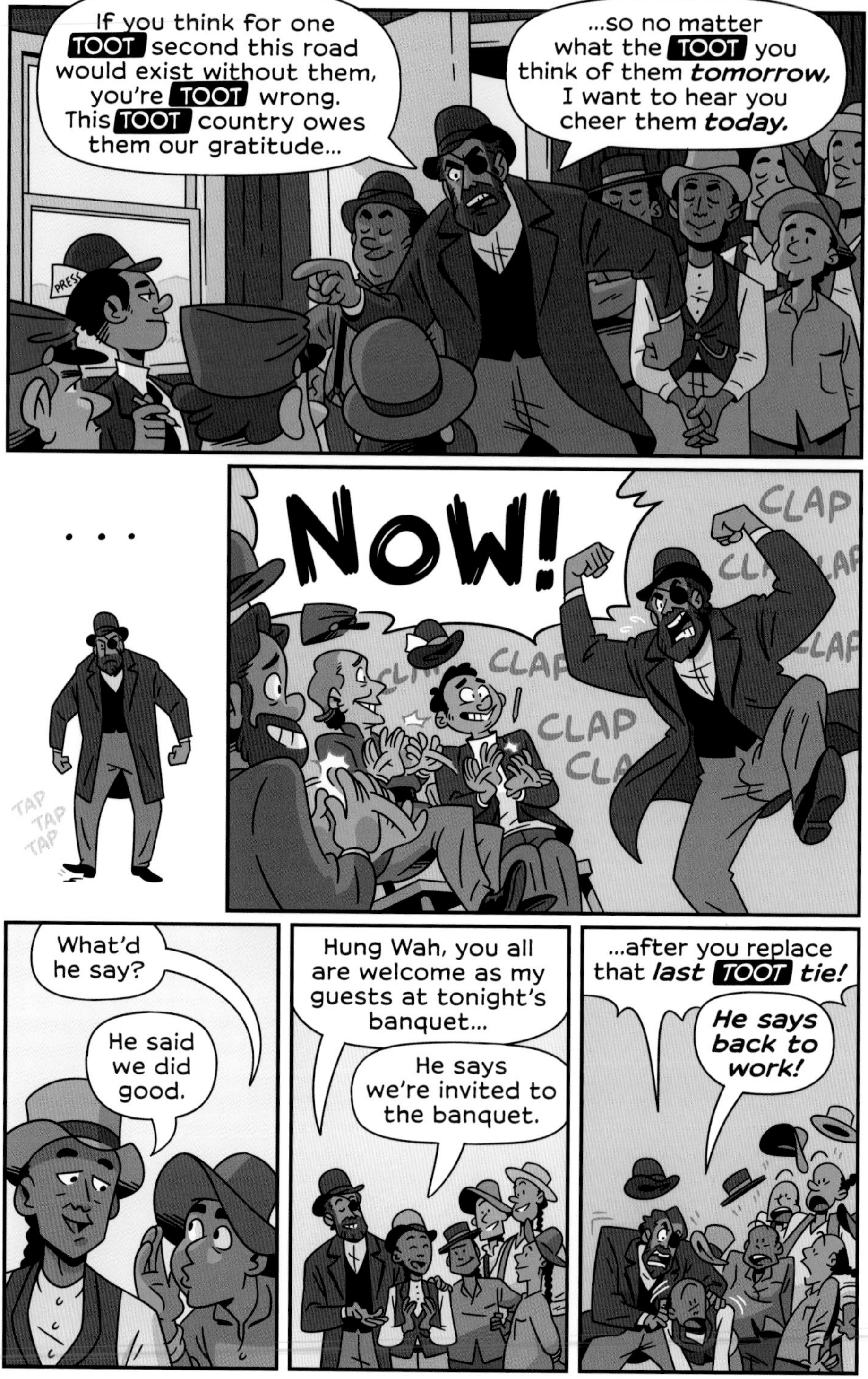
If you think for one TOOT second this road would exist without them, you're TOOT wrong. This TOOT country owes them our gratitude...
...so no matter what the TOOT you think of them *tomorrow,* I want to hear you cheer them *today.*
PRESS
. . .
TAP TAP TAP
NOW!
CLAP
CLAP
CLAP
What'd he say?
He said we did good.
Hung Wah, you all are welcome as my guests at tonight's banquet...
He says we're invited to the banquet.
...after you replace that *last* TOOT *tie!*
*He says back to work!*

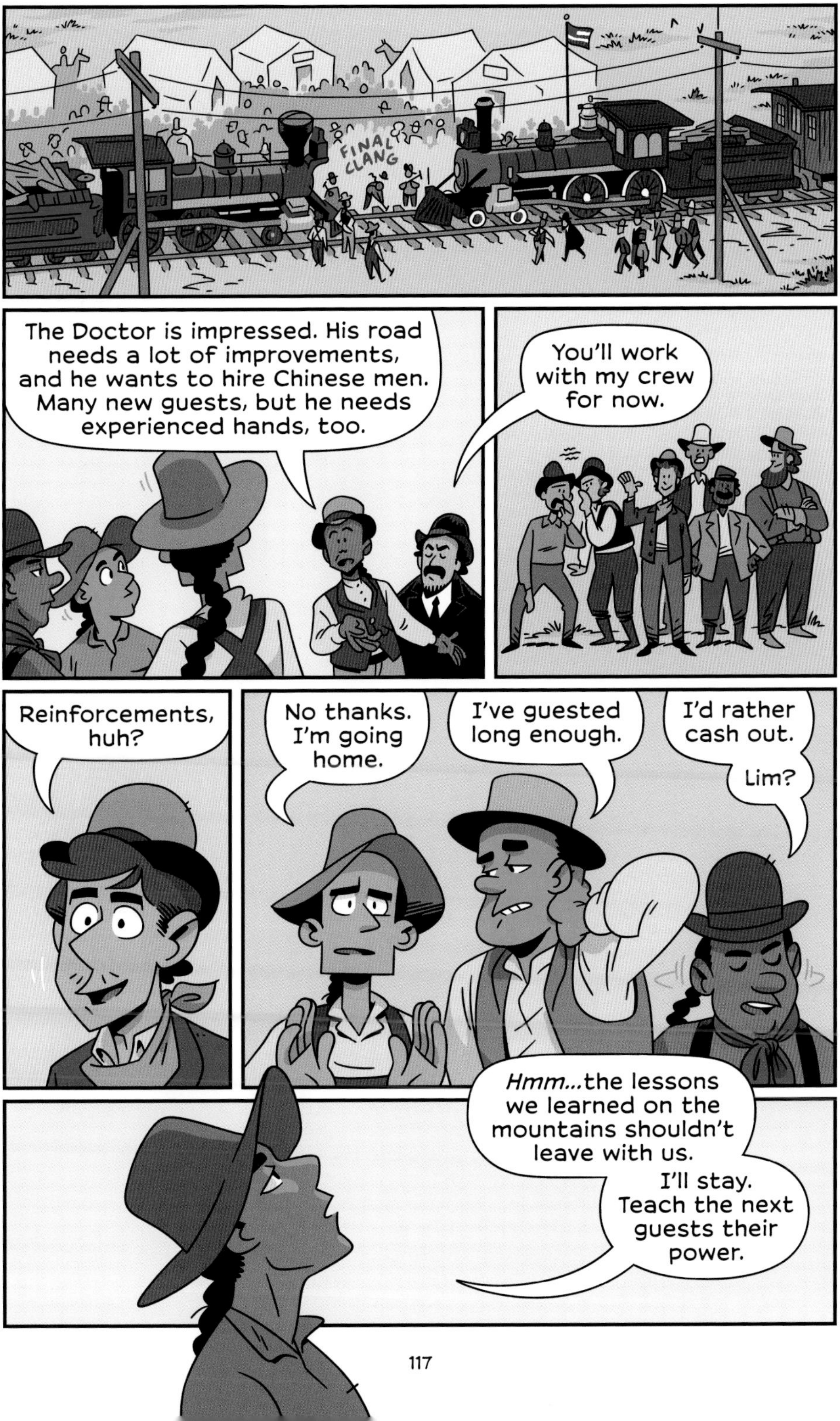
FINAL CLANG
The Doctor is impressed. His road needs a lot of improvements, and he wants to hire Chinese men. Many new guests, but he needs experienced hands, too.
You'll work with my crew for now.
Reinforcements, huh?
No thanks. I'm going home.
I've guested long enough.
I'd rather cash out.
Lim?
*Hmm...*the lessons we learned on the mountains shouldn't leave with us.
I'll stay. Teach the next guests their power.

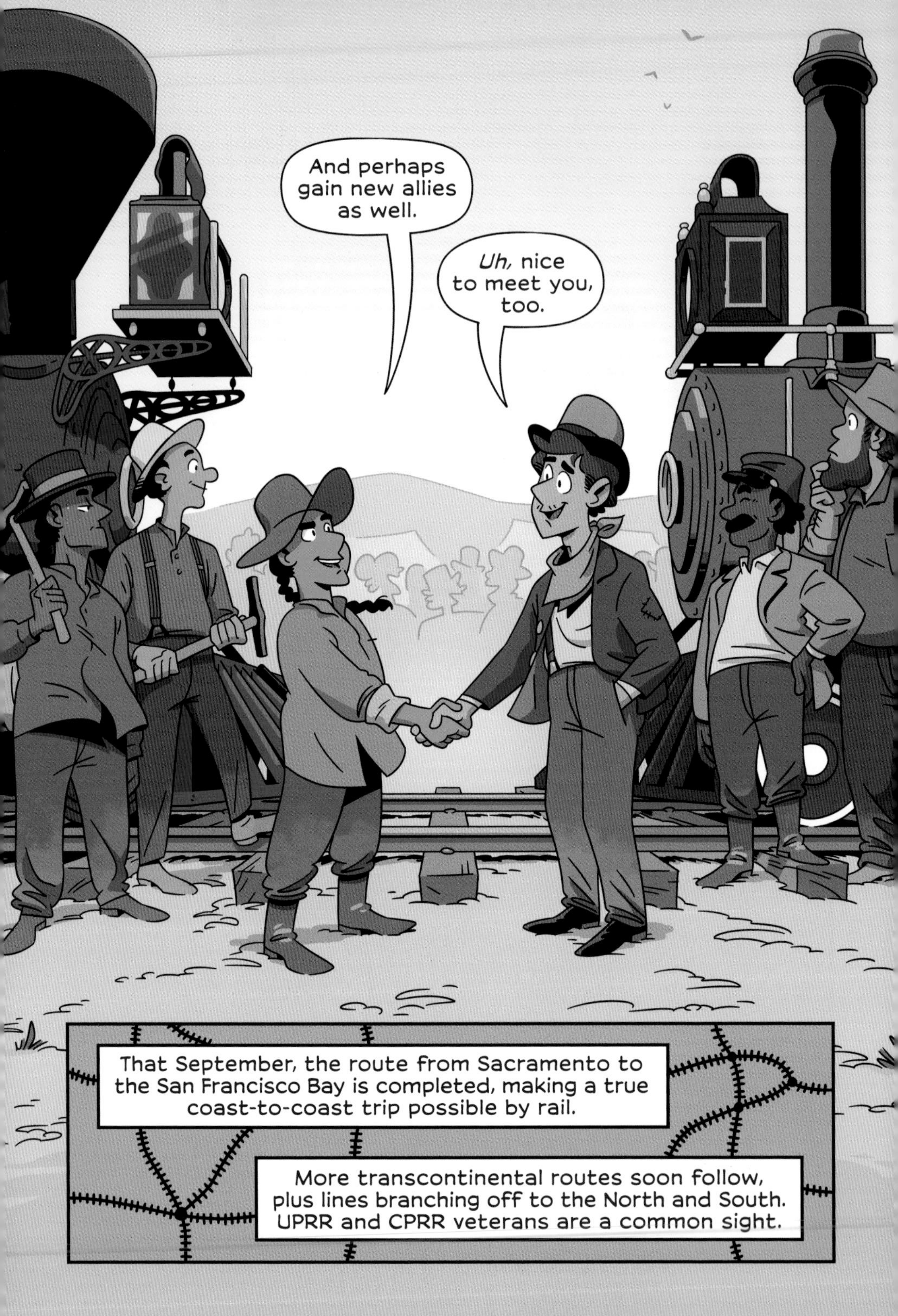
And perhaps gain new allies as well.
*Uh,* nice to meet you, too.
That September, the route from Sacramento to the San Francisco Bay is completed, making a true coast-to-coast trip possible by rail.
More transcontinental routes soon follow, plus lines branching off to the North and South. UPRR and CPRR veterans are a common sight.